Narrating Political Reconciliation

South Africa's Truth and Reconciliation Commission

CLAIRE MOON

LEXINGTON BOOKS

A division of
ROWMAN & LITTLEFIELD PUBLISHERS, INC.
Lanham • Boulder • New York • Toronto • Plymouth, UK

Published by Lexington Books
A division of Rowman & Littlefield Publishers, Inc.
A wholly owned subsidiary of The Rowman & Littlefield Publishing Group, Inc.
4501 Forbes Boulevard, Suite 200, Lanham, Maryland 20706
http://www.lexingtonbooks.com

Estover Road, Plymouth PL6 7PY, United Kingdom

Copyright © 2008 by Lexington Books
First paperback edition 2009

British Library Cataloguing in Publication Information Available

Library of Congress Cataloging-in-Publication Data

Moon, Claire, 1966–
  Narrating political reconciliation : South Africa's Truth and Reconciliation Commission
/ Claire Moon.
      p. cm.
  Includes bibliographical references and index.
  1. South Africa. Truth and Reconciliation Commission. 2. Reconciliation—Political
aspects—South Africa. 3. Truth commissions—South Africa—Evaluation. 4. South
Africa—Politics and government—1989–1994. 5. South Africa—Politics and
government—1994– 6. Apartheid—South Africa. 7. Human rights—South Africa. I.
Title.
  DT1974.2.M66 2008
  968.06—dc22   2007038130

ISBN: 978-0-7391-2127-6 (cloth : alk. paper)
ISBN: 978-0-7391-4045-1 (pbk : alk. paper)
ISBN: 978-0-7391-4046-8 (electronic)

Printed in the United States of America

⊖™ The paper used in this publication meets the minimum requirements of American
National Standard for Information Sciences—Permanence of Paper for Printed Library
Materials, ANSI/NISO Z39.48–1992.

Narrating Political Reconciliation

For Martin and Christian

Table of Contents

Acknowledgements

I gathered many debts in the writing of this book which began life as a PhD thesis in the Politics Department at Bristol University. I owe thanks to Terrell Carver and Richard Little for supervising the project, to Bristol University for a generous scholarship and to my parents for helping me out at critical times.

The ideas for this book developed out of conversations with a number of people, and for those I would like to thank especially Emilios Christodoulidis, Costas Constantinou, Mervyn Frost, Michal Ben-Josef Hirsch, Vivienne Jabri, Chris Goto-Jones, Ronnie Lippens, Debbie Lisle, Scott Veitch and Andy Schaap.

The arguments presented here draw upon published and unpublished work. Chapter two has been published as 'Narrating Political Reconciliation: Truth and Reconciliation in South Africa', *Social and Legal Studies,* 15:2 (2006). Chapter five draws in part upon the article 'Prelapsarian State: Forgiveness and Reconciliation in Transitional Justice', *International Journal for the Semiotics of Law,* 17:2 (2004), and upon a discussion of the therapeutic state which first appeared in a book chapter 'Reconciliation as Therapy and Compensation: A Critical Analysis' in *Law and the Politics of Reconciliation* (Veitch 2007). The discussion of the *Khulumani vs Barclays et al* case in the conclusion to this book also appears in that same book chapter.

Current colleagues in the Department of Sociology and the Centre for the Study of Human Rights at the London School of Economics and Political Science have contributed to and challenged my thinking about reconciliation. Notable amongst these are Claire Alexander, Conor Gearty, Nikolas Rose and Paul Rock, but most especially Stan Cohen, who has provided enormous inspiration, encouragement and support for my work. I am also grateful to my students, past and present, who always question my ideas and put me right on many things.

My biggest debt and deepest gratitude is to Martin McIvor. His tenacious intellect, boundless knowledge, curiosity and love simultaneously pushed me in my thinking and sustained me in innumerable other ways during the writing of this book.

Introduction
Reconciliation and the Governance of Political Transition

What use, young man, does telling stories have, if not that of erasing from memory all that is not origin or end?

> Ricardo Piglia, *Artificial Respiration* (Durham and London: Duke University Press, 1994).

This book reflects upon the role played by South Africa's Truth and Reconciliation Commission (TRC), which began its public work in 1996, in the construction of reconciliation as a widespread and hegemonic discourse of political transition. The TRC is the indisputable *locus classicus* to which innumerable subsequent instances of reconciliation politics have referred, and it constitutes the analytical lens through which many cases prior to South Africa have been viewed and reviewed by both practitioners and researchers. The TRC was remarkable for bringing into the political domain the more usually private rituals of apology, remorse and atonement, gestures of the formal acknowledgement of past atrocity perpetrated by the state and its agents on the one hand, and opponents of the apartheid regime on the other. It also marked the beginning of an international transitional justice industry distinguished by a proliferation of truth commissions, transitional justice institutes and research centers. This industry was, in its early days, characterized by exuberant plaudits for the truth commission, a then relatively new although rapidly developing, institution. A 'first wave' of influential writings echoed the enthusiasm of practitioners. It promoted the value of 'pragmatic' responses to past violence such as amnesties and truth-telling, and justified a move away from the criminal justice paradigm and its emphasis on punishment, features which rapidly became central to a phenomenon that is now known widely as transitional justice (see Asmal, 1997; Hayner, 1994 and 2001; Kritz, 1995; Mamdani, 1997; McAdams, 1997; Rotberg and Thompson, 2000). Since then, this enthusiasm has, necessarily, been tempered by more critical evaluations of the aims, assumptions and achievements of transitional justice in general, and truth commissions in particular (Borneman, 1997; Humphrey, 2002; Mendeloff, 2004; Wilson, 2001).

Simultaneously with this new phenomenon of political praxis, the study from the mid 90s of the TRC in particular and truth commissions more generally generated transitional justice as a then new, although now thriving, academic sub-field of the disciplines of politics, law, anthropology and sociology, which connected most forcefully to the particular field of human rights. The TRC generated enormous international political and academic enquiry into transitional justice. It promoted a renewed fascination with previously existing truth commissions, notably Argentina and Chile, as well as inspiring new research agendas located within the broader concerns surrounding conflict resolution and democratization processes.

The Reconciliation Industry

South Africa's TRC has provided the undisputed driver of a proliferating politics of reconcilation. Underpinned, broadly, by the mechanisms of transitional justice—amnesty and truth-telling—reconciliation is now not just a familiar trope governing transition, but is an *expected* response in certain contexts to past atrocities and state crimes such as torture, extra-judicial killing and disappearances. Since the TRC's highly publicized operation, reconciliation has become a ubiquitous and proliferating transitional discourse to the extent that it is now a settled norm governing political transitions. A veritable industry of reconciliation, unleashed with considerable force by the South African experience, has contributed to its formation and consolidation as a *fin de siecle* hegemonic political discourse. This industry is comprised of a powerful set of agents, institutions and funders. High-profile individuals in the field of transitional justice, or 'expert reconcilers' include Chilean lawyer Jose Zalaquet of Chile's National Commission on Truth and Reconciliation, Alex Boraine, Vice-Chair of South Africa's TRC, and most famously, its Chair, Archbishop Desmond Tutu. These individuals, and the broader epistemic community of reconciliation experts that they are constitutive of, have contributed to the promotion of reconciliation globally, advising on the setting up of new commissions and sitting on the directorial boards of centers dedicated to facilitating and funding transitional justice and reconciliation programs in Africa, the Americas, Asia, Europe and the Middle East.

These agents are frequently attached to, as directorial or advisory members of, newly established centers founded for the promotion of transitional justice and reconciliation. For example, the Institute for Justice and Reconciliation (IJR) was set up in Cape Town in May 2000 with Desmond Tutu as its main patron and a number of the TRC's commissioners as board members. The IJR was 'self-consciously located in post-TRC South Africa'.[1] This formulation of the IJR's temporal constitution is particularly telling because it reflects the way in which the TRC has come to demarcate symbolically the singular social, political and historical event marking the boundary between South Africa's apartheid past and its more democratic present. The IJR was founded with the express purpose of promoting and charting the success of reconciliation and transitional justice in South Africa through a set of political programs and engaged policy research. One of the key research publications it produces is the 'South Africa Reconciliation Barometer', an ongoing public opinion survey which endeavors to track and measure South African attitudes towards national reconciliation.

The most visible and powerful of these new transitional justice and reconciliation centers is, however, based in the United States and it has an internationalized mandate. The International Center for Transitional Justice (ICTJ) was established in 2001 in New York and opened a second unit in Cape Town in 2004. The ICTJ features some of the most prominent reconciliation experts on its Board of Directors, including Boraine and Jose Zalaquet, former head of Chile's Truth and Reconciliation Commission.[2] The ICTJ was founded to 'promote justice, peace, and reconciliation'[3] and boasts a 'diverse and specialized global team' dedicated to shaping transitional justice policy by conducting seminars for senior national and international policymakers, and to producing new research on transitional justice and reconciliation including legal and policy analyses and strategic research for justice and truth-seeking institutions, non-governmental organizations and governments.

Such institutions, and reconciliation research and practice more generally, receive substantial financial backing from well-endowed philanthropic foundations. Reconciliation as a national political project, object of foreign policy and as a subject of academic enquiry now generates attractive fellowships and internships, and is a magnet for the funds of bodies such as the Carnegie Endowment for International Peace and the Ford and Rockefeller Foundations. In addition, its consolidation as an interdisciplinary intellectual field of enquiry has been marked most recently by the birth of a new academic journal, the *International Journal of Transitional Justice* in the Spring of 2007, which claims that transitional justice is 'an academic discipline' in its own right, a claim that, although erroneous, is indicative of the power and reach of this relatively new idea and set of practices.

The story told here about the emergence of reconciliation as a new transitional norm does not, of course, trace its genesis to South Africa alone. Its contemporary appearance began, roughly, in the early 1980s when the process of acknowledging and accounting for state crimes became especially relevant in the context of three sets of historical and geo-political changes.[4] First, it was intrinsic to a number of transitions from military regimes in Africa and Latin America; second, to the disintegration of the Soviet Union and the concomitant collapse of communist regimes in Eastern Europe; and third to the demise of apartheid in South Africa. The influence of the end of the Cold War and the bipolar order that it involved is implicated, to a greater or lesser degree, in all three contexts. The specific transitional contexts within which the question of dealing with the past has arisen have been twofold: first, in transitions from various forms of military regimes and dictatorships to more democratic orders; and second in transitions from civil conflict to peace. Aside from the geo-political contexts within which reconciliation politics has played out, it is also a mark of the increasing significance of international human rights regimes that the question of 'dealing with the past', of establishing the truth about, and accounting for past horror, has today become so crucial a feature of the governance of these particular transitional moments. The truth commission has become the most important institutional location of reconciliation since the early 1980s, and in particular over the last decade, and its rise since South Africa's TRC is nothing short of remarkable. In a prescient article in 1994 Priscilla Hayner wrote about fifteen truth commissions in Uganda, Bolivia, Uruguay, Zimbabwe, The Phillipines, Chad, Southern Africa, Germany, Rwanda and Ethiopia. She constructed and articulated the moral, political and practical parameters of this new truth commission phenomenon, a phenomenon that had been mostly clearly defined by three important early cases in Argentina (1983), Chile (1990) and El Salvador (1992) (Hayner, 1994). Hayner's research simultaneously contributed to the appearance of this new political phenomenon *as* a phenomenon which, as one of the key figures on the research team of the ICTJ, now heading up its International Policymakers Unit, she was later to play an important role in proliferating and lending to it a particular normative force. Since the mid-1990s when Hayner was writing and the South African TRC began its work, the number of truth commissions in existence has more than doubled. In the wake of South Africa's TRC, and modeled upon it, many new truth commissions were set up to investigate past atrocities including, amongst others, Guatemala (1996), Ecuador (1996), Sierra Leone (2000), Peru (2000), South Korea (2000), Uruguay (2000), Ghana (2001), Timor Leste (2002), Serbia and Montenegro (2002), Morocco (2004) and Liberia (2006), whilst at the time of writing, another truth process is in the process of being constituted in the Democratic Republic of the Congo. In many of these cases, the ICTJ has provided resources, expertise advice, technical assistance and funding to local actors and government agents to facilitate the setting up of these commissions and to develop the mechanisms and principles that would best 'produce' or facilitate reconciliation in each case.

The politics of reconciliation that have been instituted in these contexts have emerged primarily out of compromises between, on the one hand, old and new regimes, and on the other, parties to conflict. In these contexts reconciliation is pitched between and attempts to answer to what are frequently understood to be roughly incompatible, indeed conflictual, imperatives: the 'moral demands of justice', on the one hand, and the 'political demands of peace' on the other. These imperatives are understood to be in tension with one another precisely because the former (justice) requires the punishment of perpetrators, and the latter (the politics of peace) requires some form of amnesty in order to facilitate a transition from violent conflict. Reconciliation processes have attempted to mediate these objectives by deploying a truth commission to conduct enquiries into past violence, the investigations of which do not, ostensibly, threaten a fragile peace because they do not on the whole result in prosecutions. Truth commissions, typically, investigate past atrocity by soliciting testimonies from victims and offering amnesties to perpetrators.[5] They present a prime institutional site, in Stan Cohen's words, 'for the symbolic recognition of what is already known but was officially denied' (Cohen, 2001: 13). Truth commissions are concerned expressly with revealing 'the truth' about past atrocity, a truth that had long been denied, concealed or repressed. Overcoming the painful legacies of violent state repression at the collective level entails diverse and multiple strategies that that are, at least initially, supposed to be traumatic before they are finally 'liberating'. Disinterring repressed truths about past violence frequently entails opening up graves to assert that yes, against the official record a massacre did happen, and yes, here are the bodies of those who had 'simply disappeared'. These strategies are crucial first steps in the process of acknowledging what had been denied all along, setting the record straight and 'freeing' individuals and nations from the terrors traumatic legacies of the past.

Truth-telling and amnesty are often cast by their proponents as having restorative objectives, as being directed towards reconciling old enemies and reinstating the nation-state as the central moral and political community. But they are problematic insofar as such practices have been a repudiation of 'justice as we know it' and have come to represent a 'justice compromised', although a justice that has necessarily been compromised for pragmatic reasons. It has now become a truism that something must be sacrificed in the process of seeking justice during political transition if democracy is to be forthcoming. This sacrifice is retributive justice, which is frequently subordinated to the broader objective of establishing political order. The memory of past atrocity, and the type of justice that accompanies it, are thus hitched to the evolution of a democratic polity, eventually becoming a footnote to a future more democratic order.

Transitional recollections of past atrocity have, at particular points in its history, especially in the Latin American context, gone under the injunction *Nunca Mas!* ('never again'), indicating that, whilst retrospective, memory work is oriented ethically towards the future prevention of the conditions under which gross violations might come to be perpetrated, yet again. Thus memory is charged with a preventive mandate in which the past is seen as a repository of recoverable lessons by which the future might be guided.[6] The purported value of collective retrospection lies in the assumption that humanity might learn from its mistakes and make positive attempts to prevent the repetition of conditions giving rise to the perpetration of atrocities in the first place. On this account, the past is endowed with a moral gravity which demands a response in the present.

Narrating Reconciliation in South Africa

Any analysis of the evolution of the reconciliation industry and the norms and assumptions that it has generated demands, as a starting point, a critical and theoretically rich engagement with the South African case. The most central of these assumptions, include the following: that truth leads to reconciliation, that truth heals, that there can be no reconciliation without an account of past atrocity and that amnesty best furthers reconciliation because retributive justice disturbs rather than promotes it, and potentially threatens a return to violence.[7] How, this book asks, are these assumptions made to appear to be self-evident? Why, for example, is it now widely assumed that revelations about past atrocity in the present will lead to some form of reconciliation in the future? Could there not, instead, be a causal and linear relationship between truth-telling and calls for justice or resurgent violence because truth may, rather than serve reconciliation, be inflammatory?

Whilst powerful, the truth claims generated by the TRC in particular and the wider industry in general are anything but evident in political practice, and important cases challenge and contradict them, as John Borneman has pointed out in his analysis of retributive justice in Eastern Europe (Borneman, 1997). The present book is concerned, primarily, with showing how these truth claims came into being with such force, and it does this by putting forward a discourse analysis of the South African case. Specifically, it demonstrates how the relationship between three distinct constituents of reconciliation—past atrocity, present truth-telling and future reconciliation—were constructed, indeed narrated, by the TRC as existing in a causal, linear, and inevitable relationship with one another.

The book reflects upon the uniquely constructed and constraining function of reconciliation by putting forward a distinctive theoretical account that differs from prevalent approaches because, first, it shows how reconciliation is constructed and not inherent—that is to say that it is grounded in particular social, political and historical conditions and emerges at particular junctures in time—and second, it demonstrates the various ways in which reconciliation is a thoroughly *political* practice rather than a purely moral or normative one because it is put in the service of new power elites with the primary purpose of underpinning state-making and political legitimacy by such new regimes.

The kind of analysis advanced here is necessary because it makes evident the relationship between reconciliation and power, between governance and the construction of new national subjects, unities and political discourses. This kind of investigation is also necessary in order that we might understand how reconciliation has acquired such a high degree of political purchase and epistemic power, and why it has been so rapidly reproduced in diverse political contexts. Despite the fact that much analysis has been generated of the TRC in particular and of reconciliation more broadly, there is still a paucity of *theoretical insight* into its workings, and much of the work already done is premised on a limited understanding of precisely how *political* reconciliation is. This lack is filled out by the insights and critical claims made in this book, which are adumbrated by a discourse analytic account.

This book takes as its starting point the idea that reconciliation is a story or narrative about transition that legitimizes, in the South African context as well as others, certain political decisions (such as amnesty) and proscribes others (such as punishment), and brings into being particular protagonists (or subjects and agents, namely 'victims' and 'perpetrators') as central to that story. This story, by definition, attempts to unify disparate and, sometimes, conflicting social, political and individual perspectives on the past, and this book investigates the particular ways in which this unity is constructed, with a special focus on how political transition is narrated with the effect of producing the nation as its central subject, a subject that evolves *as if* in a linear and developmental trajectory from past violence to future reconciliation, and each stage of this process—truth-telling, confession, remorse, forgiveness, healing and reconciliation—*is made to appear* as if each were the natural and inevitable consequence of the stage or process preceding it. That is to say, for example, that forgiveness is the inevitable outcome of truth, that trauma *will* be laid to rest and healing occur as a consequence of making testimonial, and that reconciliation *will* follow confession. Whilst this book shows how this reconciliation narrative is sometimes contested, a point it explores in particular in the concluding chapter, its primary aim is to illuminate the workings of the formal story, and to demonstrate how the TRC attempted to produce a unifying narrative that endeavored to transcend the divisions of the past and provide a new template script upon which divergent accounts of South Africa's history might be made commensurate.

At this juncture, I should point out the distinction between, firstly, a *narrative approach* towards understanding political process, an approach that this book takes, and secondly, the *role of narrative* in the transformation, construction and maintenance of political meaning in practice, which is the object of analysis of this book. To take the first of these points, this book looks at the way in which the TRC story wove what it took to be the relevant elements of South Africa's past, present, and projected future, into a particular relationship that was organized towards securing a reconciliatory outcome, or closure. By recourse to narrative theory, this books shows how narrative form orders the events it relates in a particular way, an order that is intrinsic to its internal structure. Narrative mode places constraints on meaning and drives towards coherence and homogeneity. This book shows how narrative, with particular reference to the TRC's reconciliation story, as a discursive form is ideological and closure orientated, producing self-disciplining social subjects who introject archetypal plots and act accordingly, imagining themselves as actors situated within given master plots (White 1973, 1978 and 1987). However this drive to closure and homogeneity is in conflict with a second narrative aspect of the TRC. The TRC's approach to truth was thoroughly predicated upon *different* stories or accounts of apartheid violence and opposition to it, from victims and perpetrators of that violence, and had, simultaneously a pluralizing thrust because it invites thousands of perspectives on the past, not all of which, inevitably, concorded with the overall story about reconciliation that the TRC sought to tell.

The TRC held in tension these two apparently opposing perspectives on narrative—that narrative is closure-oriented on the one hand, but that it is also plural and open because there is never a single story about the past that can be told—because these views are reflected in its seemingly contradictory processes. A narrative approach tells us much about the work of the Commission, that it has both an ideologizing and homogenizing function but that there is also something inherently open-ended about its recognition that there are, ultimately, different stories to tell about the past. This contradiction, as I see it, arises out of a tension between the homogenizing *discourse* of national unity and reconciliation, on the one hand, and the pluralizing *process* of the TRC on the other. A unitary version of the past was held in tension with multiple perspectives on that past. The TRC produced a struggle around the meaning(s) of reconciliation by virtue of this tension between rhetoric and procedure.[8]

The Argument

An understanding of narrative structure is necessary in order to flesh out the question central to this book: how did the TRC narrate reconciliation? First, it narrated a *past* conditioned by political violence perpetrated by the state and its agents, and those in opposition to the state. It then narrated the *present* as a 'confessional' story through which the truth about this violent past would emerge out of victim testimonials which contained the 'truth of suffering', and remorseful perpetrator accounts. This present narrative also worked to construct and compel the protagonists of South Africa's violent history as either 'victim' or 'perpetrator'. The confessional story aimed to lay the foundations for a future story about reconciliation and national unity, where a nation 'made sick by lies', as Michael Ignatieff put it, would be made well again (Ignatieff, 1996). The third and final dimension of this story deployed religious and therapeutic narratives, directed towards a *future* condition of reconciliation which the TRC sought to establish. As such, reconciliation as the immanent closure of the TRC story worked itself back into the unfolding events to organize the way in which the events of the past are related within the individual testimonies. Calls for reconciliation, confessions of wrong-doing and offers of forgiveness, are all articulations of reconciliation as closure, which had the material effect, crucially, of closing off the possibility of a retributive response to past atrocity.

Chapter one is a scene-setting chapter and it contextualizes the emergence of the TRC. It does so by discussing the various narratives, international and national, which coalesced to inform South Africa's transition from apartheid, and which converged to produce reconciliation as the key metaphor governing its transition. The purpose of this chapter is to show how the institution of reconciliation as transitional discourse was contingent and not given. At the international level, I look first at the distinction between, and debates about, retributive and restorative approaches to dealing with past atrocity, and at their material institutionalization. Retributive approaches to crimes against humanity have usually been the preserve of international justice, and have found their institutional expression in the war crimes tribunals of Nuremberg and Tokyo, and, more recently, in the International Tribunals for the former Yugoslavia (ICTY) and Rwanda (ICTR). This trend reached its apotheosis with the inauguration of the International Criminal Court (ICC) in 2002, a permanent body set up to deal with the crimes of genocide, war crimes, and crimes against humanity committed on or after July 2002. By contrast with retributive approaches to atrocity and their institutionalization, truth commissions have adopted what has been described as a more restorative approach to past horrors and have emphasized amnesties over punishment, but have supplemented a focus on perpetrators with an attempt to recognize the experiences of victims. Where for war crimes tribunals, the perpetrators of past atrocity are the key protagonists, truth commissions attempt to focus upon the suffering of victims and bring them to visibility as a strategy of restorative justice. In addition, where war crimes tribunals have normally been underpinned by international institutions, truth commissions are primarily an instrument of the state and work under its aegis.

This chapter moves on to evaluate the certain social, political, and historical dimensions of South Africa that conditioned the emergence of the TRC. It begins by enquiring into the background to the political negotiations at which the National Party insisted, and the ANC agreed, that there would be no punitive response to the crimes of the former regime. I examine how human rights discourse in the peace process both conditioned, but became subordinate to, the post-apartheid nation-building imperative and process. I then move on to present an account of the importance of reconciliation as a politico-theological discourse in South Africa from the mid-1980s onwards by examining the *Kairos Document*, which contained a statement about a 'just' reconciliatory response to the perpetrators of apartheid violence, and from which the TRC later departed in significant ways with its own distinctive version of reconciliation (Kairos Theologians, 1985). Following on from this, I incorporate a discussion of how the TRC deployed alternative cultural terms to reconciliation in order to legitimize and condone it, with the effect of constructing reconciliation as something 'authentically African'. The key term here is *ubuntu*, the Xhosa idea which was used by the TRC to be roughly commensurate with the term reconciliation. This part of the analysis demonstrates how reconciliation, legitimized by the stated imperative to 'unify' the nation, rather than to exact retribution and risk alienating the white minority, came to govern the spirit and processes of transition in South Africa. The point of drawing attention to the political and historical conditions under which reconciliation appeared is to elucidate the contingency of the emergence of reconciliation as a particular political 'truth' at this point in South Africa's history.

Chapter two sets out the discourse analytic framework within which is situated the broader argument in this book about how reconciliation is narrated. It presents an account of the work of Michel Foucault and Louis Althusser on truth, power, the state and subjectivity, and shows how these perspectives illuminate a political understanding of the work of the TRC (Althusser, 1993; Foucault, 1972, 1973 and 1977). In particular, the chapter demonstrates how the TRC constructed and called into existence the subjects (victims and perpetrators) and objects (gross violations of human rights such as torture and extra-judicial killings) of its enquiry, which, combined, furnish the particular truth claims central to reconciliation. My aim here is to show how these categories were actually brought into being by the Commission itself, rather than being categories that pre-existed its inauguration and investigations, and to elucidate my general purpose which is to situate the TRC as a key historical moment in the emergence of reconciliation, and to account for the ways in which reconciliatory truths emerging from South Africa have become powerful and binding internationally.

The second part of chapter two adds to the political discourse analytic account a *narrative* account of reconciliation, and draws upon the work of Hayden White and Frank Kermode in order to show how a consideration of narrative *form* is crucial to our understanding of reconciliation as closure (Kermode, 2000; White, 1973, 1978 and 1987). A narrative analysis provides special insights because the TRC constituted a specific act of narration of the political history of South Africa, and sought to close off its violent past and inaugurate a new post-apartheid political beginning. White and Kermode help to demonstrate that that reconciliation has a particular narrative performance that is structured by the internal 'dynamic unity' of narrative itself. The theoretical insights developed in this chapter permit an investigation of the technologies by which reconciliation is made to appear as if it were an inevitable political process. Firstly, a discourse analysis confirms reconciliation as a politically constructed and complex discourse comprised of various declarations, practices and rituals—verbal and non-verbal—by taking in the official sites of articulation of its premises and principles including legal documentation, the declarations of officials and the official report ensuing from the TRC work. The chapter demonstrates how the investigatory practices of the TRC are powerfully productive. For example, the TRC 'truth-finding engine' is shown to yield a particular historical narrative, and the ritual of the confessional is the key public site through which the new political subjects of South Africa were constructed.[9] By concentrating upon the official texts, the production of victim and perpetrator truths, and their reproduction in the public sphere through the hearings, this analysis shows how these texts functioned to interpellate, enforce, and discipline the central subjects of the new South Africa.

Chapter three takes up the first part of the core argument of the book. It enquires into how the TRC narrated South Africa's violent *past* by interrogating the historical construction of political violence presented by the Commission's official documentation. In this chapter I show how the TRC Report situates the period of the past that the TRC was mandated to investigate from 1960 to 1994 within a historical horizon that reaches back through three centuries, a period it narrates as being marked overwhelmingly by violent oppression and conflict. The central political effect of this narrative is threefold. First, it renders an account of the genesis of the nation that is commensurate with the origins of apartheid. Second, it gives force to the reconciliatory contention that a restorative response to past violence is much more likely to settle and end violence, as opposed to a retributive response which might, so the claim goes, perpetuate violence. And third, it excludes a proper discussion of the period of so-called 'black on black' violence between, primarily, the Inkhatha Freedom Party (IFP) and African National Congress (ANC) in the early 1990s because this did not fit within the broader morality tale the TRC sought to tell about South Africa's past. This chapter delineates the technologies of reinforcement of this story, showing how this history is once narrated in the TRC Report, and then repeated in tabular format in order to emphasise the elements of the story that the TRC wants to highlight as relevant to its own investigations.

The chapter then discusses how this presiding narrative was brought to bear upon and frame the individual testimonies. I show how the core committees of the TRC, The Human Rights Violations and the Amnesty Committees solicited testimonies and discuss the process by which testimonies were 'captured' and broken down into a taxonomy of violations by the TRC data management system, Infocomm, in order to demonstrate the particular ways in which the TRC's narrative of reconciliation transformed and maintained meaning through emplotment. The TRC re-interpreted apartheid violence, its meaning and context, through the framework of human rights violations arising out of the political conflict of the past, which became the ordering principle of South Africa's new historical narrative. This narrative connected people, events and organizations by mapping out a network of relations between the three across a given period of time. The interpretation rendered in this chapter illuminates the way in which reconciliation sought unity within and between these diverse elements, making commensurate divergent perspectives on the past by constructing a universe of comprehensibility through which seemingly incommensurable views and experiences were mediated and synthesized. I show how the TRC reinterpreted the apartheid past and reformulated history anew in order to found a new political and moral order in South Africa by narrating apartheid violence, and violent resistance to the regime as the salient truth of South Africa's history, resulting in its chief indictment: that apartheid was a 'crime against humanity'.

Chapter four takes up the second key aspect of the production of reconciliation by exploring how the TRC, in reflecting upon its violent past, constructed a *present* conditioned by the confessional through which the 'sins' of the past were to be purged and a future reconciliation to be instantiated. The argument draws upon the work of Foucault on the confessional to investigate the TRC amnesty hearings which were the central technology through which the TRC sought to instill repentance and remorse in the confessing subject (Foucault, 1978). The public ceremonial of the amnesty hearings functioned in order to interpellate and discipline perpetrators and to constitute 'truth' as the object of the confessional. Further, the argument develops this point to show how victims were encouraged, in their exchanges with Commissioners, to forgive perpetrators who had confessed, and as such the confessional served to structure the script upon which victims also related their own accounts of suffering, since it was often incumbent upon the victim to offer forgiveness to a perpetrator in return for the confession and as a final absolution for the original harm.

Chapter five takes up the final part of the story to explore reconciliation as a political trope that is oriented towards the *future* constitution of community. It shows how reconciliation in South Africa was filled out by theological and therapeutic interpretations of the effects of atrocity and their amelioration, and in particular by the discourses of forgiveness and healing. The metaphors of national sickness and healing are currently some of the most under-explored discourses of reconciliation processes, and yet they underpin some of the most powerful assumptions made by reconciliation: on a therapeutic account, that truth-telling will provide catharsis and relief and that it will 'lay the past to rest', and on a theological account, that forgiveness will follow a confession and thus allow victims and perpetrators of past violence to co-exist.

The book concludes with a discussion of how the final TRC Report, presented to the South African nation in 2003, constitutes a cathartic 'book of confessions', documenting the creeds and catechisms that were foundational moral tenets of the new political order. It discussion how these have been taken up internationally on two main fronts: firstly in the multiplication of new truth recovery projects which take as their touchstone the South African experience, and secondly in the emergence of a new 'right to truth' which is finding its way into the United Nations' legal and moral lexicon. However, the conclusions also enquire into a simultaneous front of *contestation* of the terms and legacy of the TRC which has opened up on the domestic front in South Africa by looking at the *Khulumani* reparations case, the pursuit of which were deemed necessary by the TRC's largely unfulfilled promise of reparations to victims.

By combining the insights of discourse analytic and narrative approaches, this book facilitates two fundamental political insights. First, it shows how reconciliation *constrains* in that it constructs power relations and is productive of political processes. The TRC's narrative structuration of South Africa's past, present and future is implicated in this constraint by its rendering of past events, produced under the aegis of 'truth' and in the service of reconciliation. Second, this combination of approaches allows an understanding of those moments where narrative *fails* to constrain, where there is a discrepancy between those who conform and those who do not. These are moments that make apparent the way in which the TRC forces a unity between conflictual and disparate elements. The book argues that whilst there were, inevitably, important refusals to engage with the narrative of the Commission, the central norms of the TRC still provided the basis of opposition, and hence of connection, to its terms.

The incommensurability of accounts of past violence produced a clash of narratives with particular results. Early refusals to co-operate came from sometimes surprising quarters. Whilst the TRC was widely considered to be pro-ANC it encountered considerable difficulties in getting the ANC to co-operate with its investigations. Many ANC officials stated publicly that they considered that the TRC should be a forum for perpetrators from the former regime to give their accounts of the past in return for amnesty. The ANC, it argued, had already conducted investigations into the perpetration of abuses within its camps in Angola, Zambia, Tanzania and Uganda, which, it argued, should exempt its members from the TRC investigations. The ANC argued that the TRC would merely replicate rather than add anything to their previous findings. Tutu's response to this was to threaten to resign from the Commission in mid-1996 unless the ANC co-operated, after which the ANC distributed amnesty applications to its members and encouraged them to apply. An additional problem emerged later when the ANC finally made extensive submissions but made them collectively rather than individually, against the stipulated rules of the amnesty process. The ANC sought to claim collective responsibility for the actions of its armed wing, arguing that it had been fighting a just war of liberation. However, the principle of collective responsibility proposed by the ANC meant that there were fewer applications from its members, and hence fewer amnesties granted, than there were from, for example, the Freedom Front, the Pan African Congress (PAC), and even the extreme right Afrikaner Weerstandbeweging (AWB). However, the low numbers of applications from the ANC were matched by those from the other key political protagonists, the National Party (NP) and from members of state security forces.

Both de Klerk and P.W. Botha, former State President and long-standing Defense Minister, refused, and de Klerk continues to refuse, to accept full responsibility for the activities of the security forces. They claimed that abuses were 'transgressions' perpetrated by a few 'rotten apples' rather than having ensued from state policies designed to eliminate systematically opposition to the regime. They denied that orders were given, for example, to assassinate key opponents of apartheid and blamed the liberation movements for some of their own actions, notably, the planting of land mines across the country, and ANC 'necklacing' of alleged government informers in the townships. The South African Defense Force (SADF) also used deflective strategies in its submissions and concentrated on placing the blame for violations on ANC operations. However, important submissions from a few key individuals in the NP widened the debate and generated access to more information. The former South African Police Commissioner Johan van der Merwe, and former Minister of Defense Magnus Malan, claimed responsibility for those under their command and revealed information about security force covert operations.[10] However, de Klerk withdrew the NP from the TRC proceedings in May 1997 citing discrimination against the NP on the part of the TRC and threatened legal action. The IFP also argued that the Commission had turned into a political witch hunt against opponents of the ANC. Just before the Report was due to be formally presented to President Mandela in October 1998, both the ANC and de Klerk threatened legal action if the allegations made against them were not removed. The ANC were unsuccessful in their request but de Klerk's indictment is still omitted from the final version of the Report, what stands in its place is an ominous black box, speaking volumes in its silence.

Reconciliation in South Africa is by no means settled, but is continually haunted by its legal 'other', the specter of retribution. Retribution continually threatens the plausibility of the reconciliation narrative because it was constantly invoked as the transitional path that was being negated in favor of reconciliation and restorative justice. Whenever retribution was invoked by the TRC it was compared unfavorably with the more 'equitable', 'moderate', and 'rational' model of restorative justice, to the extent that retribution in South Africa has largely been discredited through its constant, and erroneous, invocation as being akin to vengeance. This argument has been emphasized in Richard Wilson's excellent anthropological study of the TRC. He documents the way in which reconciliation primarily served the needs of the political elites, noting that the impact of the TRC in the urban districts of Johannesburg was limited because popular notions of justice in the townships was thoroughly predicated on the principle of retribution which has, historically, attempted to maintain social order in the face of wider social alienation (Wilson, 2001: 188). The prevalence of popular justice was also indebted to the fact that black South Africans rarely took their complaints to the official courts and Wilson argues that continued high levels of urban violence are continuous with such well-established traditions of township justice, but have also been exacerbated by a culture of impunity generally perceived to have been one, deeply problematic, effect of the work of the TRC.

Reconciliation is under increasing threat in South Africa as thousands of victims still await reparations ten years after the TRC began its work. This outstanding issue has generated much criticism of the TRC, particularly as the restorative process granting reparations and rehabilitation to victims was cast as the key moral pillar structuring its mechanisms. Victims disappointed with the compensations process of the Reparations and Rehabilitation Committee of the TRC are already presenting a powerful disturbance of the moral order and quasi-legal norms that the politics of reconciliation has instituted and sought to settle. For example, in November 2002 two victim support groups, Khulumani and Jubilee South Africa, lodged a lawsuit in a federal court in New York on behalf of victims of state-sanctioned torture, murder, rape, arbitrary detention and inhumane treatment (*Khulumani, et. al. v. Barclays National Bank, et. al.* Case No. 02-CV5952, S.D.N.Y. 2002). The groups argue that the dozens of European, American and Asian corporations who collaborated in the murder, torture and forced labor of black South Africans during the apartheid years need to be brought to account and forced to make reparations to individuals. Banks, oil companies and IT manufacturers are put forward by the lawsuit as crucial agents of violence during the apartheid era because they sustained the regime with loans, goods and markets and thus supported the conditions under which apartheid was allowed to flourish.

The lawsuit represents a contestation of the TRC's presiding narrative which concentrated instead upon the political struggle between various parties and violations perpetrated in the context of the political struggle. By contrast, the lawsuit highlights yet another story about South Africa's past which implicates more forcefully than did the TRC the role of multinational corporations in sustaining the apartheid regime and exploiting its repressive order for their own profit through the use of cheap and forced labor. This story is elided by the TRC's investigations because it could not be integrated within the overall story about *party political violence* that the TRC argued was integral to South Africa's violent history. International corporations represent different moral agents, or protagonists, from those engaged more directly in political struggle and as such, the interests of these agents alter considerably the kind of historical narrative that might be written about South Africa. The Khulumani lawsuit reflected the necessity of seeking justice for those who were not the victims of party political violence, but of the daily injustices of apartheid. The lawsuit attracted much criticism from proponents of the TRC who argued that South Africa made a collective decision to close the past era of apartheid rather than turn it into a jackpot for ambulance-chasing lawyers, thus discrediting the demand for monetary reparations as 'immoral'. That the case was discredited by some political elites in South Africa is testimony to South Africa's fear of deterring foreign investment. Foreign investment, argued the justice minister Penuell Maduna, worked to benefit not just individual victims but the entire population (Carroll, 2002). However, South Africa is not alone amongst states coming to terms with violent pasts in failing to implicate international agents, political and corporate, in the perpetration of human rights abuses. These agents have been ignored by the vast majority of truth commissions and reconciliation processes to date in part because reconciliation is a nation-centered discourse which seeks primarily to reify the identity of the national community, and does not seek to apportion responsibility beyond its own territorial boundaries.

Reconciliation has emerged as a new transitional ideology which demands further and local critical enquiry into its political effects. In order locate and understand this ideology, what is needed in order that the debate about reconciliation might be furthered and deepened—instead of broad surveys and taxonomies—is a *specific* analysis of each invocation of reconciliation in which reconciliation is recognized as a particular narrative which emerges at the intersection between a plethora of international and national social and political imperatives and circumstances. Work on this area would need to take into account the specific ways in which reconciliation is informed, animated, understood and interpreted within the context and circumstances of its deployment and would need to develop theoretical frameworks that aim to elucidate and illuminate the particular, and political, workings of each case. The aim of this should, in part, be concerned with countering progressivist views on truth commissions which deem later commissions inherently more sophisticated than previous ones by virtue of 'lessons learned'. This progressivism is tenuous at best, and at worst elides the specificity of the politics of reconciliation, which generates local and particular meanings that are not merely replicated and 'improved upon' by each subsequent case. It is in this critical spirit that this book is written, and I hope that this work might be read as a contribution to a new mode of critique of, and debate about, this complex and intriguing recent political phenomenon.

Notes

1. For this IJR statement and others see http://www.ijr.org.za
2. Also sitting on the Board is Richard Goldstone former Justice, Constitutional Court of South Africa and chief prosecutor of the UN International Criminal Tribunals for the former Yugoslavia and Rwanda.
3. See http://www.ictj.org/en/about/mission/
4. Although reconciliation has achieved a particular and noteworthy power in the context of post-Cold War state-building, it is not an entirely new political discourse. Indeed, as Jon Elster argues, transitional justice practices have a much longer and richer historical heritage than current analyses allow, going back as far as classical Greece and the English and French restorations (Elster, 2004).
5. There are multiple ways in which amnesty has been used to promote reconciliation and any enquiry should evaluated within the specific context in which the amnesty was instituted, and heed taken of the particular form it took, whether individual, blanket, in exchange for truth as in the case of South Africa, issued prior to the commission in

question as in Chile, or as a response to the findings of the report as was the case in El Salvador.

6.   The alleged relationship between remembering and prevention is one that, whilst widely assumed and promoted, has not been established empirically, as David Mendeloff argues (Mendeloff, 2004). However, whilst Mendeloff's criticisms are important, it is difficult to imagine how a strict and causal relationship between the two might be established empirically. It is perhaps enough to suggest at this point that this is an underexplored assumption that is foundational of much of the work of truth commissions.

7.   This latter assumption about the relationship between retributive justice and resurgent violence has received special interest in light of Saddam Hussein's execution for crimes against humanity.

8.   The text of the Report itself, however, does not present a completely synthetic narrative account. It appears as a patchwork of different narratives, from historical overviews to legal discussions and individual testimonies, and seems to lack an overarching narrative dynamic within which all the disparate elements are unified. However, I argue that it is the concept of reconciliation, underpinned by its attendant precursor, truth, which provides a unifying force that *attempts* to bring together and make sense of the disparate elements in relation to one another. These concepts were iterated and reiterated in various sites including official declarations, the legislation founding the TRC, the public amnesty and human rights violations hearings and the Report.

9.   The metaphor of a 'truth-finding engine' is coined by Michael Lynch and David Bogen in their discussion of the Iran-Contra hearings (Lynch and Bogen, 1996).

10. The only other security minister other than Malan who sought amnesty was Adriaan Vlok, former Minister of Law and Order who has, controversially, since been put on trial for his role in the attempted murder in 1989 of the then secretary-general of the South African Council of Churches, Reverend Frank Chikane. The trial took place in August 2007 and Vlok was given a suspended prison sentence.

Chapter One
Dealing With Past Atrocity: The TRC in Context

You think that just because it's already happened, the past is unfinished and unchangeable? Oh, no, the past is cloaked in multicolored taffeta and every time we look at it we see a different hue.

> Milan Kundera, *The Book of Laughter and Forgetting* (Harmondsworth: Penguin, 1983).

The increasing force of the discourse of 'dealing with the past' has been evidenced by its appearance in a more unusual site. In Piedrafita de Babia, a village in the mountains of Leon in the north of Spain, a mass grave containing the secrets of Spain's civil war was disinterred in July 2002. Sixty-five years after the gruesome event took place in 1937, relatives of the dead gathered to witness the removal of the skeletons of fourteen men. Their skulls bore jagged pistol holes at the back, the trace of summary execution. These disinterrals represent one important way in which the secretly buried and 'forgotten' details of the violent Falangist campaign against Republican opposition are finally coming to light, twenty-eight years after Franco's death (Tremlett, 2002).

These events are surprising because post-Franco Spain, notably, has been conditioned by a deliberate and continuous 'politics of forgetting' the events of the civil war, a forgetting that has been widely regarded as a successful political coup. Limited by a political 'pact of oblivion', the governance of Spain's transition to democracy was defined by a selective amnesia. This amnesia entailed several decisions on the part of the government which included the refusal to conduct purges or trials, the avoidance of public references to Franco and the destruction of memorials venerating his memory. Of those pro-Franco memorials that remained, memorial counterpoints were erected to challenge the old history. The period of the civil war was officially re-narrated as Spain's 'tragedy', a story that displaced the predominant Francoist account that had privileged Falangist forces by narrating theirs as a victory of 'right' over 'wrong', of 'good' over 'evil'. The purpose of this post-Franco political forgetting was to found a new political legitimacy that appealed to a democratic future *without* first engaging with the problems of the past (Rigby, 2001: 39–61).

This political forgetting represents a strange incongruity with the contemporary proclivity for disinterring the past. Spain's tentative first steps towards recovering it's 'lost history', placing it on public record, restoring the names of the victims and their families, and ultimately permitting a public discourse around the concealed details of the Spanish civil war, are not as yet being undertaken by the government but by a group of relatives of the deceased, assisted by a team of international volunteers.[1] Indeed, in an inversion of the conventional colonial relationship and as a consequence of Latin America's own efforts to scrutinize the past, Spain drew upon the expertise of forensic anthropologists from Guatemala, practised in unearthing the awful excesses of their own political past, to unearth and interpret anew Spain's buried history.

That this process is taking place in Spain at all, and indeed right now, is yet another indication of the power of international narratives about dealing with past atrocity, and it is within the horizon of their rise that I provide an account here of the imperative of reconciliation that conditioned South Africa's own process of accounting for its past. I locate the institution of South Africa's Truth and Reconciliation Commission as an effect of transitional narratives about human rights framed by the tropes of 'reconciliation', 'restoration', and 'healing', then operative (albeit tentatively) within international and national spheres, which the TRC in turn consecrated and reinforced. In tracing out the different narratives leading to the inception of the TRC, I seek to locate its genesis at the intersection between both global and local narratives. In so doing, this chapter looks first at governing international narratives of transition, second at national narratives, and finally at the way in which these converged to condition the remit, institutional structure, narrative parameters, and guiding concepts of the TRC itself.

Presiding International Narratives

Retribution and restoration were the two authoritative legal narratives that came to govern the contemporary predilection for dealing with the past. Around the time of the inauguration of South Africa's Truth and Reconciliation Commission, debates about addressing past human rights violations frequently turned upon the construction of a sharp dichotomy between retributive and restorative (to which reconciliation was, then, alleged to be akin) styles of justice, and their relative merits in establishing new politico-moral orders. Retribution and restoration answer differently to the question of how to acknowledge present suffering incurred by past human rights violations. Where retribution is, broadly, directed towards punishing perpetrators, restorative or reconciliatory justice attempts instead to compensate victims for spiritual and material losses whilst simultaneously rehabilitating perpetrators through the use of amnesty, and 're-humanising' them via the confessional mode of self-disclosure.

Broadly speaking, retribution narratives have found their institutional expression in criminal tribunals which have concentrated on punishing the perpetrators of gross violations of human rights, and reconciliation narratives have come to be embedded in truth commissions, bodies which have concentrated on acknowledging victim suffering. Both are vehicles through which previously repressed information about human rights violations is brought to light, and redress, whether punitive or compensatory, exacted. Criminal tribunals and truth commissions are both institutional locations of international discourses on human rights, and represent the sites of materialization of a meta human rights narrative of 'progress' that today is one of the key drivers of political transitions and democratization processes. However, the establishment of information about past human rights violations have frequently been primarily instrumental to state legitimacy rather than being fundamental priorities in their own right, and has entailed 'sacrificing justice for truth' (Gutmann and Thompson, 2000: 22), and refuting the moral and legal 'duty to prosecute' (Orentlicher, 1991) established by the Nuremberg precedent. The dichotomized debate around the relative merits of retributive and restorative styles of justice prevalent at the time of South Africa's TRC, and indeed compounded by it's own political circumstances and justificatory discourses, contributed to an entirely dualised way of thinking about issues central to transition: peace vs justice, restoration vs retribution and the privileging of national political order over international legal imperatives. These dualisms thoroughly informed the appearance of the truth process in South Africa and have proven to be particularly resilient in spite of more recent combined approaches—mixing the retributive with the restorative—to dealing with the past (Teitel, 2003).

Retribution

Recent years have witnessed an increased and reinvigorated relationship between human rights (where the perpetration of atrocities is concerned) and the rule of law. This relationship was initiated and has been further consolidated by the establishment of a number of mainly ad hoc international criminal tribunals. From the Nuremberg and Tokyo trials some fifty years ago to the contemporary International Criminal Tribunals for the former-Yugoslavia (ICTY) and Rwanda (ICTR), the issues of asserting human rights through the rule of law, and specifically through the mechanism of retributive justice, have been concomitant. Retributive justice is predicated on ascertaining individual moral responsibility for violations in order to bring those responsible to legal account.

A further development of this deepening relationship between human rights and the international legal order has seen the relatively recent ratification of the International Criminal Court (ICC) in 2002, mandated to try individuals for the crime of genocide, crimes against humanity such as enslavement, deportation, torture, murder and rape and war crimes. The narrative of accountability for past violations of human rights now extends its remit to heads of state, with varying effects, but these are agents for whom indemnity was previously the rule. A landmark case brought by Spanish citizens in December 2000 charged Augusto Pinochet with responsibility for human rights violations during his rule in Chile. In the Spring of 2002 in Belgium, another case was brought by a group of Palestinians against Israel's current leader, Ariel Sharon, who was charged with genocide with respect to the Sabra and Shatila Palestinian refugee camp massacres in Lebanon 1982. The case was unsuccessful, ruling immunity in the case of a sitting prime minister. Most recently in July 2002, an Argentinian judge issued an arrest warrant for Argentina's ex-president, Leopoldo Galtieri, for human rights violations perpetrated by his regime between 1982–1983.

These examples have followed on from a growing imperative for knowledge about human rights violations to enter the public sphere, recognition and accountability to be established, and the punishment of those found to be directly guilty or indirectly implicated in the perpetration of abuses. Retributive mechanisms have interpreted these issues through the mandate of international human rights law, which maintains that those responsible for gross human rights violations must be brought before a court of law and held criminally accountable for their actions. This principle is enshrined within a corpus of international law which includes conventions on genocide and torture and which maintain that signatory governments must punish violators of the principles of the respective conventions.[2] Additionally, the Universal Declaration of Human Rights and the International Covenant on Civil and Political Rights both constitute the rights of victims of crimes as deserving of effective redress in the form of punishment.

Such post-1945 developments have firmly placed retributive justice on the map of political transitions from conflict to peace. Along with establishing accountability, retribution carries with it the moral mandate of deterring criminality, and preventing a repetition of violations in the future. The necessity of retributive measures is insisted on by some, such as John Borneman in his research on post-communist Eastern Europe (Borneman, 1997). Borneman asserts that 'a successful reckoning with the criminal past obligates the state to seek retributive justice and that a failure to pursue retributive justice will likely lead to cycles of retributive violence' (Borneman, 1997: 6). However, that retributive measures are central to effective transitional justice is an assumption that was thrown into question by the vogue for reconciliation, which suggests, by contrast, that punishment is in fact more likely to promote vengeance and further cycles of violence, than to aid in their cessation.

Reconciliation

In parallel with this internationally invigorated retributive narrative, however, a concurrent master narrative of the late twentieth century emerged. A new 'romance with remorse and with reparation, memory and healing—of the individual and the social body' (Scheper-Hughes, 1998: 26) powerfully repudiated the retributive imperative and was conditioned by the ideal of reconciliation which was frequently set by its proponents in opposition to the punitive demands of retribution.

One manifestation of this narrative has been a flourishing of the political apology, which has inserted itself with some force into the scene of transitional justice in particular, and into recent political life more generally. This 'politics of regret' (Olick and Coughlin, 2003: 37–62) has been widely pervasive, going beyond the particular transitions from conflict, as seen in El Salvador, Guatemala and Sierra Leone, or the democratization processes of Argentina and Chile, instead lodging itself within a broad range of reflective junctures and reparatory gestures in the life of the nation that have been designated to deal with 'historical injustice', frequently towards indigenous populations such as in the U.S., Canada and Australia. The apology has been utilized as an atonement strategy by states seeking to make amends for repressive policies or atrocities of the past, addressing a range of issues including slavery, war crimes and the legacies of colonial rule. Japan and the U.S. have been among the most prolific issuers of apologies for past wrongs, although these apologies often have been issued in restricted ways that either deflect complete responsibility or obviate any material consequences that might flow from such an apology, namely, actual and meaningful (for the victims, and where requested) *financial* reparations. Japan has made official although limited apologies for wartime atrocities in Nanking, to the (inappropriately named) Korean 'comfort women', and in October 1998 the Japanese Prime Minister Keizo Obuchi issued a written apology to President Kim Dae Jung for abuses perpetrated during Japan's thirty-five-year occupation of South Korea. The U.S. under Bill Clinton offered apologies on a whole range of issues, national and international in dimension. In 1993 he endorsed an 'Apology Resolution' for the role of the U.S. in the overthrow of the Kingdom of Hawaii in 1893. In 1997 Clinton openly considered a public apology for slavery in what has become an ongoing and fiercely contested debate, although notably, his intervention appeared to some as an attempt to deflect calls for financial reparations for slavery—far more costly and committed than a verbal apology (Torpey, 2004). In the same year, Clinton apologized to the black male victims of the notorious forty-year Tuskegee Experiment in Alabama on the long-term effects of syphilis, between 1932 and 1972. In this experiment, medical researchers enrolled four hundred black, male, syphilis sufferers with the false promise of free health care and despite the treatability of the disease, the men received no medication to prevent its deleterious effects. Elsewhere, France's Jacques Chirac apologized in 1995 for the French role in the persecution of Jews under German occupation; Britain's Tony Blair in 1997 for the English role in the Irish potato famine; and in 2000 Australia's John Howard apologized for the decimation of the Aboriginal population. Australia even has a state sanctioned 'Sorry Day' to consecrate state remorse for federal policies that separated forcibly Aboriginal children from their families. Most recently in Northern Ireland, the IRA issued an unprecedented apology to the families of non-combatants who were killed during thirty years of violence (Cowan and Watt, 2002). Examples of apologies in transitional justice include South African F. W. de Klerk's 1993 apology for apartheid; former Guatemalan President Álvaro Arzú in 1998 for atrocities perpetrated against indigenous Guatemalan citizens during the country's thirty-six-year civil war; and former Chilean President Patricio Aylwin's apology to the victims of the Pinochet regime in 1991 on presentation of Chile's Truth and Reconciliation Commission's final report to the nation.

In light of these and other episodes, it has been suggested that the end of the last century is memorable precisely for what the Nigerian writer Wole Soyinka has called a *fin de siecle* 'fever of atonement' (Soyinka, 1999: 90). A wave of public contrition has accompanied national attempts to acknowledge and emerge from the legacies of past injustice, to which these numerous examples attest, and this has contributed to the appearance of new national narratives of healing the individual and social body. The public theatricality of the apology lends dramatic force to this particular narrative. Roy Brooks, who has investigated this apologetic proclivity in some detail, argues that political apologies are much more complex than the mere 'canonization of sentimentality'. For Brooks, public displays of accountability and remorse have a profound impact upon society, improving the 'national spirit and health' and consequentially raising its 'moral threshold'. Roy Brooks argues that apologies make a crucial contribution towards establishing and acknowledging accountability for past wrongs, and most importantly, apologies create the possibility of a future free from repeated abuses (Brooks, 1999; 3-12). However, the apology is a highly contentious and problematic mode of redress for a number of reasons, and not least because its proliferation in recent political life has been widely lauded. Accounts like Brooks' lend credence, problematically, to a teleological account of the moral maturation of a Western political sensibility, of which the proliferation of political apologies is regarded to be clear and strong evidence.

Political apologies are one prominent technique of reckoning with past wrongs in order to constitute 'new moral orders'. This is an enterprise that has seen the emergence of truth commissions as prominent and complex formal mechanisms. To date, this propensity has been realized most forcibly by South Africa's TRC, which institutionalized and reified the politics of remorse to spectacular effect. But this apparent propensity for remorse and apology, both within national and international relations, has itself been articulated within the discursive horizon of human rights talk which demands accountability and recognition for past wrongs. Processes of democratization in Latin America from the mid-1980s and Eastern Europe from 1989, for example, were conditioned by imperative of human rights within which respect for human rights was constituted as the antidote to authoritarianism. Human rights discourses were materialized through human rights legislation pivotal to institutional transformation and the importance of establishing the rule of law in the wake of transition from authoritarianism.

Truth commissions have become a primary site through which remorse is publicly performed, and the political antecedents of South Africa's TRC, most notably in Latin America, lent authority to and legitimized the South African decision to favour a restorative approach over a retributive one for past crimes. It is important at this juncture, then, to situate the TRC as flowing from its histori-cal antecedents and to review the work of some of the previous commissions. This brief synopsis is not exhaustive, nor does it intend to give the impression that there have been no other prior investigations which might well fall within the rubric of what is today understood by the term 'truth commission'. My aim here is to reflect what has been constituted by the predominant literature as the historical lineage and antecedents of the TRC, and, more importantly here, to chart the geo-political emergence and conditions of this narrative of reconcilia-tion as a governing story about transition.

Truth commissions have operated with a variety of mandates and effects in a diversity of political circumstances and contexts, from Uganda to the Philip-pines, Argentina, Chile, El Salvador and Guatemala. As I have already argued in the introduction to this book, Priscilla Hayner, in a seminal article, provided the first generic study of the 'truth commission' phenomenon with the effect of con-secrating the study of truth commissions as a particular research field (Hayner, 1994). Since the advent of the South African TRC, the term 'truth commission' is commonly used retrospectively to describe commissions of enquiry that were not necessarily at the time known as such. The constitution of a field demands an authoritative typology which Hayner duly provides, although I would depart from her analysis to urge caution about over-generalizing the relationship be-tween these various bodies which were instituted within and responsive to, widely varying social, political, historical, and cultural circumstances. Indeed, Hayner's research itself is constitutive of the increased interest in, and the domi-nation of the study of conflict resolution and transition by questions of restora-tive justice and reconciliation and it has played a key role in the production of (sometimes problematic) truth claims within the field.

Hayner's typology delineates four principle features common to truth com-missions. Firstly, they are investigatory bodies that focus on a strictly delimited period of the past. Secondly, they do not focus on a specific event, as do 'com-missions of enquiry' but attempt to portray a pattern of human rights abuses or violations of international humanitarian law over a pre-specified time period. Thirdly, commissions operate for a limited and pre-determined period of time, cease to exist with the submission of their findings, and are not instigated as a permanent body for the monitoring of continuing violations. And fourthly, they are vested with authority through its governmental sanction, or through sponsor-ship by an international organization such as the United Nations as in the case of El Salvador. Truth commissions have mainly been instigated during or immedi-ately after political transition either from one regime to the next, or in the wake of the settlement of civil conflict and investigations have most frequently been carried out by taking testimonies from victims, perpetrators and other relevant witnesses. Although in only a few of the cases was an amnesty law passed which explicitly prevented trials, prosecutions have not been part of the work of truth commissions to date only in the Bolivian and Argentinian cases were there trials resulting from the commission findings.

The earliest identified truth commission, according to Hayner, was set up in Uganda under the auspices of Idi Amin. The *Commission of Inquiry into the*

Disappearances of People In Uganda since 25 January 1971 investigated the practice of 'disappearances' by the military. The proceedings of the commission were public—an important feature that has characterized a number of African commissions although, notably, has been absent from many of the Latin American cases—and it succeeded in placing on historical record an official recognition of violations perpetrated by the military. In the early 1980s, the first Latin American commissions were instituted in Bolivia (1982) and Argentina (1983). The Bolivian commission worked immediately following change to a more democratic regime and was charged with investigating disappearances under the former regime.[3] The Argentinian Commission, the *Comision Nacional para la Desaparicion de Personas* was the first to receive significant international attention.[4] It is still widely considered to be one of the most important commissions alongside subsequent ones in Chile and South Africa. The commission was sponsored by President Alfonsin to investigate disappearances between 1976 to 1983 under the previous military regime and its investigations led to the publication of a famous report, *Nunca Mas* (Never Again). The pocket-sized report became a national best-selling book, its revelations reputedly forming the subject of 'everyday conversation' in bars, on beaches and in offices.[5] Subsequent to the work of the commission, a number of prosecutions of high-ranking military officers took place, and the effects of the work of the commission are still being felt today, with continued, although ad-hoc, investigations into allegations of abuse during the period of military rule.

That the Bolivian and Argentinian investigations focused on the practice of disappearance is reflective of the way in which this particular violation was broadly endemic in those contexts, although not exclusive to them. This is worth commenting upon because a later commission in Uruguay in 1985, following in the wake of the Bolivian and Argentinian commissions, was also mandated to deal with disappearances at the hands of the former military regime.[6] However, the resulting report documented few disappearances and excluded any investigation of torture and extra-judicial imprisonment, both of which were more common than disappearances in Uruguay. The effects of the commission were minimal due to the restricted and non-representative scope of its investigations. This was a clear exercise in political legitimation which sought to replicate the paradigm of previous investigations in other countries by way of demonstrating the willingness of the new order to 'do something' about Uruguay's violent past. However, the fact that the specific violations that were investigated were of marginal relevance to the previous regime, this was more an exercise in sanctioning the new regime rather than a serious attempt to address past state crimes. It did not represent a genuine attempt to redress and repair the wrongs of the past, a charge that has more recently been leveled against a commission instigated in Algeria in 2000. Such examples reflect negatively upon the burden of precedent where a truth commission may be instigated in order to signal a regime's willingness to deal with the past and develop a human rights culture without any genuine attempt to address the legacy of the specific context within which violations took place. Indeed, a truth commission is becoming an almost mandatory requirement of any state in transition. It is, as such, an instrument through which any democratizing state signals to the national and international community that it is incorporating human rights concerns into its political remit and on these grounds attempts to secure recognition and legitimization from outside as well as from within its borders.

Other commissions prior to the TRC included yet another in Uganda in 1986, but this time under the aegis of President Museveni who investigated violations under Milton Obote's regime.[7] And in the same year a Presidential Commission on Human Rights was established in the Philippines by Corazon Aquino to look into state crimes between 1972 and 1986 under the former military regime.[8]

However, it was not until the Chilean National Commission for Truth and Reconciliation, or Rettig Commission, began its work in 1990 that the narrative of 'truth and reconciliation' was explicitly invoked by such an investigation. This narrative framed the scope of the commission's investigations, precluding trials given that 'reconciliation' rather than 'retribution' was the central organizing trope. However, as happened later in South Africa, the discourse of reconciliation was mobilized in part to justify the Commission's inability to prosecute those it found guilty of violations, because it was constrained by and enduring military amnesty that had been instituted by Pinochet himself. Mandated to investigate human rights abuses resulting in death or disappearance during military rule under Pinochet between September 1973 and March 1990, the commission focused on abuses resulting in death or disappearance during this period. Upon presentation of the report to the public, President Aylwin apologized to the victims and families on behalf of the state and called upon the army to acknowledge its role in the perpetration of violations. Assassinations followed the submission of the report and its circulation was prevented for fear of further ramifications, but a Reconciliation and Compensation Corporation was set up to continue the work of the commission and to ensure reparations to victims. However, the commission had one clear shortcoming for which it was heavily criticized by international human rights organizations. It failed to investigate cases of abuse that did not result in death or disappearance, a limit which precluded living victims from having their complaints considered, and which, arguably, hindered the process of national reconciliation which the commission claimed to instigate and promote.

The Chilean commission provided perhaps the most important precedent to South Africa's TRC, influencing both its political discourse and also the scope of its investigations. But between Chile and South Africa, a number of other commissions began work in Chad, Honduras, Haiti, and El Salvador. These commissions primarily looked at violations perpetrated under a previous regime and limited the remit of their investigations to the former authorities and institutions. Rarely, and notably, did a commission investigate the role of international agents in the violations it uncovered. One exception is the commission held in Chad in 1991 which implicated the U.S., France, Iraq, and Egypt in the sponsorship of military training, and went further to prove that a U.S. advisor had worked closely with security personnel at a centre where political prisoners were regularly tortured and killed.

Transitional governments have aimed to address past atrocity through a variety of measures, most of which have been conditioned by local circumstances, as the example of Chile suggests. The implementation of one, another, or a combination of approaches are contingent on the political, historical, and cultural conditions of their inauguration. For example, lustrations or purges have been a common feature of transition in Eastern Europe following the collapse of communist regimes.[9] Aveizer Tucker attributes the Eastern European 'tendency' towards lustrations *not* to what has been described as a 'culture of vendetta' but to something intrinsically 'amnesiac' in post-communist societies where, in his view, traditions, historical identities, and memories were subordinated to a broadly unifying ideology (Tucker, 1999: 73). In similar vein, Vaclav Havel blamed the 'mechanization' of the individual under communist regimes for the absence or loss of individual moral accountability, a 'condition' which, arguably, militates against the alleged reflexivity of reconciliatory politics (Havel in Tucker, 1999: 67). More interestingly, Tucker criticizes the 'liberal saving messianism' of westerners keen on retroactive justice and the universal application of cultures of democratization and human rights as 'necessarily' appropriate to all conditions and contexts of transition. In Eastern European and other contexts, the individualization of guilt and the removal of those responsible for violations from office perhaps make more sense in redressing past wrongs than the wide-scale cathartic drama of confession, forgiveness, and atonement seen in South Africa.

Around the time of the appearance of South Africa's TRC, reconciliatory and retributive narratives were generally dichotomized in these contexts rather than them being simultaneously enacted, the institution of the one mode of justice often precluding the possibility of the other and decisions for one method pitched against the failings of the other. Reconciliation was predominantly understood as being outside and beyond retribution. Reconciliation and retribution seemed to exclude one another, and yet each is conditioned by the other, is made possible, indeed only makes sense through by the presence, or threat, of the other. The problems with such an exclusive conceptualization of justice were multiple. For example, must victims forgo material and spiritual reparations if retribution is the order of the day? And why cannot limited criminal trials further, rather than impede, reconciliation?

Whilst both retributive and reconciliatory narratives currently condition post-atrocity political change, political expressions of the 'need' for reconciliation appear preponderant. That this is the case is primarily indebted to a political imperative of nation-building where human rights talk has become the rubric of pragmatic political compromise rather than that of moral principle and individual accountability, as Wilson has argued (Wilson, 2001: 228). Political compromises have framed the terms within which a number of truth commissions have worked, many of which were instituted as part of political settlements between conflicting parties. Where truth commissions have been instituted as part of a political settlement, they have often been charged with the tasks of 'affirming human dignity' and preventing the repetition of violations rather than punishing perpetrators. As such, truth commissions, arguably, have dislocated human rights from the very legal mechanisms through which rights were previously materialized and enforced. Reconciliation narratives have thus, arguably, promoted the detachment of human rights from legality, and have become a general moral discourse that primarily underpins political legitimacy through an appeal to 'national unity' whilst conveying human rights as the paramount transitional concern. Within this schematic, nation-building was once presented as being compromised by retribution, which, as argued in South Africa, threatens to further divisions rather than forge national and political cohesion. As such in the case of South Africa's TRC, the organizing trope of reconciliation served to place human rights as subordinate to, or in the service of, national unity.

Presiding National Narratives

Whilst South Africa's TRC was conditioned by international discourses on human rights and the global proliferation of truth processes which pitched themselves between the debate about retribution and reconciliation, it simultaneously emerged out of a confluence of national narratives and political decisions. Primary amongst these were the narratives of human rights and nation-building that issued from, and were delimited by, the political negotiations and the establishment of an interim constitution in the early 1990s.

Background and Political Negotiations

As Richard Wilson has argued, it is important to look at the rise of human rights discourse in the peace process between 1985 and 1994 in order to understand how human rights became the face of, and simultaneously subordinate to, nation-building in South Africa. According to Wilson, it was during this period that the discourse of rights provided the language that provided the basis of later agreement between the main parties to the conflict, the ruling National Party and the African National Congress. As Wilson notes, human rights, problematically, provided the 'language not of principle but of pragmatic compromise, seemingly able to incorporate any moral or ideological position'. Human rights discourses circumvented issues of race and ethnicity which had been central to apartheid reasoning and 'came to be seen less as the language of incorruptible principles and more as a rhetorical expression of an all-inclusive rainbow nationalism' (Wilson, 2001: 5). This shift to a broadly unifying rhetoric of human rights was conditioned by changes in the conflict, compounded by international pressure on the apartheid regime, towards the end of the 1980s, making a shift towards negotiations possible. The armed conflict had reached a stalemate in which a clear victory of one key party over another was unlikely and the NP took a different line on its stated ideological commitment to 'eradicating Communism', a shift which took place in the context of such international changes as the withdrawal of Soviet-backed Cuban troops from Angola and the fall of the Berlin Wall.

During the 1990s South Africa was transformed from white minority rule to a multi-racial democracy. President F. W de Klerk unbanned the ANC, Pan African Congress (PAC), and the South African Communist Party (SACP) in February 1990 in order for multi-party negotiations to proceed. Nelson Mandela was released from prison and indemnity was granted to formerly exiled ANC members so that they could return to South Africa to participate in the process. Resistance movements formally changed their commitment to violent opposition to the regime, and the National Party finally agreed to the idea of a constituent assembly. The unbanning of the parties, the suspension of armed struggle, and continued and intense international pressure for a political solution were key factors in precipitating political negotiations. According to Mary Burton, commissioner to the TRC, 'that was the moment of public recognition by the rulers of the time that the system of apartheid could no longer withstand the continued assault of international resistance and international rejection' because the 'price being paid, in economic and societal terms had become too high' (Burton, 1998). Negotiations were dominated by issues of power-sharing, management of transition and the shaping of the future, but also central to the negotiations were persistent questions about how to deal with human rights violations perpetrated under the old regime.

The ANC, led by Nelson Mandela, and The Inkatha Freedom Party (IFP) representing the Zulus of Natal led by Chief Mangosuthu Buthelezi, negotiated a new multi-racial constitution with the white government and in 1991 all remaining apartheid legislation was repealed. The Convention for a Democratic South Africa (CODESA) talks between the government, ANC, IFP, and others lasted until 1992 during which a transitional constitution was drafted and power given to a multi-racial Executive Council. These moves faced opposition from both the extreme Afrikaner parties on the one hand, and from the large Zulu minority represented by the IFP on the other, who feared that their interests would be subordinated to those of other groups. The whole process was dogged by persistent violence between ANC and IFP activists and during the period from 1990 to 1994, negotiations to establish a new constitutional order saw more than sixteen thousand violent deaths resulting from this particular conflict (Guelke, 1999; Howarth and Norval, 1998). The TRC might have been initiated in the wake of negotiations but was conducted in the midst of some of the worst political violence between the IFP and the ANC where a state of near civil war between their respective supporters in KwaZulu-Natal persisted. In March 1994 a state of emergency was declared and conflict between the two groups continued throughout the 1990s.

An Interim Constitution was agreed upon and enacted by Parliament in December 1993 which facilitated the first democratic elections, outlined the conditions for transition to democratic rule, and stated that the foundations of South Africa's new democracy would rest upon the investigation and redress of abuses perpetrated during the apartheid regime. This investigation was to be predicated upon the amnesty agreement made during the peace talks, an agreement which constituted a pragmatic attempt to involve all parties in the process. The adoption of an amnesty provision by the Interim Constitution made the first democratic elections possible and was followed in 1995 by the promulgation of the Promotion of National Unity and Reconciliation Act (no. 34 of 1995) inaugurating the TRC. The seeds of the TRC are sown in the final clauses of the Interim Constitution of South Africa Act (no. 200 of 1993), cited below, in which provision of amnesty was formalized:

> This Constitution provides a historic bridge between the past of a deeply divided society characterized by strife, conflict, untold suffering and injustice, and a future founded on the recognition of human rights, democracy and peaceful co-existence and development opportunities for all South Africans, irrespective of color, race, class, belief or sex.
>
> The pursuit of national unity, the well-being of all South African citizens and peace require reconciliation between the people of South Africa and the reconstruction of society.
>
> The adoption of this Constitution lays the secure foundation for the people of South Africa to transcend the divisions and strife of the past, which generated gross violations of human rights, the transgression of humanitarian principles in violent conflicts and a legacy of hatred, fear, guilt and revenge.
>
> These can now be addressed on the basis that there is a need for understanding but not for vengeance, a need for reparation but not for retaliation, a need for ubuntu (the African philosophy of humanism) but not for victimization.
>
> In order to advance such reconciliation and reconstruction, amnesty shall be granted in respect of acts, omissions and offences associated with political objectives and committed in the course of the conflicts of the past. To this end, Parliament under this Constitution shall adopt a law determining a firm cut-off date which shall be a date after 8 October 1990 and before 6 December 1993 and providing for mechanisms, criteria and procedures, including tribunals, if any, through which such amnesty shall be dealt with at any time after the law has been passed.
>
> With this Constitution and these commitments we, the people of South Africa, open a new chapter in the history of our country.

Dullah Omar, the Minister of Justice at the time, defended his decision to make an amnesty provision but not to pass an amnesty law because this would have granted blanket amnesty to all those found guilty of human rights abuse as defined in the legislation. Omar claimed that an amnesty law would bypass the victims of violence, and that the forgiveness of perpetrators that an amnesty law might symbolize would go against attempts to 'restore the honor and dignity of the victims and give effect to reparation' (Omar, 1998). Omar further stated that the question of amnesty was to be located in a broader context within which the recognition of the 'wounds' of the people could take place without making the distinction between 'ANC wounds, PAC wounds, and other wounds'. He remarked that 'many people are in need of healing, and we need to heal our country if we are to build a nation which will guarantee peace and stability'. Instead, the amnesty provision demanded that amnesty be granted upon the consideration of *individual* applications which, he argued, had the best chance of facilitating reconciliation on an individual and a national level. The amnesty provision was formally and explicitly attached to the TRC's reconciliatory aim, and was the principle mechanism through which the redress of past violations was to be instituted. Omar's comments, echoing the postscript to the Constitution, invoke human rights but simultaneously subordinate them to the imperative of nation-building, implying that individual healing and national healing (or rather, national unity) were to be ineluctably conjoined.

The political discourse of reconciliation emerged through the Interim Constitution as the discursive regime that would characterize not only the TRC but the wider discourse of political transition in South Africa. Three documents, the Interim Constitution, the Promotion of National Unity and Reconciliation Act, and the TRC Report, share a rhetorical intimacy in which the discourse of national 'healing' of past 'wounds', the emphasis on reconciliation, on 'turning the page' on the past and opening a 'new chapter' in South African history are repeated, thus serving to reinforce the discursive limits of transition and to enforce and normalize the underlying assumptions of the TRC.

In April 1994 the first democratic elections voted in the ANC and South Africa's thirty million black population was finally admitted to the parliamentary system which had been fully established for whites since 1930. The ANC won sixty-three per cent of the vote in an overwhelming electoral victory, the National Party twenty per cent, and the IFP ten per cent. Mandela became president with de Klerk vice-president, and from 1994 to 1996 a coalition government led by Mandela oversaw the instigation of the TRC, until the withdrawal of the National party from the coalition in 1996. After such a strong victory, the ANC was in such a position of political strength that it was largely able to dictate the terms of transition. These were conditioned in the first instance by the ideal of national reconciliation, an ideal that was to be furthered by a confrontation with the past and the retrospective establishment of truth in an attempt to secure a sense of justice for violations arising out of the conflicts of the past. 'Justice' was to be approximated without resorting to retributive measures, largely precluded by the continued strength of the security and military forces dominated by the old order, which would almost certainly have disrupted the process if prosecutions had been threatened.

A key task the TRC faced was that of re-narrating past violations as an effect of a legitimate political struggle between liberation movements and successive apartheid regimes because South Africa's political transition did not emerge out of a revolution in which the liberation movements were victorious and a 'victor's justice' against the former regime could be exacted. The nature of the political settlement in which all parties were involved precluded calls, mainly from the ANC, for criminal trials but it was widely accepted that an examination of past abuses must be conducted as a key part of the political transition (see Boraine, 2000: chapter one). Kader Asmal, prominent architect of the TRC, argued that retributive justice manifest by criminal trials would not serve the interests of the 'new' South Africa given the fragile and complex circumstances conditioning the political negotiations:

> I. . . say to those who wear legalistic blinkers, who argue that immunity would be an affront to justice that they simply do not understand the nature of the negotiated revolution that we lived through. We must deliberately sacrifice the formal

trappings of justice, the courts and the trials, for an even higher good: Truth. We sacrifice justice, because the pains of justice might traumatize our country or affect the transition. We sacrifice justice for truth so as to consolidate democracy, to close the chapter of the past and to avoid confrontation (Asmal cited in Onyegbula, 1999).

Thus a retributive model of justice was subordinated by the TRC to the ideal of 'truth recovery' that was to be facilitated by the incentive of amnesty.

The paradox of what Asmal described as South Africa's 'negotiated revolution' was at the heart of governmental and public debates that took place preceding the formal inauguration of the TRC, particularly with respect to the question of justice. Two important public discussions on dealing with the past were organized by the Institute for Democracy in South Africa to encourage debate around the issues at the heart of the TRC. Issues discussed included the value of 'truth revelation', 'reconciliation', amnesty, and the notion of 'just war'.[10] Participants included scholars and human rights experts from Eastern and Central Europe and Latin America, many of whom had actively participated in other truth-recovery initiatives, and who reflected on their own experiences of transition in order to inform the South Africa debate. In the latter debate, the majority of participants were South Africans and discussions focused more specifically on the case of South Africa. That these public debates took place at all reflected on the strength of civil society in South Africa. Commissioner Mary Burton notes that many NGO leaders were at this time absorbed into national, provincial, and local government after the elections. Although their weakened the organizations for a period of time it had the advantages of allowing their concerns to be reflected at the level of government (Burton, 1998: 2).

Of particular concern to debates about what a commission should aim to achieve was the idea of justice and especially the idea of restorative justice with its emphasis on reparations to victims, as opposed to retributive justice. The pivotal issue upon which these debates turned was the question of whether to include an amnesty provision which ultimately formed the fundamental mechanism of the TRC. However, the amnesty provision, outlined in the postamble to the Interim Constitution, was a forgone conclusion, justified by the TRC as being subordinate to the 'higher good' of 'truth' with the result of compelling the effects of the decision against criminal trials and figuring amnesty as an 'inevitable' precondition of the political settlement. However, the public debates made it appear as if amnesty was up for discussion by putting forward the relative merits and dismerits of different types of justice, and what might best be appropriate in the South African case. The provision for amnesty was the outcome of the limited powers of the ANC to call for prosecutions although all parties eventually agreed upon the demand for truth in exchange for amnesty.[11] This meant that all parties to the violations would be subject to scrutiny by the TRC although the ANC had already addressed the issue of violations within their own camps through the mechanism of internal enquiry on two earlier occasions and initially opposed the suggestion that the TRC should subject the ANC to the same scrutiny as the NP.[12]

Reconciliation and *Kairos*

Reconciliation was not a new political discourse in South Africa in the early 1990s but it had a particular resonance within the history of opposition to apartheid, a resonance that, notably, was contrary to the way in which the TRC finally formulated and instituted reconciliation as a transitional ideology. However, the TRC's version of reconciliation was undoubtedly influenced by its former incarnation, in no small part due to the fact that the TRC's chairperson, Archbishop Desmond Tutu, had been involved in calls for reconciliation from the mid-1980s.

As a socio-theological discourse, reconciliation had figured largely in publications issued by the various churches which had explored the relation between theological principles and the social and political conditions of South Africa under apartheid. The Kairos Document of 1985 was the most significant of a number of such statements and it inspired other such appeals in Central America and Europe (Kairos Theologians, 1984).[13] Kairos is critical of the concept of reconciliation and is worth looking at in some detail because it presents a prescient critique that can be used to evaluate and understand the TRC brand of reconciliation that subsequently emerged. Kairos was signed by one hundred and fifty-one black and white South African theologians of different religious denominations drawn from the Roman Catholic and a variety of Protestant churches, and reflected the ideas of around fifty black pastors working in the townships in and around Johannesburg.[14] It provided a theological comment on the political crisis in South Africa and critiqued theological models that underpinned the activities of the Church in relation to various social and political problems. Kairos took to task state (ab)use of theological concepts and Biblical texts through which it (the state) sought to justify, even sacralize, the apartheid regime. In addition, Kairos blamed the official, although contested, opinion of the church in South Africa claiming that it opposed apartheid in too limited a fashion by concentrating on three principle ideas drawn from the Christian tradition; the principles of reconciliation, justice, and non-violence, the first two of which were, later, to form the core principles of the TRC. The document claimed that 'Church Theology', the official line of the church, applied these principles to the situation in South Africa with the effect of silencing revolutionary opposition to the regime. Kairos developed an alternative theological model as a basis of opposition which was manifest in its doctrine of 'Prophetic Theology' which was set up as a challenge to 'State Theology' and 'Church Theology'. 'Prophetic Theology' expressed an extant commitment to the ideals of liberation theology, to social analysis, resistance to the regime, and to an absolute rejection of the official line of the church. It argued against the moral legitimacy of a tyrannical regime and implicitly condoned violent resistance as a rightful response to violence perpetrated by the state. Ultimately, it warned against the church becoming a 'third force', stating that it should alternatively identify with the ideals of justice and liberation and oppose the perpetration of state violence: 'the church must avoid becoming a "Third Force". . . between the oppressor and the oppressed. . . programmes must not. . . run counter to the struggles of those political organizations that truly represent the grievances and demands of the people (Kairos Theologians, 1984: 29).

These debates were later iterated by the TRC and were manifest particularly in its indictment of the right-wing Christian churches for their role in propagating 'state theology'.

Of particular interest here is Kairos' powerful repudiation of reconciliation which, it claimed, had assumed the status of an authoritative discourse that had 'been made into an absolute principle that must be applied in all cases of conflict or dissension'. Kairos distinguished between 'true reconciliation' and 'counterfeit reconciliation', the latter being a reconciliation that 'allows the sin of injustice and oppression to continue.' It concluded with the assertion that 'no reconciliation is possible in South Africa without justice'. The document sets up peace and justice in opposition to one another and shows how 'counterfeit reconciliation' serves peace at the expense of justice and indicates the readiness on the part of the perpetrator (that is, the apartheid state) to receive absolution without any attendant sense of obligation, nor a manifestation of such, towards the victim. In turn, counterfeit reconciliation requires victims to renounce the struggle against oppression and the pursuit of justice for the sake of peace. The imperative of peace, propagated by the official church, thus silences calls for justice by emphasizing national unity via the discourse of reconciliation. By contrast, Kairos states that 'true reconciliation' is served only by justice in the more conventional, or retributive, sense. Kairos questions in particular the Christianity of the principle of reconciliation where parties to the conflict in question are unequal:

> There are conflicts. . . in which one side is right and the other wrong. There are conflicts where one side is a fully armed and violent oppressor while the other side is defenceless and oppressed. There are conflicts that can only be described as the struggle between justice and injustice, good and evil, God and the devil. To speak of reconciling these two is not only a mistaken application of the Christian idea of reconciliation, it is a total betrayal of all that Christian faith has ever meant. Nowhere in the Bible or in Christian tradition has it ever been suggested that we ought to try to reconcile good and evil, God and the devil. We are supposed to do away with evil, injustice, oppression and sin – not come to terms with it. We are supposed to oppose, confront and reject the devil and not try to sup with the devil (Kairos Theologians, 1984: 17–18).

This construction of conflict through the absolutes of 'good' versus 'evil' constitutes the struggle against apartheid as a 'just war', a figuration which again emerged later during the work of the TRC during its discussions of whether violent resistance by the ANC and other groups was 'just' by international standards. By indicting the principle of reconciliation espoused by the official church, Kairos assured those engaged in the struggle of the absolute rightness of their cause and by implication, of the absolute evil of the apartheid state and its agents. It simultaneously demonized the regime and sacralized the cause of those in opposition to it, defying any 'reconciliation' of the two. The Kairos view resonates with other radical theological perspectives on reconciliation, which contrast reconciliation with justice, revolution and institutional change (see Maluleke in Cochrane, 1999). This bifurcation of counterfeit reconciliation and justice is clearly at odds with the TRC's later formulation which privileges notions of reconciliation, restorative justice and healing over that of retributive justice which more clearly assigns culpability and punishment to perpetrators. Where liberation theology founds reconciliation on retributive justice, the TRC, conversely, subordinated the experiences and claims of victims and perpetrators to the notion of reconciliation. The TRC effectively silenced black theological perspectives on the process beyond those participating as 'mere informants for mainly white male researchers and commentators' (Maluleke in Cochrane, 1999: 101). The absence of black critical voices was an effect of the way in which the TRC's homogenizing discourse excluded narratives of particular experiences. Experiences of forced removals and pass laws, the result of institutionalized violence, for example, were effectively censored by the TRC's mandate to deal with only with 'gross human rights violations' such as torture, extra-judicial killings and abduction. This had the effect of marginalizing particular perspectives, including radical theological ones, from the process of reconciliation with the effect that they were also precluded from properly participating in the process of assigning meaning to the new South Africa.

Kairos argued that Christians under apartheid had a special responsibility for social change, an assertion that was repeated during the work of the TRC. Indeed, one commentator stated at the TRC's hearings that South Africa's past was only partly about apartheid, security laws and so forth, but that 'it was also about Christian triumphalism' (TRC 1998: 4 (3) 78). The later lengthy submissions by the faith communities to the TRC testifies to the important role of the church both in supporting and resisting the regime.[15] Some faith communities, especially amongst the English-speaking churches, defined themselves as 'consciences of the nation', whereas others defined their responsibilities as being directed primarily towards their own members (TRC, 1998: 4 (3) 58).

After Kairos, key figures within the church including Archbishop Desmond Tutu called upon the church to confess their guilt for apartheid. A number of statements and conferences followed the publication of Kairos calling for repentance on behalf of the churches. Amongst these were the National Initiative for Reconciliation in 1985, the South African Council of Churches Soweto Conference on 'Confessing Guilt' in 1989, the Rustenburg Conference of Churches in 1990, and the Cape Town Consultation of the World Council of Churches member churches in South Africa in 1991. The sedimented effect of these calls for repentance was that 'the faith communities and their members helped shape the consciousness within which the idea of the TRC was nurtured' (Cochrane, 1999: 4), and consequently the TRC's enterprise was captured and conveyed by theological discourse. The special institutional hearings of the TRC called to account not only the business, legal, health, media, and prison sectors for their social and political roles during apartheid, but also the faith communities, who were enjoined to testify and submit a report. Clearly, the TRC attributed to the faith communities a special moral authority from which issued a greater burden of accountability. It was this special responsibility to which the Kairos theologians had made their earlier appeal, and which was echoed by the submissions of the faith communities to the TRC. Those in the faith community held to account for involvement in the regime, if morally superior to other agents, were to be held more accountable for their actions.

The Kairos understanding of reconciliation was never incorporated into the work of TRC because justice was defined differently in order to suit the political constraints of the negotiations out of which the amnesty provision arose. The narrative of justice and reconciliation deployed by the TRC, whilst conditioned by theological interpretations, emphasized forgiveness over revenge and as such was closer to Kairos's version of counterfeit reconciliation.

Ubuntu

Although reconciliation was the pivotal metaphor of national unity in transitional South Africa, the TRC introduced a concurrent 'Africanist' discourse of *ubuntu*, a Xhosa term. *Ubuntu* had been invoked by the Interim Constitution in 1993, reiterated by Archbishop Tutu prior to, and throughout the human rights violations hearings of the TRC, and was also later enshrined in the official documentation ensuing from the Commission and cast as one of the key principles guiding its work. The TRC interpreted *ubuntu* as a principle given to restorative justice, emphasizing reparations and rehabilitation of victims, and forgiveness rather than punishment, of perpetrators. According to the Constitution, *ubuntu* calls for 'the need for understanding but not for vengeance, a need for reparation but not retaliation, a need for *ubuntu* but not for victimization'. Against the punitive drive of retribution, *ubuntu*, it was argued, established individual identity as inextricably located within the community through the idea that 'people are people through other people'. As an organizing trope of the TRC, *ubuntu* stressed the centrality of community, social cohesion and solidarity to identity and humanity, and simultaneously opposed the principle of retribution because it was seen to violate those principles. At the heart of *ubuntu* lies the assumption that the extent to which we treat others as if they were less than human, is commensurate with the extent to which we dehumanize ourselves. Thus the 'restoration' of a social harmony that restores the other and elevates the self through the practical application of forgiveness rather than revenge, of *ubuntu*, promises to move society beyond a cycle of violence. This interpretation of *ubuntu* suggests that the identities of victims and perpetrators are inextricably tied to one another.

Consequently, *ubuntu* inculcated, through the TRC, human rights as reconciliation and precluded the possibility of the redress of violations by retributive judicial processes. Throughout the TRC's public hearings, human rights and reconciliation were broadly subsumed within the discourse of *ubuntu* which performed as an important political and quasi-legal concept that framed individual testimonies about past human rights violations. *Ubuntu* performed a legitimizing function for the restorative path taken by the TRC and, as Wilson argues, worked as 'an ideological concept with multiple meanings which conjoins human rights, restorative justice, reconciliation and nation-building within the populist language of pan-Africanism' (Wilson, 2001: 13). *Ubuntu* was designated as the site of an 'authentic' black South African identity through Tutu's constant appeals to, and reiteration of, its principles. When one woman at the TRC hearings articulated her forgiveness of her son's killers, Tutu remarked 'you make me so proud, Mama, to be a black person like you', and also that 'what the world lacks, black people have' (Krog, 1999: 111). Through *ubuntu* human rights was embedded within specific cultural articulations of identity.

However, whilst it has been argued that Tutu's *ubuntu* theology provides a distinctive identity for black South Africans in its appeal to 'ancient African concepts of the harmony between individual and community' (Battle cited in Krog, 1999: 110), *ubuntu* is problematic not least because of its constitution of a distinctive and inherent black African identity. *Ubuntu* is also problematic because the articulation of that identity as intrinsically forgiving effectively silenced black calls for retribution. On the TRC's terms, how could one be an 'authentic' black South African and demand retribution for those who murdered a son, for example?

Tutu's statements and writings are the principle locus of the articulation of *ubuntu* that laid claim to an authentic version, not only of black identity, but also to the law as restoration rather than retribution (Tutu, 1999: 34–36). Tutu used *ubuntu* to pitch 'African' against 'Western' values remarking that 'retributive justice is largely Western', but that the African understanding of justice is 'far more restorative—not so much to punish as to redress or restore a balance that has been knocked askew' (Tutu cited in Minow, 1998: 81). The ideological impetus of such an appeal to 'African values' served to articulate and enforce the idea that post-apartheid justice would not be impelled by vengeance, or even by its 'weaker' legal figuration, retribution. Further, *ubuntu* dichotomized two types of justice that positioned 'African' *ubuntu* and reconciliation against 'Western' vengeance and retribution with the effect of precluding any consideration of legal retribution as a potential *agent* of reconciliation. The constitutional right of citizens to due process was short-circuited by the amnesty provision such that a strong justification of the decision to grant amnesty was required. *Ubuntu* provided that justification by designating *ubuntu* as a 'uniquely African form of compassion' but one that arguably, in the TRC's hands, 'compromised justice and the state's abrogation of the right to due process' (Wilson, 2001: 11). In sum, the discourse of *ubuntu* was used to make appealing to black South Africans the reconciliatory version of redress for human rights violations by seeking recourse to local cultural values and favorably position them in opposition to 'foreign' Western judicial principles (Wilson, 2001: 13).[16] *Ubuntu* conditioned the closing appeal of the Interim Constitution that laid the foundations of the TRC, but such was its hegemonic force that it was not simply restricted to shaping and justifying the principles of the Commission but proliferated in other institutional spheres. For example, *ubuntu* was a principle extensively drawn upon within the first Constitutional Court judgment on the death penalty in 1995, in which it was used to redefine justice against the principle of revenge (Wilson, 2001: 10).

The key political effect of reconciliation and *ubuntu* was to redefine human rights such that human rights became subordinated to national political imperatives that favored 'national unity'. This meant that the 'recognition' rather than punishment of perpetrators of violations was accorded a higher priority than the establishment of justice on an individual case basis (Wilson, 2001: 3). As such, a peaceful transition from apartheid rule without the threat of disruption from, primarily, the military and security sectors of the former regime, was privileged over the pursuit of redress for violations through existing legal mechanisms. As a result, the TRC's configuration of restorative judicial principles arguably threatened to undermine rather than contribute to the secure establishment of institutional, and particularly legal, reform.

The Truth and Reconciliation Commission

The principle task of the TRC was to facilitate South Africa's transition from the divisions instituted by apartheid rule to national unity. The discourse of national unity was animated primarily, as previously argued, by the narrative of reconciliation which drew upon both national and international sources of legitimation and performed as a new moral foundation for the nation.

Following the Promotion of National Unity and Reconciliation Act of 1995, President Nelson Mandela announced the names of the seventeen commissioners who would co-ordinate the operations of the TRC. Mandela appointed a broadly representative committee in order to assist his decision. Civil society organizations, political parties, churches and individuals participated by nominating candidates and monitoring the hearings that were held as part of the appointment process. Almost three hundred people were nominated and after the public hearings, a list of twenty-five names was submitted to the President who consulted with the Cabinet and party leaders in order to decide on the final seventeen commissioners. The appointed commissioners went through a rigorous and open process of selection, with the provision that not less than fifteen of them should be South African citizens, broadly representative of the South African community, and appropriately qualified for the task at hand.[17] Two religious leaders were appointed to the most important posts, Desmond Tutu as chairperson and Alex Boraine as deputy chairperson. Their influence was crucial to the ethical and spiritual dimension of the TRC's work. Amongst the commissioners who were selected as representative of various 'interests'—national, ethnic, racial and gender-based—were ten men, seven women, seven Africans, six whites, two coloreds, and two Indians drawn from various professions including law, human rights, and the clergy. Although the selection was broadly approved there were some objections, most notably from F. W. de Klerk and Mengosuthu Buthelezi who disapproved of the appointment of Tutu to Chair. They argued that the TRC could not be an impartial adjudicator of South Africa's violent past with Tutu at it's helm, since it could only be an instrument of ANC policy and therefore primarily constitutive of ANC interests.

The Commission was inaugurated on 16 December 1995 and began its work in the same month. The first of the public hearings took place on 15 April 1996. marking the beginning of two years during which South Africans were exposed through television broadcasts of the hearings on a regular weekly basis to revelations about past abuses. The Commission worked from November 1995 to October 1998 taking testimonies from victims and perpetrators in regional 'courts' for the period of around thirty-three years under scrutiny, from March 1960 to December 1993. The TRC received around twenty-one thousand victim statements and around eight thousand applications for amnesty for acts the supplicants claimed to have committed, authorized or failed to prevent. Around ten per cent of these testimonies were made publicly. In addition the TRC received statements from the former State President P. W. Botha, political parties, a number of civil institutions and organizations, the armed forces and others.

The public hearings on human rights violations concluded with the Chemical and Biological Warfare Programme hearings on 31 July 1998, and on 29 October, around one year after the original deadline, Desmond Tutu presented the Report of the Truth and Reconciliation Commission to President Mandela. It was the result of nearly three years of investigations by the TRC. The Report was handed over amidst fears that litigation claims would prevent its publication. In the days leading up to its submission, F.W. de Klerk and the ANC both requested that indictments be removed from the Report. de Klerk was successful in his request and the allegations related to him were removed from the Report. The Report concluded that apartheid was a crime against humanity, that former president P.W. Botha, Winnie Mandela, and Inkhata Freedom Party leader Buthelezi were accountable for gross human rights violations and that most South African businesses benefited in various ways from the apartheid system and had committed human rights violations. The TRC held the NP government ultimately accountable for extra-judicial killings and the State Security Council for atrocities perpetrated by the security forces. The state was identified as a key perpetrator of abuses as the TRC stated that the apartheid government, its civil service and security forces were primary perpetrators both within the domestic boundaries of the state and across the Southern African region within which South Africa was a key player in the 'war against communism'. The TRC proposed assistance in the redress of apartheid's legacy of poverty through a new taxation dispensation. It also recommended the prosecution of those responsible where amnesty had not been sought or had been denied.

Objectives of the Commission

The stated objectives of the TRC categorically define its work as oriented towards national unity. The determining objective of the commission, as defined by the Promotion of National Unity and Reconciliation Act, was the promotion of 'national unity and reconciliation in a spirit of understanding which transcends the conflicts and divisions of the past'. As a function of the pursuit of reconciliation, the TRC identified four key objectives. The first of these aimed to establish as 'complete a picture as possible' of the causes, nature, and extent of gross human rights violations from 1 March 1960 to 10 May 1994. This narrative about the past conflict was constructed out of a consideration of the antecedents, circumstances, factors, and context of the violations as well as the perspectives of the victims and perpetrators which were established by individual investigations and public hearings, and receives fuller discussion in this book in chapter three. Secondly, the TRC was mandated to grant amnesty to those making a 'full disclosure' of all facts relating to violations perpetrated committed with a political objective with respect to furthering reconciliation and 'transcending' past conflict. Thirdly, the commission was charged with establishing and revealing the fate or whereabouts of victims and with the 'restoration of human and civil dignity' to victims by granting them the opportunity to relate their personal accounts of abuses suffered. Further, the commission aimed to recommend reparative measures where considered due. And the fourth and final objective entailed the compilation of a comprehensive Report of the findings and to make recommendations of measures to be taken to prevent the repetition of such violations in the future. That these objectives specifically preclude the possibility of retributive justice is in part testimony to the prior amnesty provision rather than to any preference of one method of justice over another. The ideological framework of reconciliation thus serves to cover over and justify the pragmatic decision to grant amnesty to perpetrators.

Concepts and Principles

The work of the Commission was underpinned by an explicit set of 'concepts and principles' directed towards achieving the broad aims of the TRC. These included establishing the civil and human rights of victims, making reparations to victims, uncovering the 'truth' about past violations, making an official historical record of them, and finally restoring 'moral order' to society through the establishment of a human rights culture and respect for the rule of law. The TRC argued that without the guiding discourses of 'reconciliation', 'truth', and 'ubuntu', what it called the 'philosophical, religious, and moral aspects' of the Commission, the TRC would be an 'empty legal vessel which would do a great deal of harm and achieve nothing' (TRC, 1(5) 1). The most important of these, reconciliation, was defined by the TRC as both 'goal and process', where the 'journey' towards reconciliation must also be 'conciliatory' in nature. The TRC identified different levels of reconciliation: reconciliation with 'painful truths' about the past, reconciliation between victims and perpetrators, reconciliation at a community level both within and between different ethnic and racial groups, national unity and reconciliation, and reconciliation through the redress of socio-economic inequalities. However, the different sites of reconciliation were subordinated to the locus of its prime articulation: the nation.

The complexity surrounding the construction of a new truth about the past emerged out of the public debates prior to the inauguration of the Commission. The construction of a coherent truth about the past upon which to found a reconciliation between the various parties to the conflict(s) of the past, was inevitably likely to be fraught with difficulty. As a political effect of the 'recognition' that a unified truth about the past was unlikely to be palatable to all, the TRC distinguished four types of truth. These manifold truths were defined as 'factual or forensic truth', 'personal and narrative truth', 'social truth' and 'healing and re-storative truth' and are discussed in more detail in chapter four of this book. This multiple definition of truth could be interpreted as inherent to the TRC's attempt to portray of 'as full a picture as possible' of violations within the given period. But was also, and perhaps more importantly, a function of its political mandate to 'reconcile' and to find as much ground for commensurability as possible be-tween varying accounts without attempting to adjudicate between these compet-ing truths. This taxonomy of truth fed into the assumed and determining relation-ship between truth and reconciliation central to the TRC.

The TRC provided justifications for the decision not to hold criminal trials, arguing that in a 'fragile transitional context there are strong arguments for the adoption of a truth commission rather than Nuremberg-type trials' (TRC, 1 (5) 71). The TRC balanced this proposition against the idea of criminal trials which would have been costly, financially, politically, and in terms of time. It argued that fewer trials would be held as a result which would impede the emergence of a broad historical pattern of violations, the recovery of which was purported to better found a type of 'social justice'. The TRC also stated that the decision did not concern a trade-off between amnesty and criminal or civil trials, but the choice made by the TRC was one which prioritized 'full disclosure' of the de-tails surrounding violations and of hearing as many cases as possible within the time allowed. Thus it constituted its decision as one which is *not* conditioned by the choice for restorative justice and against retributive justice, but rather as one that was *for* maximizing the truth.

Structure of the Commission

A national office in Cape Town co-ordinated the operations of the regional of-fices in Cape Town, Johannesburg, East London and Durban. The three commit-tees stipulated by the Act were also established: the Committee on Human Rights Violations, the Committee on Amnesty and the Committee on Reparation and Rehabilitation.

The Committee on Human Rights Violations was mandated to aid the truth recovery process by taking statements from survivors and families of victims, establishing the identities of perpetrators and the circumstances of perpetration and selecting representative cases to be presented at the public hearings. In se-lecting cases for public hearings the TRC took into account the nature of the abuse in the community or district and put cases forward which were considered to be roughly representative of the community or district experience. The hear-ings were divided into Event Hearings, Special Hearings, Institutional Hearings and Political Party Hearings.

The Event Hearings took testimony from both victim and perpetrator and were selected as 'window cases' which, by providing an insight into a particular event, were designed to reflect more generally on a wider pattern of violations. Affected communities and their representatives were afforded the opportunity to speak about collective experiences of abuse, 'thus offering a more global perspective of human rights abuse' (TRC, 1998: 1 (6) 37).[18]

The Special Hearings were set up to establish patterns of abuse experienced by individuals and groups, and to focus particularly on the experiences of 'vulnerable persons'. Hearings were held on children and youth, women, and conscripts to compulsory national service.

The Institutional Hearings sought evidence from various professions, institutions and organizations about the role they had played in perpetrating, opposing, or facilitating abuses. These hearings dealt with the broader social and institutional context within which individual violations had been made possible and attempted to portray, in a very limited fashion, the *systemic* conditions of party-political violence. To this end the TRC conducted investigations into the health sector, the judiciary, the media, the business sector, the penal system and faith communities.

The Political Party Hearings allowed the parties to give their perspectives on the causes and nature of the conflicts of the past with accounts stating involvement in, or culpability for, gross violations. These hearings were conducted in two phases, the first of which saw the parties make submissions with the Commission only asking clarificatory questions, and in the second phase, the TRC put substantive questions to the parties based on the submissions and on evidence gathered by the Investigative and Research Units. Of those who made statements, less than one-tenth testified publicly. The Report points out that 'it is important to stress that all the statements received the same degree of attention. . .' and 'in order to provide this attention, it became necessary to curtail the public hearings and focus on the mass of statements and on making findings in every case' (TRC, 5 (1) 38).

The Committee on Amnesty was empowered to grant amnesty after a public hearing in every case, to those found responsible for perpetrating gross violations of human rights *with a political objective* within and beyond the borders of the state. Amnesty had to be applied for on an individual, rather than a group, basis in order to facilitate 'full disclosures' of the offence 'associated with a political objective committed in the course of the conflicts of the past' (The Promotion of National Unity and Reconciliation Act, No. 34 of 1995). The individual applicant was not granted amnesty if considered to have been acting alone, but only as a member of a known political party or employee of the state. The effect of this particular narration was to institute human rights violations as conditioned by party political conflict and to exclude *individual* admissions of accountability which did not fit within the new official history of the conflict.

The Committee on Reparation and Rehabilitation received applications for reparations from those individuals claiming to have suffered a gross human rights violation. It considered matters referred to it by the TRC, the Committee on Human Rights Violations and the Committee on Amnesty, and was the only one of the three Committees not to hold public hearings. After considering each application and any supporting evidence, the Committee decided whether the deponent could be classified as a 'victim' and if so, whether to make recommendations for reparations.[19] The Committee secured counseling and medical help for victims where necessary and provided special support for those giving public testimony in the form of advice and accompaniment during the hearings. In making recommendations for the future prevention of violations, this Committee was most explicitly concerned with setting out provisions on the basis of 'lessons learned from the past.'

The TRC embarked upon a public information process in order to facilitate the solicitation of testimonies, and the TRC relied heavily upon the support of non-governmental organizations and faith communities in this campaign. Public meetings and discussions were held on the subject of the TRC and its work as a means of disseminating information about the Commission and of encouraging people to come forward and apply for amnesty or to register a victim deposition. Individuals were trained as statement-takers to record testimonies given by those who came to the TRC offices or to one of a number of registration points. They were drawn from a cross-section of society and between them spoke the eleven languages of South Africa. A statement form was designed for the purpose of formalizing and recording the testimonies which were translated where necessary and recorded in English in order to be processed onto a database. In total, around 21,300 petitions for gross human rights violations were placed with the TRC and 7,124 from people requesting amnesty for abuses they committed, authorized or failed to prevent. Only about ten per cent of the statements were heard in a public context.

The seven volume report issued by the TRC reflects the extensive investigations carried out by the three committees. It also, arguably, constitutes a 'biography of the nation' during the period under investigation and incorporates fragments of publicly-given testimonies which are taken to be paradigmatic narratives of abuses perpetrated within a particular region or the nation as a whole.

Conclusions

I have argued here that South Africa's reconciliatory narrative emerged out of a confluence of international and national narratives which partly conditioned and framed the political negotiation of amnesty during talks between, primarily, the ANC and NP in the early 1990s. It was this important agreement upon which the incorporation of a reconciliatory rather than a retributive narrative turned, and to which the discourse of national unity, which emphasized the 'restoration' of both victims and perpetrators, was integral. By way of justifying this decision the TRC drew upon, to use an Althusserian formulation, the 'always-already there' national discourses of reconciliation and *ubuntu* that circulated in various spheres of social, political, and religious life. These principles emerged through public debates prior to the inauguration of the TRC about which narrative—reconciliatory or retributive—should shape South Africa's transition. At the national level, discourses within South Africa on the importance of building a culture of human rights and accountability played to, and were conditioned by, presiding global narratives of human rights to which had been attached both retributive and reconciliatory narratives, all subsumed under the paradigmatic platitude of 'dealing with the past'. These had become hegemonic discourses within which other transitions from conflict to peace and from authoritarian to democratic rule were framed, and indeed they were discourses that South Africa was about to play a crucial role in perpetuating and securing the predominance of.

Notes

1. Amongst them were elderly members of the international brigades who voluntarily assisted the Republican movement against Franco. Notably, the group called upon the UN to oblige the government to take on the task of disinterring the graves. The UN has previously been involved in such actions in Guatemala and El Salvador.

2. Namely, the Convention of the Prevention and Punishment of the Crime of Genocide (UN 1948/1951) and the Convention Against Torture and other Cruel, Inhuman or Degrading Treatment or Punishment (1984/1987).

3. The Bolivian commission investigated disappearances from 1967 to 1982 but excluded any investigation of other types of violations such as torture and extra-judicial detention. It documented around one hundred and fifty-five cases within the given time period and managed to locate some human remains. The commission did not complete its work as it was dissolved due to lack of resources and political support. Consequently, no report emerged from the enquiry.

4. Also known as CONADEP or the Sabato Commission after the author Ernesto Sabato who led the enquiry.

5. The Argentinian commission documented around nine thousand disappearances, investigating detention centres, police stations, and clandestine cemeteries. Exiles returned from abroad to testify and a televised report on the findings was broadcast. The report recommended further judicial enquiries and financial and social reparations for those disadvantaged by the repressive measures of the previous regime, in particular children and relatives of the disappeared. It suggested that abduction should be enshrined within law as a crime against humanity, and promoted the instigation of education programmes with the aim of encouraging and promoting human rights cultures within the military, police, and civil institutions. It also concluded that judicial procedures for investigating violations should be strengthened, and that repressive laws still in operation should be repealed.

6. In the same year Hayner identifies another commission in Zimbabwe in which a commission of enquiry was conducted into government repression of alleged dissidents in Matabeleland where around 1,500 civilians were killed in 1983. A report was produced in 1985 but kept confidential although the defence minister subsequently apologised for the killings and torture in 1992. Admissions of specific accountability have still not been made and the government continues to prevent compensation claims by refusing to recognise the deaths. That Hayner mentions this enquiry at all within the framework of her own typology is odd. The enquiry investigates a *particular episode* rather than a national pattern of abuse and thus does not properly accord with her own definition of what constitutes a truth commission.

7. The commission concentrated on the practices of arbitrary arrest and detention, torture, and killings perpetrated by security forces under Obote's government from December 1972 to January 1986. As with the previous Ugandan commission, many of the hearings were publicly made. Law reform with regard to detention without trial was ac-

cepted and a permanent human rights commission was established in its wake. No reference was made to the previous commission although part of the period of investigation overlapped with the investigations already carried out by the previous enquiry conducted under Amin's auspices.

8. The commission justified its decision only to investigate abuses perpetrated by army personnel arguing that violence perpetrated by insurgents could be dealt with through the existing legal system and did not require a special enquiry. The report was not completed and the commission investigations were limited by the fact that a number of implicated military personnel maintained a high profile due to their role in the coup against former President Marcos, and also by the continuing war against insurgents.

9. The most notable was in Czechoslovakia where a lustration law came into operation in 1991 with the aim of purging the legislative, executive, and judiciary branches of the government, the military, police, security services, and media, state industry and banking sectors. The Panev Law in Bulgaria in the following year in December 1992 resulted in the removal of around ninety per cent of government administrators. Lustration laws were also effected to remove individuals from office in Poland and Lithuania and often provided incentives for confessions with lenient sanctions.

10. The first of these debates was entitled 'Justice in Transition: Dealing With the Past', and the second 'Truth and Reconciliation' and the discussions were widely publicised and distributed in South Africa. These discussions were published in ensuing collections by Boraine et al (1994) and Boraine and Levy eds. (1994).

11. The Justice Minister, Dullah Omar, threatened to withdraw immunity from prosecution for seventy-three ANC members in order to compel agreement to the inclusion of amnesty into the proceedings. Immunity had initially been granted in order to allow the members to return to South Africa to participate in the negotiations in the early 1990s.

12. These were the Motsuenyane and Skwekyiya Commissions. The first of these enquiries was criticised for its lack of independence, and the second one set up as a response to these criticisms. The TRC investigated again the violations already looked into by the ANC during these two enquiries.

13. Following its publication, a Central American Kairos Document was issued in 1988 calling upon churches and Christians in the U.S. to withdraw support for U.S. involvement in Latin America and to renounce colonialism and imperialism. And in 1996 a Kairos Europa network was established and a document published in 1998 calling upon faith communities, trades unions, social movements and individuals to work for social, political, and economic change in Europe.

14. The majority of signatures came from the Anglican, Roman Catholic, Methodist, United Congregational and Dutch Reformed Mission churches out of around 30 different denominations.

15. I am using the concept of 'church' here in a very broad sense to include *all* denominations of faith. For details of the submissions by the faith communities to the institutional hearings see TRC 1998: 4 (3).

16. Wilson also notes that *ubuntu* undermines the TRC's claim that human rights would have no cultural or ethnic dimensions in South Africa.

17. The names of those appointed were published in the Government Gazette on 15 December 1995 (*Government Gazette,* South Africa, no. 16885) in order to underline the transparency of the proceedings. They were Archbishop Desmond Tutu (Chairperson), Dr Alex Boraine (Vice-Chairperson), Ms Mary Burton, Adv Chris de Jager, the Revd Bongani Finca, Ms Sisi Khampep, Mr Richard Lyster, Mr Wynand Malan, the Revd Dr Khoza Mgojo, Ms Hlengiwe Mkhize, Mr Dumisa Ntsebeza, Dr Wendy Orr, Adv Denzil Poltgieter, Dr Mapule F. Ramashala, Dr Fazel Randera, Ms Yasmin Sooka and Ms Glenda Wildschut. Of these, Wynand Malan dropped out of the proceedings due to his

objections to the procedures and principles of the Commission. He remained as an observer to, but not participant in, the TRC meetings, and his criticisms of the Commission are fully included in the fifth volume of the Report. Within weeks of the appointment of the commissioners, more staff were appointed and four regional offices opened in order to register and process individual testimonies.

18. The TRC identified the following events for particular investigation: the 1976 Soweto student uprising; the 1986 Alexandra six-day war; the KwaNdebele/Moutse homeland incorporation conflict; the killing of farmers in the former Transvaal; the 1985 Trojan Horse ambush by the security forces in the Western Cape; the 1986 killing of the 'Gugulethu Seven' following security force infiltration of ANC structures in the Western Cape; the 1990 Seven-Days war resulting from IFP-ANC clashes in the Pietermaritzburg area; the Caprivi Trainees, trained by the South African Defence Force (SADF) and deployed in KwaZulu-Natal as a covert paramilitary force in 1986; the 1960 Pondoland Rebellion against the imposition of the Bantu Authorities Act; and the 1992 Bisho Massacre in response to an ANC national campaign for free political activity in the homelands.

19. There were five classifications of reparations: an Individual Reparation Grant, which was part of an individual financial grant; Symbolic Reparation, which usually included burials and commemorations of individuals or events; Community Rehabilitation Programmes; Institutional reform with the intention of preventing a repeat of abuses; and Urgent Interim Reparations for those considered in need of immediate assistance whilst waiting for the full reparation to be decided and granted.

Chapter Two
Constructing Reconciliation: A Discourse Analysis

Men. . . to make sense of their span. . . need fictive concords with origins and ends, such as give meaning to lives.

> Frank Kermode, *The Sense of An Ending: Studies in the Theory of Fiction* (Oxford: Oxford University Press, 2000).

The previous chapter situated the emergence of South Africa's TRC at the juncture between global and local narratives about dealing with the past. It positioned the TRC's appearance as an effect of of international legal discourses on retributive and restorative modes of dealing with past atrocity, and simultaneously of local discourses on human rights, reconciliation and *ubuntu*, all discourses it was about to play a critical role in promoting and reinforcing. The discussion turns, in this chapter, to a discourse analysis of the TRC's official documentation and some of its depositions in order to show precisely *how* and *to what effect* the TRC story about reconciliation was constructed, and presents a distinctive theoretical lens that combines aspects of political discourse analysis with strands of narrative theory. The aim of this chapter is to further a thorough and theoretically grounded approach to the politics of reconciliation in South Africa by scrutinising the subjects, objects and material practices that flowed from the TRC's particular assumptions and practices. This approach presented here is one that could readily be applied to the politics of reconciliation in other contexts because it is one that is attentive to the particularities of any case, and is designed to facilitate an understanding of what, politically, is permitted within the reconciliation process and what is excluded by it.

The argument here turns on two crucial assumptions. The first is that *discourse* constitutes and naturalizes the subjects and objects of political life. In describing the implications of this assumption I draw upon the work of Michel Foucault and Louis Althusser. The second, and related, assumption is that *narrative* is a special discursive form, the structural features of which have specific political effects that are not illuminated by a more general discourse analytic approach. In making this argument extant I draw upon two key theorists of narrative, Hayden White and Frank Kermode, who are chosen because they highlight the ideological dimensions of narrative and thus render an approach that is particularly apposite to any analysis of narrative in political life.

The invocation of narrative theory here fleshes out and renders more specifically applicable some of the general claims of political discourse analysis; while the insights of political discourse analysis highlight the political contexts and effects of governing narratives that most narrative theory, on its own, is blind to. The combination of these two theoretical premises, each supplementing the other, furnishes a uniquely appropriate and powerful approach to understanding the story about reconciliation told by the TRC, and illuminates its particular political effects.

Political Discourse Analysis

Foucault and Althusser combined provide a distinctive and insightful approach to the political dimensions of reconciliation in South Africa, and I have taken up two powerful aspects of their work, one methodological the other conceptual, in order to disinter specific aspects of the workings of the TRC: Foucault's archeological method, and Althusser's concept of the ideological state apparatus, which I discuss in turn below.

Taxonomies of Violations: a Foucauldian approach

Foucault's 'archaeological' method seeks, primarily, to historicise the emergence of specific discourses over time and to account for the way in which certain discourses become powerful, binding, and sustained at particular historical junctures (Foucault, 1973, 1977 and 1978). In a second and related feature of his analysis, Foucault shows how discourses discipline subject positions within a constellation of power relations. For Foucault, discourse is constitutive of, and materialised through, social and political relations and identities, which are embedded within and emerge via non-discursive practices such as institutions and policies. For example, medical discourses discipline the subject categories of 'patient' and 'doctor' and legal discourses 'judge' and 'criminal' within a specific and hierarchical relationship governed by institutional forces, conventions and arrangments.

Foucault analyses the sets of statements, or discourses, which constitute powerful claims to truth by societies at certain points in time and identifies the rules of formation governing their appearance. He describes the emergence of, and the relations between, particular statements within specific historical contexts and is concerned with the connection between 'discursive practices' and 'non-discursive' activities and institutions. In drawing out this connection, Foucault details the way in which 'discursive formations' comprise four constituent aspects (Foucault, 1972):

1. The *objects* about which statements are made;
2. The *enunciative modalities* or positions from which subjects speak;
3. The *concepts* which govern discourse;
4. The *strategies* or *theories* that flow from particular discursive formations.

These four aspects comprise the particular *rules* governing a discourse and are constitutive of the authority, indeed hegemony, of a discourse at a particular point in time. These four rules provide a fruitful technique of analysis of South Africa's reconciliation discourse in the following ways:

The Objects of the TRC

First, Foucault accounts for the construction of objects within discourse 'by relating them to the body of rules that enable them to form as objects of a discourse and thus constitute the conditions of their historical appearance' (Foucault, 1972: 48). The first of these rules comprises the social relations in which certain practices or symptoms (for example, 'neurosis', 'psychosis', or 'dementia') become the objects of scientific (medical) investigation. The second set of rules consists of the 'authorities of delimitation' invested with the power to adjudicate to which discursive formation belong certain objects.

Foucault argues that discursive practices *constitute* their objects of enquiry rather than the objects of enquiry being *prior to* the discourses that 'contain' them. As such, his arguments help to elucidate an account of the contingency of the TRC's story about the past, which in turn attests to the political context in which the truth about South Africa's violent history was (re)constructed.

As discussed in the previous chapter, the language of human rights facilitated and conditioned the political negotiations in 1991, appearing to 'transcend' or in some way obviate the ideological positions of the key parties thus enabling multi-party talks to proceed. In addition, the demand made by the NP that all parties to violence should be investigated led to the TRC positing 'gross violations of human rights' perpetrated by all parties to South Africa's violent struggle between 1960 and 1994 as the central objects of its investigations. In so doing, the TRC identified, defined, and quantified precisely which categories of violations were central to its investigations, such as 'killing', 'torture', 'abduction', 'severe ill-treatment' and so on. It placed a further limitation on which violations were to be investigated by stating that only violations perpetrated with a 'political objective'—that is, facilitating the investigation of *all* party political violence—could qualify as a gross violation of human rights and thus be legitimate objects of investigation. As such, *'* 'authorities of delimitation', were not simply restricted to the officials of the TRC but can be traced back to the actors engaged in the peace negotiations in the early 1990s, and to their specific demands, with most importance being place upon the NP insistence upon the amnesty provision and requirement that all parties be subjected to the same scrutiny. As a result, 'violations perpetrated with a political objective' were delimited as the common denominator around which a multi-party scrutiny could take place. This in turn meant that responsibility for violations would not appear to be the sole preserve of the former regime but would be apportioned to all political parties who had utilised violent means of waging their campaigns.

The political effect of this delimitation was to elide other potential histories of South Africa which may have claimed to be equally 'true' and 'complete' without rendering an account of politically motivated violations. For example, prior to the ascendancy of international discourses on human rights that shaped South Africa's reconciliatory process no-one would have seen the history of South Africa as a history or series of 'human rights violations'—not the National Party nor the security forces, of course, but neither the ANC nor much of the black majority who might instead have narrated South Africa's history as one of, for example, oppression, exploitation, cruelty, just war or revolution. Significantly, structural violence was crucial to apartheid's project of 'separate development' and was not included in the TRC's main appraisal of past violations of human rights although it did figure as a 'contextual' scenario within which gross violations of human rights were perpetrated and flourished. Yet many thousands more people were victims of such structural violations than of the political violations the TRC sought to compensate and 'reconcile'.

The notion of "a human rights violation" in this context is thus an example of a discursively constructed object in the Foucauldian sense, in that it is defined by its place within a discourse which is circumscribed by the conditions, social, political, and historical, of its emergence.

Enunciative Modalities of the TRC

Second, Foucault describes the appearance of the subjects of discourse as a function of 'enunciative modalities'. This refers to the way in which certain subjects of a discourse are endowed with the authority to speak, often because of their recognised training and concomitant 'expertise', such as judges and doctors. The authority of their declarations is constituted by two things: the institutional site, and the authorised professional position from which they speak. Truth claims are an effect of the declarations of such subjects being empowered to make authoritative statements (Foucault, 1972: 50–55).[1] Subjects do not independently produce, but are constituted by discourse and they in turn reproduce the particular assumptions of the discourse within which they are constituted, thus ensuring its hegemony, continuity and also, crucially, the invisibility of its reproduction.

The enunciative modalities of the TRC's discourse are made evident by its designation of the subject positions of 'victim' and 'perpetrator', authorised to speak the 'truth about the past'. Victims and perpetrators were elected as the key

agents and witnesses of South Africa's history of 'human rights violations'. The force of 'truth' was endowed upon those testifying by the institutional site of their declarations, the public hearings of the TRC which were widely disseminated by national media.

Notably, 'victim' and 'perpetrator' constitute the subject positions from which authoritative and binding statements about South Africa's violent past were made, but these are over-determined subjects that are not exclusive or fundamental but are contingent upon the new narrative about past violence. Given that the constitution of victim and perpetrator is an effect of the TRC's *particular* historicization of the South Africa's apartheid past, it is probable that under different political circumstances these subject positions would have been occupied by different individuals. If, for example, the ANC had been fully able to dictate the terms of the transition and had held members of the former regime to account at a criminal tribunal, it is unlikely that ANC members would have been identified as perpetrators. Or perhaps an investigation might have also enquired into the 'bystanders' and the 'beneficiaries' of apartheid, thus adding further categories of subjection. As such, different subjects would be assigned the authority to speak by virtue of their constitution within another, different, politico-historical discourse about the past.

A further and specific account of subjectivity is rendered by Foucault in the *History of Sexuality* that is of special relevance here. In this book Foucault puts forward an account of subjectivity as a function of the confessional (Foucault, 1978: 58–63).[2] Through the confessional, human agents are implicated in their own subjection, such that subjection appears to be voluntary, or even willed. The confessional is an invisible function of power and domination such that 'the obligation to confess is now relayed through so many different points. . . that we no longer perceive it as the effect of a power that constrains us' (Foucault, 1978: 60). As such, perpetrators appear to collude in their own subjection as perpetrators by performing a public ritual of confession to the TRC—as, indeed, do victims collude in their own subjection as victims by 'bearing witness' to suffering. The confessional as a site of subject production is of special importance to the TRC and receives further and more detailed consideration in chapter four of this book.

Concepts of the TRC

Third, Foucault outlines the set of rules governing the production of 'concepts' within a discourse that is comprised of a 'field of statements' governed by rules which stipulate the proper order of appearance and relation between the respective concepts that are constitutive of the 'reality' they claim to reflect (Foucault, 1972: 56).

Foucault's understanding of the workings of 'concepts' can be usefully applied to understanding the way in which the official discourse of the TRC organised human rights violations into sets and subsets by a 'coding frame', the purpose of which was to taxonomize systematically in order to quantify and attribute 'gross violations of human rights' as follows:

HRV CATEGORY	CODE	DEFINITION
Killing	KILLING	A killing is when a person dies, in one of three ways: Assassination is the killing of a *targeted person* by a person or group who *developed a secret plan or plot* to achieve this. A person is targeted because of their political position. Execution is capital punishment (death sentence) imposed and carried out by a legal or authorised body such as court of law or tribunal. Victim is aware of death sentence. Perpetrators are the state, homeland governments, or security structures of political movements. Killing is all other deaths, including a killing by a crowd of people.
Torture	TORTURE	Torture happens in *captivity* or in *custody* of any kind, formal or informal (for example, prisons, police cells, detention camps, private houses, containers, or anywhere while the individual is tied up or bound to something). Torture is usually used to get information, or to force the person to do something (for example, admit to a crime, or sign a statement), but it is also used for punishment, degradation, and systematic breakdown of an individual. It includes mental or psychological torture (for example, witnessing torture, or telling the person that their family is dead).
Severe Ill-treatment	SEVERE	Severe ill-treatment covers attempted killing and all forms of inflicted suffering causing *extreme*

		bodily and/or mental harm. It tends to take place outside of custody (for example, injury by a car bomb, or assault at a rally), but a person can be subjected to severe ill treatment in custody too (for example, a single server beating, or tear gas in the cell).
Abduction	ABDUCTION	Abduction is when a person is forcibly and illegally taken away (for example, kidnapping). It does *not* mean detention or arrest. Arrest is not a gross violation of human rights (see *associated violations*). If the person is never found again, it is a disappearance.

*'HRV' = 'human rights violation'.

(TRC, 1998 5 (1), Appendix 1)

Following this broad categorisation, each HRV (human rights violation) category—'killing', 'torture', 'severe ill-treatment'—is broken down into further, more detailed subsets as follows:

KILLING	**CODE**	**DEFINITION**
Beaten to death	BEATING	Beaten to death by being hit, kicked, punched, specifying description of part of body assaulted, if known (e.g. feet, face, head, genitals, breasts), or object used (e.g. sjambok, baton, gun, rifle, stick, rope, whip, plank, beat against wall).
Burnt to death	BURNING	Killed in a fire or burnt to death using petrol, chemicals, fire, scalding, arson. This does *not* include

		'necklacing' or petrol bombing.
Killed by poison, drugs or chemicals	CHEMICALS	Killed by poison, drugs, or household substance such as bleach or drain cleaner.

A further fifteen categories of 'killing' are delineated in addition to thirteen categories of 'torture', sixteen categories of 'severe ill-treatment', two of 'abduction' and fourteen of 'associated violations'. This coding frame was used by the TRC to organise, categorise, and hierarchize the details of tens of thousands of testimonies which were then fed into the TRC's Information Management System, *Infocomm*.

The political effect of this categorisation was to synthesise divergent testimonies about the past around the narration of related violations, and to construct human rights violations as occurring within a 'political context' which was concordant with the overall historical narrative about past violence that the TRC wished to tell—that is, as occurring within the framework of party-political violence. For example, the description of 'killing' explicitly invokes the *political* contexts within which killing occurs and speaks of 'targeted persons', 'plots', 'plans', 'assassinations' and 'capital punishment'.

The disciplinary effects of this categorisation are well-illustrated by an imaginative inversion. By substituting 'murder' for 'killing' an assertion of *individual* agency and accountability for violations is more powerfully evoked, which might legitimise a *retributive* process that would attempt to apportion individual culpability, rather than the *restorative* one favoured by the TRC, and one which attempted to make sense of individual actions within the broader violent party-political contest.

Strategies of the TRC

Foucault puts forward a fourth set of rules to describe the way in which certain 'strategies', themes or theories flow from a particular discourse and which are comprised of the organisation of the objects, types of enunciation, and concepts (Foucault, 1972: 64). The application of these rules to this empirical case enable us to understand reconciliation in South Africa as a particular social and political construction arising out of a convergence of social, political and historical factors that produced its own authoritative truth claims about transition from apartheid.

Reconciliation in South Africa was a strategy of political transition that derived its authority from its construction of the objects, subjects and concepts of the discourse and the sites from which it was articulated. It engaged particular constellations of speaking authorities, evidence bases and concepts such that other interventions were excluded or quite simply never emerged. For example, reconciliation organised the subjects (victims and perpetrators), objects (human rights violations), types of enunciation (confessional and testimonial), and concepts (gross violations of human rights, truth, reconciliation) in relationship to one another. The effect of this organisation was to allow specific acts of reconciliation to emerge by providing a general template-script of what reconciliation should consist of and involve, that is, confession, testimony, forgiveness, amnesty and so on, into which particular individuals could fit themselves as reconciled 'victims' and 'perpetrators'. However, the TRC did not make it possible, nor provide a language within which people could say 'I am not reconciled', or 'I do not forgive you', or 'I want you to be punished', or 'I want to be punished', or 'I do not confess or apologise for what I did' or 'I do not recognise this process'. Simply put, it did not facilitate or recognise non-reconciled outcomes as possibile responses to the truths about the past that the TRC produced.

We can also use Foucault's analysis to point to a 'failure' of reconciliation on the part of the TRC. Particular instances of reconciliation, such as individual 'reconciliation events' would seem perfectly illustrative of Foucault's general account of 'strategies'. Yet the TRC did not provide the official forum through which victim-perpetrator encounters, which might seem to be the perfect examplar of a reconciliation event, could be enacted.

In sum, Foucault's work facilitates an account of reconciliation as an intrinsically political project that is constitutive of power, truth, and subjectivity. Reconciliation discourse, by constituting its objects, subjects, concepts, and strategies, governs the production of knowledge and statements of 'fact' and 'value' and maps out the relations of power between those subjected to, and constituted by, its disciplinary force.

Althusser and the TRC as Ideological State Apparatus

To this Foucauldian account of the TRC, I want to add a consideration of Louis Althusser's work on ideology and subjectivity. Althusser's formulation of ideology as an element of the 'state apparatus' represents a more compelling (for this study of the TRC) account of the institutionalisation of power than that rendered by Foucault, for whom power is more complex, emanating from a diffuse and intricate network of locations. As Slavoj Zizek notes, Althusser's ISA (Ideological State Apparatus), in order to be able to call into being the individual, 'always-already presupposes the massive presence of the state' (Zizek, 1994: 13). Thus Althusser accounts more forcefully than Foucault for the production of subjectivity as an effect of centralised power, of special relevance to an interpretation of the political performance of the TRC (Althusser, 1993). Zizek argues that by contrast, Foucault fails to engage with 'ideology' as power which means that he cannot draw out the concrete mechanisms of power's workings.[3] Nevertheless the continuities and resonances joining Foucault's account of 'discourse' to Althusser's of 'ideology' are suggestive and taken together, they can provide a complementary account of the political workings of discourse.[4]

For Althusser, ideology is not independent of, or apart from, the social world, nor does it simply reflect its 'realities'. Rather, ideology is constitutive of society in that it produces material effects, important amongst which is the construction of human subjectivity. As such, Althusser regards ideology as necessary function of society, a social practice that provides individuals with social and political identities that are embodied in social institutions and rituals that in turn bolster particular belief systems. It ultimately functions to secure the reproduction of a 'social formation' by effecting an 'imaginary' resolution of 'real' social antagonisms. For Althusser these antagonisms are, primarily, class antagonisms generated by the relations of production, where ideology functions to secure social reproduction under such conditions. However, I would depart from Althusser by arguing that such antagonisms are not *always* reducible to class antagonisms, and with this in mind wish to suggest in the following argument that Althusser's insights, whilst specific to a class analysis, can usefully be transposed and deployed to understand the resolution of antagonisms that reconciliation seeks to secure.

Two aspects of Althusser's writings are relevant here: first, his account of the embodiment and enactment of ideology in material institutions; and second, his exposition of human subjectivity as a material effect of ideology through the function of the 'interpellative hail'.

Ideology as Material Practice

Althusser understands ideology as a fundamental force in the reproduction of society. It is a social 'practice' which produces human subjectivity, constitutes social and political identities, beliefs and outlooks that are embodied in social institutions and their attendant rituals. Ideology renders stable and seamless the social order; it functions to cover over discontinuities, discrepancies, and contradictions. So crucial is this political function, and so firmly does Althusser wish to insist upon its institutional materiality that he makes the unusual and startling terminological move of designating ideology and its embodiments (Church, family, media, etc.) as *part of the state* or in his terms 'the state apparatus'. For Althusser, ideology binds together a social formation no less materially than do the police, courts, and army. It is in his notion of the ISA that Althusser's account of subjectivity makes a compelling theoretical framework through which to interpret the workings of the TRC, a temporary institution that specifically constructed and called into being the subjects of political violence that underpinned and moralised South Africa's democratic transition.

In Althusser's account, any perception of reality is always already an act of interpretation which draws upon, and is legitimised by, a prior collective discourse which is itself produced by a combination of material and social conditions and institutionalised in ISAs (Althusser, 1993: 16–17).[5] Ideology materialises through ritual practices that find their formal articulation in institutions. For example, religious practices appear to the believer and others as fundamentally an expression of an inner conviction: the Church is made manifest by its attendant rituals of, for example, baptism, confession and prayer; the ritualistic expressions of the institution make its inner manifestation—'faith'—

external, material and observable. However, rituals are legitimised by and through the institution. They do not simply *reflect* an inner faith but are intrinsic to its material constitution. In Althusser's words 'the existence of the ideas of [a subject's] belief is material in that his ideas are his material actions inserted into material practices governed by material rituals which are themselves defined by the material ideological apparatus from which derive the ideas of that subject' (Althusser, 1993: 43). This point is nicely captured by Zizek, who writes that ISAs 'designate the material existence of ideology in ideological practices, rituals and institutions . . . the "external" ritual performatively generates its own ideological foundation' (Zizek, 1994: 12–13). These insights into the relationship between ritual, faith and its institutionalisation illuminate the way in which the TRC politicises the outer enactment or performance of 'inner' psychological and faith-based processes such as remorse, forgiveness and reconciliation. As an ISA the TRC is a material institution replete with tribunals, formal procedures and rituals. Althusser refers to Pascal's 'kneel and you will believe' which parallels the TRC's implicit 'testify, take part, follow our procedures, and you will be reconciled'. Moreover, the very notion of an Ideological *State* Apparatus seems particularly applicable to the TRC which was even in the most basic legalistic sense a state organisation, established by South African law, with the explicit purpose of securing social unity and legitimising the new regime through the deliberate construction of a new, inclusive national identity.

The Ideological Interpellation of Subjects

The materialisation of ideology in everyday life is manifest in Althusser's 'interpellative hail' through which human subjectivity is constituted (Althusser, 1993: 44–51). Althusser argues that 'the category of the subject is only constitutive of all ideology insofar as all ideology has the function. . . of "constituting" concrete individuals as subjects' (Althusser, 1993: 45). Following on from this, a double constitution takes place where the functioning of ideology is only extant in its functioning in the material forms of its existence, that is, embodied within the subject called into being by ideology. Central to this materialisation is the process of 'recognition' by which the subject is brought into being. Althusser uses the example of two friends meeting in the street, one of whom addresses the other 'hello, my friend', and shakes his hand. Hand shaking and ritual addresses are material ritual practices 'of ideological recognition in everyday life' through which certain subjects—friends, acquaintances, colleagues—are recognised, called into being or 'interpellated' (Althusser, 1993: 46). Ideology functions by 'transforming' concrete individuals into subjects through the operation of the interpellative hail where the materialisation of ideology and the hailing or interpellation of individuals as subjects are simultaneous with one another.[6]

The TRC can readily be understood as an ISA because it explicitly interpellated South Africa's new political subjects through a series of legal declarations and public hearings, amongst which were the legal documentation preceding the Commission such as the Interim Constitution and the Promotion of

National Unity and Reconciliation Act, the Committees of the TRC and the ceremonies that attended the public performance of national reconciliation. Central to this performance were the subject categories of victim and perpetrator through which the new national ideology of reconciliation was materialised and enacted and accompanied by the rituals of confession, forgiveness and remorse. These rituals called into being their subjects who, by virtue of their recognition of the given subject category as either victim or perpetrator, participated in a double subjection. Their recognition of the interpellative hail entailed an acceptance of themselves within the order designated by the ideology of reconciliation. This required, for example, an acceptance on the part of the victim that a perpetrator is not punished but granted amnesty in return for truth. And at the public hearings, perpetrators were encouraged to make palpable shows of remorse and to seek forgiveness from victims.

Victims and perpetrators were also institutionalised through the discrete Committees of the TRC to which they had to give testimony. The Amnesty Committee solicited, recorded, and processed perpetrator testimonies, and the Human Rights Violations Committee did the same with victim stories. As a result, those testifying had to decide to which Committee their evidence would be submitted on the basis of whether their submission was a victim or perpetrator submission. This had to be decided *prior to* submission. In short, individuals had to decide *in advance of speaking to the TRC* whether they were speaking as 'victim' or 'perpetrator'. This fundamental division in the mechanisms of the Commission structured the identities of those submitting to its authority prior to public hearings which further reinforced, perpetuated and legitimised these already established identities as the central protagonists of South Africa's new historical account.[7]

Narrating Politics

Having put forward a distinctive political discourse analysis of the subjects and objects of the TRC's reconciliation story I turn now to the question of narrative, the internal structure of which performs precise disciplinary functions that are not captured by the analyses presented so far. Narrative, typically, imposes a trajectory upon its subjects—victims and perpetrators—and makes sense of its objects—gross violations of human rights—because it arranges actions and events in a sequential and connected relationship and embeds them within a tripartite temporal structure which consists of a well-marked beginning, middle and end. The works of Hayden White and Frank Kermode help to flesh out the ways in which an understanding of narrative *form* is fundamental to thinking through the politics of reconciliation in South Africa.

White and the Content of the Form

Hayden White argues that narrative 'entails ontological and epistemic choices with distinct ideological and even specifically political implications' (White, 1987: ix). The effect of these 'choices' is to endow upon any narrated events an 'illusory coherence' that underpins a claim to a 'secured knowledge of reality' (White, 1978: 81). Narrative makes a claim on reality insofar as it feigns 'to make the world speak itself and speak itself as a story' (White, 1987: 2).

The correspondence effect—between narrative and reality—is embedded within narrative structure. Stories situate the actions of agents within a particular socio-political order and direct their actions towards an end point or closure which effects a summation of the overall 'meaning' of that depiction. Of course, no sequence of events really does just end or become resolved, so narrative closure comes to signify the constructed transition 'from one physical or social space to another' (White, 1987: 23), such as the transition from apartheid to multi-party government in South Africa.

Closure provides the central principle by which a teleological significance is assigned to preceding events, with the effect that narrative transforms its subject(s) into a 'totality evolving in time' because it comprises a temporal unity that delineates a beginning, middle, and an end. This temporal unity underpins the claim to an 'authentic' representation of 'what actually happened' because in order to sustain the mimetic effect—the correspondence between the narrative and the real—events must, according to White, be narrated according to the chronological ordering of their occurrence. They must also be 'revealed as possessing a structure, an order of meaning, that they do not possess as mere sequence', an effect secured by closure or resolution (White, 1987: 5). Narrative endows 'reality' upon the events related because the events appear on the one hand to be subordinated to a particular order of moral existence, and on the other they elicit meaning from their place within this order. For example, the TRC's narration of a history of 'gross violations of human rights' perpetrated with a 'political objective' is subordinated to the principle of reconciliation, and violations elicit meaning from their place within the moral order that reconciliation (as closure) institutes. Narrative 'possesses a content prior to any given actualization of it in speech or writing, or rather a "content of the form"' (White, 1987: ix), and it is this feature that secures its ideological effect, conditioning relations between events narrated by being *prior* to them.

White cites Hegel to suggest historical narrative not only displays a particular form but also presupposes a particular content through which materialises a socio-political order or legal system 'against which or on behalf of which the typical agents of a narrative account militate' (White, 1987: 13). The questions of law, legitimacy, and authority are thus central to narrative, the closure of which exacts the force of a moral judgement on the events it relates. But what White does not illuminate in Hegel is the explicitly political question of the relationship of narrative to the state. Hegel notes that the appearance of the state as a continuous and stable entity is an *effect* of official historical narratives that document its emergence: 'It is the State which first presents subject-matter that is not only *adapted* to the prose of History, but involves the production of such history in the very progress of its own being' (Hegel, 1956: 61). In Hegel's view, narrative—'the prose of History'—is fundamental to the production of the unity and continuity of the state, an endeavour to which the narrative of reconciliation in South Africa is also manifestly directed.

In general, White's work investigates narrative as a universal 'deep structure' of historical consciousness and historical representation in order to disclose the repressions inherent in the construction of knowledge and authority that are, in part, an effect of narrative structure itself. In so doing, he reflects primarily upon historiography because, he argues, it provides an especially fruitful locus of any deliberation on narrative because narrative is the instrument 'with which the conflicting claims of the imaginary and the real are mediated, arbitrated, or resolved in a discourse' (White, 1987: 4).

This observation is pertinent to the politics of reconciliation which mediates a contest between the imperatives of the real and a desire for the imaginary. The TRC negotiated the relationship between the real (violent conflict) and the imaginary (future reconciliation), by narrating a causal and linear relationship between them. Its narrative was roughly organised around the following stages in its story: a past conditioned by violent conflict, a present marked by the confessional, and testimonial, and a future reconciliation. In three important sections of the Report, explored in detail in chapter four, the TRC narrates and re-narrates South Africa's history as a history overwhelmingly conditioned by violence. The Report asserts the necessity of placing the investigated events within a broad historical context because the TRC 'tells only a small part of a much larger story of human rights abuse in South and southern Africa' (TRC, 1998: 1 (2) 3). It states that the wider story is conditioned by two main factors that shaped the national history: 'violence and the law, and the relationship between them' (TRC, 1998: 1 (2) 4).

The first of these accounts appears prominently as the 'scene-setting' chapter in the first of the six volumes, which recounts the political and historical perspective within which 'gross human rights violations' during the investigated period from 1960 to 1994 took place. This narrative takes in almost three hundred and fifty years of violations, reaching back to the mid-seventeenth century. It is organised into three national historical 'phases': the first presenting a backdrop of three centuries of violent and oppressive practices in South Africa and focuses upon the struggle between the Afrikaners, of Dutch descent, and all other ethnic groups living in South Africa during this period; the second phase is marked by the inauguration of the National Party in 1948 which marked the formal instantiation of apartheid and investigates the violent foundations of its laws and regulations; and the third phase marks out the time span of the TRC's investigations beginning with the Sharpeville Massacre in 1960 and ending with the legal inauguration of the TRC in 1994. This latter period is narrated as one of 'intensified conflict' and is portrayed primarily as a political contest between the National Party and the African National Congress.

By situating the mandated period within a historical context of violence reaching back some three hundred years the TRC narrates a linear, causal, and cumulative effect of the perpetration of gross human rights violations. The resultant and central political effect of this narrative is to render an account of the genesis of the South African nation that is commensurate with the origins of apartheid. The Report thus enters contentious historiographical debates about the inception of apartheid. The term 'apartheid' is often used to designate practices of governance and control used three hundred years ago and also refers to the laws and policies inaugurated by the National Party from 1948. The TRC acknowledges that the inauguration of the NP in 1948 represents an intensification and formalisation of apartheid but not a departure from previous practices of governance. The effect of this is to suggest that the success of the NP in 1948 did not constitute a 'rupture' to a previously different political order, but by contrast, represented the continuation of a long history of violent oppression in which the NP were only recent protagonists. The *continuity* of violence governs the TRC's narration, authorising the necessity of reconciliation.

The TRC's history conveys the message that 'violence has been the single most determining factor in South African political history', but that, and crucially, only a reconciliatory politics could provide the necessary moral and lasting closure of violence, the inauguration of which symbolised a new order of existence coinciding with transition to the new regime (TRC, 1998: 1 (2) 68). This is a redemptive narrative in that it offers to the victims of human rights violations the hope of deliverance from their traumatic experiences, and to the perpetrators, the narrative offers a warning that contains, even although it does not actualise, the possibility of retribution.

That the new regime in South Africa sought to re-narrate the past at all is testimony to a political contest in which *at least* two versions of the past could have been narrated. In the absence of such a contest, there would be no real reason to undertake the authority of rendering a 'true account' of 'what really happened'. The authority of the narrative rendered thus functions as 'the authority of reality itself' (White, 1987: 20).

Kermode's 'Sense of an Ending'

Kermode pushes an interpretation of closure further. He explores the ways in which apocalyptic fictions, or 'fictions of the end', condition our experience of living in time, where closure emerges out of crisis and is a response to the desire for order and meaning (Kermode, 2000). For Kermode, crisis and closure are the conditioning features of narrative which itself functions as the fundamental discursive technology through which we make sense of the world and of our place within it.

Kermode suggests that 'the ending' conditions the unfolding of a story from its very beginning. He suggests that the end is *immanent* rather than simply imminent in the story itself because narrative emplotment 'imposes a meaning on the events that make up its story level by revealing at the end a structure that was immanent in the events all along' (Kermode, 2000: 20). Reconciliation as the prefigured closure of transition thus shapes the new official history *from its very beginning* in both symbolic and material ways, both as an imaginary condition of co-existence, and as a disciplinary discursive construction.

Reconciliation as closure functions not only at the level of the official narrative told by the TRC, but as a powerful trope governing individual testimonies. Jeffrey Benzien, a former security policeman in the 1980s, stood before the TRC in 1996 to confess to the killing of Ashley Kriel and to torturing other ANC activists. He was present at the TRC to tell the 'truth' about violent state security operations in exchange for amnesty. He related how he had developed a torture technique which became known as the 'wet bag', involving placing a wet cloth bag over the head of a restrained suspect and closing it tightly around the neck, and how he had used this technique in order to 'extract information' from Kriel amongst others. Benzien prefaced his confession with the following 'reconciliatory' declaration:

> Firstly, I apologise to any person or persons whom I have harmed and I specifically apologise to the families of Ashley Kriel for the death of their son and brother. . . Life is precious and judged *ex post facto*, and based on today's political situation of reconciliation, his death was unnecessary. . . It is now reconciliation, forgive and forget at its best (*TRC Amnesty Hearing*, Benzien, Cape Town, July 14, 1997).

Benzien's apology explicitly invokes reconciliation as the desired end point towards which his revelation is directed. In his testimony, Benzien mentions that the reconciliatory spirit in which he offered his 'truth' had been already reciprocated by some of Kriel's family members who had stated that they would not oppose his amnesty application. Reconciliation, thus, conditions and structures Benzien's 'confession'. Indeed, Benzien's testimony appears on first reading to resonate with White's understanding of narrative as a powerful system of meaning production 'by which individuals can be taught to live a distinctively "imaginary relation to their real conditions of existence"'. The TRC's narrative conditioned individual testimonies to the TRC in order to make commensurate those accounts with the overall story about reconciliation it sought to tell. This had the effect of inculcating amongst many participants 'an unreal but meaningful relation' to the social formations of reconciliation in which they were 'indentured to live out their lives and realize their destinies as social subjects' (White, 1987: x).

However, Benzien implicitly indicates the contingency of South Africa's reconciliatory narrative, and knowingly implies that he might tell his story differently under different conditions. He states that his confession is made on the basis of 'today's political situation of reconciliation', and that 'it is now reconciliation', implicitly acknowledging the contingent political circumstances out of which a reconciliatory politics emerged, and implying that he might be delivering his account on different terms had the political climate been different. Benzien's witting manipulation of the TRC narrative is still, however, a demonstration of the disciplinary power of the official story, which he makes (or is required to make) internal to his own account, as much as it is a subtle repudiation of it.[8]

Kermode's thesis allows us to see how reconciliation works back through the official narrative and conditions individual testimonies delivered to the TRC. Reconciliation works as an organising category that seeks and imposes concordance in place of contestation, conditioning the way in which South Africa's history is related in symbolic and material ways; through the discourse of forgiveness at the public hearings, and through the negation of criminal trials in favour of amnesty. Reconciliation conditions what gets told and how. It demands that a particular story about South Africa's past is told, a story of a cleavage between or violent 'splitting' of 'two' communities that requires healing. It tells of what is past, violent conflict, what is passing, truth-revelation (confession) and remorse, and what is to come, reconciliation. Thus the past and present bear the mark of future narrative closure, of reconciliation. Reconciliation is thus a transformative fiction that confers both a sequential and causal logic *and* a moral unity upon the related events.

Kermode acknowledges that the moral force of closure is thus in some way related to judgement as the hidden, organising principle of narrative itself where, as White also notes, 'the "weight of meaning" of the events recounted is "thrown forward" onto a future just beyond the immediate present, a future fraught with moral judgement and punishment for the wicked' (White, 1987: 23). As such, the TRC figures reconciliation both as narrative closure but also as a principle of judgement that seeks concordance between contending perspectives on the past. In compensation for the irregularity and contingency of 'real life', 'justice is the human order we find or impose upon it' (Kermode, 2000: 105).

South Africa's past is, of course, irreducible to a single plot as past and current contestations, including Benzien's subtle testimony, suggest. But Kermode's analysis of narrative structuration is less deterministic than his explication of closure appears to allow because he argues that closure is continually marked and disrupted by the interplay between identity and difference (Kermode, 2000: 144). This is expressed as a conflict between the overall plot and individual contestations of the plot, such that what is of real interest is 'the conflict between the deterministic pattern any plot suggests, and the freedom of persons within that plot to choose and so to alter the structure, the relations of beginning, middle, and end' (Kermode, 2000: 30).

Indeed, 'real events' disrupt the coherence that narrative sanctifies because *they do not yield themselves as stories* but are *transformed into stories*. Every story entails the inclusion of particular events, and the exclusion of other events and accounts that do not fall within the narrative *telos*. Those excluded threaten to disturb the formal (moral) coherence of the story because no single narrative can contain the range of meanings it generates or forecloses. One notable contestation of the TRC's story which illustrates this point deserves a mention here. Wynand Malan was originally appointed as commissioner to the TRC but withdrew because he objected to its premises. Malan's opposition to the TRC is included as a 'Minority Position' in the Report in which he argues against what he perceives as the TRC's antipathy to 'certain groups living within traditional or nationalist value systems who were party to the conflict', that is, NP supporters and agents (TRC, 1998: 5 (9)). Malan goes on to criticise the TRC's equation of 'reconciliation' with 'national unity', and specifically opposes the religious tenor of the TRC's work. He disputes the TRC's historical narrative by providing an alternative (NP)) narrative of apartheid violence which, he argues, was justified by the 'need for security'. The convention of the 'minority position' deployed by the TRC makes possible the inclusion of alternative narrative interventions that might be incongruent with, indeed generated by, the dominant story *without* derailing the main story the TRC wishes to tell. This convention simultaneously subordinates Malan's position to the perspective of the TRC.

Conclusions

The theoretical interpretation of reconciliation in South Africa advanced in this chapter has sought to illuminate two related arguments that reveal its political workings. First, it demonstrates the ways in which reconciliation is an ideological system of meaning that constructs and makes 'real' the subjects and objects of the political processes it governs. And second, by incorporating a narrative analysis into the general frame of discourse analysis, this discussion has shown how causality and connection between historical events and political processes is constructed and not 'found', and that what are assumed to be the regular continuities and assumptions of political life, or specifically of reconciliation in South Africa, are in part an effect of their narrative representation. It shows what, discursively, is entailed in constructing reconciliation as a response to the conflict between the moral demands of justice and the political demands of peace, a dilemma out of which many reconciliatory political projects to date have been conceived.

By combining the insights of discourse analytic and narrative approaches, this chapter facilitates two fundamental political insights. First, it shows how reconciliation *constrains* in that it constructs power relations and is productive of political processes. Second, this combination of approaches allows an understanding of those moments where narrative *fails* to constrain, where there is a discrepancy between those who conform and those who do not. These are moments that make apparent the way in which the TRC attempts to force a unity between conflictual and disparate elements of the story, as Benzien's testimony and Malan's refutation demonstrate. In fact, far from closing off the past, South Africa's reconciliation story produced new conflicts around the meaning of that past to which attest contemporary contestations of the TRC's work around the issue of reparations, discussed in the conclusions of this book. This case demonstrates one of the important ways in which the type of reconciliation projected by the TRC did not, could not, fully redeem the antagonisms of the past.

Notes

1. This formulation does not preclude the possibility that declarations by authoritative subjects are contestable and indeed contested in practice.

2. Foucault's account of subjection is extended further in his later writings and comprises a more elaborate account than I am able to present here. Foucault shows how human subjection is manifest differently according to particular historical configurations (Foucault, 1982).

3. It is important to note that Foucault deliberately excludes the concept of ideology from his own analyses. His aversion to ideology is opposed to the general understanding that ideology stands in opposition to something else, for example truth, but Foucault refuses to adjudicate between the truth or falsity of any particular discourse (Foucault, 1980: 118).

4. These continuities are not implausible given the shared intellectual milieu in which they were developed. David Macey records that Althusser and his key collaborator Etienne Balibar regarded Foucault's *The Order of Things* as helping to provide 'a general theory of ideology', whilst a brief flirtation of Foucault's with the terminology of 'Ideological State Apparatuses' reflected the influence of Althusser's essay (Macey, 1994: 197 and 300). However, many may see Foucault's work as a project that develops and departs from that of Althusser in ways that surpass or subvert its original framework. But a contrary case can be made, as suggested by Zizek, that Foucault's insights can be put to more effective use if reintegrated within a revised or "post-Althusserian" framework.

5. Althusser distinguishes between ISAs and Repressive State Apparatuses. ISAs cover religious institutions, educational bodies, the family, legal institutions, the political system and parties, trade unions, media, and cultural institutions. Repressive State Apparatuses 'function by violence' and include the government, administration, army, police, courts, and prisons (Althusser, 1993: 16–17).

6. However, this would suggest a linear temporal fixing of the 'concrete individual' as being prior to the subject. Althusser corrects his linear account by arguing that as ideology is 'eternal' it has always-already interpellated individuals as subjects such that 'individuals are always-already subjects' even before they are born (Althusser, 1993: 50).

7. Whilst this may not seem problematic, in some cases this identity division was complex. For example, *askaris* were former ANC armed operatives who were captured by the state and 'turned' through torture into state security agents, fitting into both the 'victim' and 'perpetrator' categories constructed by the TRC.

8. This is partly because the success of his amnesty application fell upon the narrative framing of his testimonial and Benzien was adept at adopting the language of the new order. As such, the amnesty provision provided a further constraint not on simply *what* could be related but *how* it could be related in order for an amnesty application to be successful. For an excellent discussion of the narrative framing of amnesty accounts see Veitch (2001).

Chapter Three
Narrating the Past: Writing South Africa's Violent History

The quest for memory is the search for one's history.

> Pierre Nora, 'Between Memory and History: Les Lieux des Mem-
> oires.' *Representations*, 26 (1989).

This chapter opens out the discussion in the previous chapter about the particularities of *how* and *to what effect* the TRC story about reconciliation was constructed. It presents the first in a sequence of three chapters that are dedicated to
unpacking the TRC's tri-partite organization of its reconciliation narrative—
from past violence, to present confessional to future reconciliation—and to
showing how these are constructed as existing in a linear, causal and seemingly
inevitable relationship with one another. As the first of these three chapters, this
one concentrates on how the TRC narrates South Africa's past. Presented here is
a reconstruction and critique of the broader historical narrative within which the
TRC interpreted and made meaningful its own, unique, account of party political
violence under apartheid from 1960 to 1994, the period of time that the TRC was
mandated to investigate. The scope of the TRC's history of South Africa is,
however, much more expansive than the mandated period, reaching back around
three hundred years. This three hundred year history is one which, at every significant juncture, is narrated as being overwhelmingly violent, and is invoked in
order to contextualize the mandated period as a consequential and ineluctable
evolution of violent social and political practices that had a long and entrenched
lineage. This chapter also shows how this history converged upon and conditioned the individual testimonies. The disciplinary effects of this broader narrative were brought to bear upon, and made to shape, the individual testimonies

from both victims and perpetrators. This narrative framing was partly an effect of the TRC's mandate and also its information management system which made necessary particular methods of solicitation and interpretation of the individual testimonies, discussed later in this chapter.

The TRC's Politico-Historical Narrative

The official documentation ensuing from the TRC's investigations constitutes a palpable attempt by the TRC to write a memoir or biography of the nation, and marks out the narrative parameters within which the Commission made individual testimonies of violence intelligible. In three important sections of the extensive official documentation, the TRC narrates and re-narrates South Africa's violent history within an overall national historical context.

The first of these accounts appears prominently as the prosaic 'scene-setting' chapter in the first of the five volumes of the final report, and it seeks to historicize the political and historical perspective within which gross human rights violations during the mandated period investigated by the TRC, from 1960 to 1994, took place (TRC, 1 (2)). This narrative takes in almost three-hundred and fifty years of violence (reinterpreted by the TRC as 'violations'), reaching from the mid-seventeenth century right up to the inauguration of the TRC in 1995. It provides the foundation upon which the ensuing chapters in the documentation build, and which deal in turn with the instigation of the TRC, its mandate, concepts and principles, methodology and processes, and the particular legal challenges faced by the TRC.

The effect of situating the mandated period within a historical context of violations reaching back some three hundred years narrates a linear, causal, and cumulative account of gross human rights violations. The key political effect of this narrative is to *render an account of the genesis of the nation that is commensurate with the origins of apartheid*. The Report as historical documentation thus enters historiographical debates contesting the inception of apartheid, which, as Aletta Norval notes, broadly contend that:

> The term 'apartheid'. . . has been used to refer both to practices which came into being more than three hundred years ago, making the history of apartheid coincide with that of South Africa, and to the more narrowly defined set of certain legislative measures that came into being with the victory of the National Party (NP) in 1948 (Norval, 1996: 1).

Whilst for the TRC, the inauguration of formalized apartheid in 1948 represented an intensification and formal materialization of apartheid, its logic of separate development had been manifest long before, if not formally so. The political success of the National Party in 1948 did not, according to the TRC narrative, constitute a 'rupture' to a previously different political order, but represented, rather, the continuation of violent repression.

The Report asserts the necessity of placing the investigated events from the mandated period within a broad historical context of violence because the TRC 'tells only a small part of a much larger story of human rights abuse in South and southern Africa' (TRC, 1 (2) 3). The wider story gives weight to that concentrated upon by the TRC because it is conditioned, the TRC argued, by two main factors that shaped the national history: 'violence and the law, and the relationship between them' (TRC, 1 (2) 4).

The National Narrative

This first narrative focuses on the struggle between the Afrikaners, of Dutch descent, and all other ethnic groups living in South Africa at different times including those of English descent. It is organized within the final Report into three national historical 'phases': the first presenting a backdrop of three centuries of violent and oppressive practices in South Africa carried out by, primarily, a succession of white settlers against the black African population; the second phase is marked by the inauguration of the National Party in 1948, an event widely considered to mark the birth of apartheid; and the third phase marks out the terrain of the Commission's investigations, the period of 'intensified conflict'—that is, of violent opposition to the apartheid regime—from 1960 to 1994. It is this latter period of conflict between government and resistance groups from 1960 to the elections in 1994 that formed the focus of the TRC's investigations and of its historical narrative.

The overall effect of this narrative is to convey the TRC's central moralizing thrust that 'violence has been the single most determining factor in South African political history' (TRC, 1 (2) 68). In this passage, the Report goes on to state that the reference to violence does not apply 'simply to physical or overt violence—the violence of the gun—but also to the violence of the law or what is often referred to as institutional or structural violence.' Whilst on one level this concords with the narrative that the TRC seeks to tell—that dimension of South African history that illuminates the relationship between violence and the law— but at the same time, this narrative is at odds with the overall story the TRC tells about political violence, primarily because structural violence is almost entirely excluded from the mandate of the TRC. As such, there is a tension between the *context* that the TRC wishes to illuminate here, and the *particular instances of violence* that occurred against this backdrop and that form the core of the TRC story. This national context is depicted as follows:

From the seventeenth century to 1948
The first phase of South Africa's violent history is traced back to violations committed in the course of the slave trade in the Cape between 1652 and 1834,[1] the wars of dispossession and colonial conquest dating from the first war against the Khoisan in 1659 and the Bambatha uprising of 1906 which saw the last armed defensive action by an indigenous group; the systematic hunting and elimination of indigenous peoples by Boer and British settlers in the seventeenth and eight-

eenth centuries; the *Mfecane* or *Difaquane* where thousands died and were displaced in a Zulu-led process of state formation and dissolution; the South African War of 1899–1902 during which British forces put Boer women and children in concentration camps during which around twenty thousand people died (in addition to which a roughly equal number of black Africans are alleged to have been exhumed from the sites of British concentration camps) (TRC, 1 (2) footnote 2); and finally the genocidal war early in the twentieth century conducted by the German colonial administration in South West Africa which resulted in the Herero people being almost completely wiped out.

This rendering makes it clear that the Commission did not deem gross human rights violations the exclusive preserve of parties to the post-1960 phase of 'intensified conflict'. In charting the historical precedents of violence, the Report constructs a succession of governments as perpetrators of varying degrees of violations. It notes that the South African Party government, consisting of mainly English-speaking South Africans, killed over one hundred strikers and onlookers during a miners' strike on the Reef in July 1913. Further, three times in 1921 and 1922 the same government orchestrated a military response to a protesting religious sect, the Israelites at Bulhoek, killing one hundred and eighty three people, and again against striking white mineworkers on the Reef in 1922 resulting in two hundred and fourteen deaths, and for the third time against the Bondelswarts people of South West Africa, a landless hunting people, who were protesting against a dog tax in 1922. One hundred civilians were machine-gunned to death from the air.

It is against this historical backdrop of violence that the TRC sets such actions as the South African Defence Force (SADF) killing over six hundred civilians and combatants in Kassanga, Angola in 1978, and the South African Police (SAP) shooting of several hundred black protestors in the weeks following the June 16 events in Soweto. Of these events the Report states that government agents were 'operating in terms of a well-established tradition of excessive or unjustifiable use of force against government opponents' which 'is not, of course, to exonerate them or the force they employed, but simply to put those events and actions in historical context' (TRC, 1 (2) 9). However, the effect of historicizing such events and actions is not simply an act of objective 'cataloguing': it is political. It is to invoke the specter of a particular history in order to justify the investigation of certain events over others in order to legitimize particular narratives over others. This narration is telling, however, in a more subtle way in that it concentrates primarily on the crimes of the powerful. This story provides a nuanced, almost counter-backdrop, to the narrative about recent violence which the TRC was forced to relate in terms of violence perpetrated by the state *and* opposing forces, and to apportion blame across the parties.

1948–1960

The Report gives much more attention to the second 'historical phase' it demarcates, which concentrates on the practices of the National Party government since its inauguration in 1948, marking an intensification and formalization of the ideology of 'separate development' or apartheid.

The National Party consolidated and extended the remit of the first South African Constitution of 1910 which already excluded the majority black population from basic civil and political rights. The Report states that 'the determination of an individual's civil and political rights by. . . skin colour. . . had its roots far back in South Africa's colonial past', but it was the policy of apartheid introduced by the NP that marked the institutionalization of racial segregation (TRC, 1 (2) 22). In the first decade or so of its existence, the regime built upon or reinstated and updated existing legislation to extend segregation into every aspect of political, economic and social life. Several key legislative acts were implemented during this time and they are highlighted by the TRC in its attempt to tell a story about the relationship between apartheid violence and the law. These were the Population Registration Act of 1950 which required the classification of every South African citizen into one of four racial categories; the Group Areas Act of 1950 which divided the entire state into areas for exclusive occupation by designated racial groups; the Prohibition of Mixed Marriages Act of 1949 and the Immorality Amendment Act of 1950 prohibited future interracial marriages and sexual contact; the Suppression of Communism Act of 1950 banned the Communist Party and provided the legislative means to 'eliminate' or proscribe all forms of dissent; the Separate Amenities Act of 1953 separated all public amenities designating them for the exclusive use of specified racial groups; the 1953 Bantu Education Act instigated a separate and inferior education system for African pupils, and finally, the Extension of University Education' Act of 1959 denied black students access to their university of choice which resulted in the creation of separate colleges. These eight acts underpinned the new apartheid order in South Africa which, combined with a powerful internal security apparatus backed by legal powers to eliminate opposition to the regime, presented a formidably imperious system of governance which still managed to possess a veneer of democratic order by making use of elections and proper legislative processes, with the effect of concentrating economic, political, and military power in white hands.

Despite the far reach of the regimes' project of 'social engineering' the Commission does not claim it to be the sole preserve of the NP, but the continuation of practices of governance already well established. For example, it condemns the post-South African War government led by Alfred Milner for its 'Anglicization schemes' in the form of the 1913 Land Act. This piece of legislation laid out the basis for the territorial segregation of whites and Africans and precipitated a massive forced removal of black Africans in which many died. This method of dispossession and discrimination had already been initiated by the British Parliament in 1909 with the South Africa Act through which were merged Britain's four South African colonies into one nation and granted juridical independence, transferring power to a minority of white voters. And again in 1936 the Representation of Natives Act further disenfranchised Cape African voters and the 1956 Senate Act deprived colored men of the vote. The Report comments that 'this latter piece of constitutional chicanery was only the end of a process of black disenfranchisement begun by the British in 1909' (TRC, 1 (2) 18).

In spite of such antecedents, the degree of segregation put into operation by the apartheid regime was unprecedented. The result was that 'while the state and other operatives were committing the murders and abductions and other violations. . . a much larger pattern of human rights violations was unfolding' (TRC, 1 (2) 43). Such violations were a direct result of the key legislation and amendments detailed, and included the forced relocation of people, the destruction of villages, traditional communities and homelands, the demolition of villages, schools, and places of worship, and the mandatory carrying of passes, affecting millions of black South Africans and some poor whites. The TRC claims that for the majority of South Africans, human rights abuses were a systematic feature of apartheid, although it was, ultimately, unable to address the wider systemic effects of the regime:

> For nearly half a century. . . the warp and weft of their experience. . . defining their privilege and their disadvantage, their poverty and their wealth, their public and private lives and their very identity, the system itself was evil, inhumane, and degrading. . . amongst its many crimes, perhaps its greatest was the power to humiliate, to denigrate and to remove the self-confidence, self-esteem and dignity of its millions of victims (TRC, 1 (2) 44).

An important critique of the elision of structural violations has been provided by Mahmood Mamdani who has claimed that by focusing on *particular* human rights violations, those that we might see as being governed by international legislation on what constitutes a 'violation' and what does not (as argued in the previous chapter), the TRC failed to address the grievances of the majority of victims of apartheid who suffered as a result of the apartheid regime's policies including the pass laws, land confiscation and education laws (Mamdani, 1996). As a result, the TRC's representation of past violence was extremely partial and did not resonate properly with the everyday lived experience of apartheid.

In the 1950s the implementation of the laws enforcing apartheid were opposed by a number of political campaigns. Most of this was in the form of non-violent resistance in the cities such as the 'Defiance Campaign' in 1952–1953, the 'Congress of People' in 1955, bus boycotts in 1956, and the campaigns against the mandatory carrying of passes in 1959 and 1960. This action was paralleled by a degree of violent action in some rural areas. By the end of the decade however, resistance was weak and the ANC suffered a split from which the more radical Pan African Congress emerged. However, neither of the organizations had a mass support base, and the support they had was concentrated in urban areas. The principle of non-violent action was abandoned by opposition groups, but even so the groups failed significantly to threaten the state.

1960–1994

During the mandated period of investigation by the TRC, the NP deployed state security forces directly to wage war on those it perceived to be its enemies. By the late 1970s the security establishment comprised three main forces, the South African Defense Force, the South African Police, and the Bureau of State Security, in addition to which were special security forces in each of the twelve 'independent homelands'. The security forces were, under President Botha in 1975, engaged in a national security policy entitled 'Total Strategy' which was formulated to deal with internal and external threats to Afrikaner domination. By the mid-1980s, many security units were operating by what was called the 'Third Force'. This Third Force acted independently of a formal chain of command and as a result caused considerable problems for the TRC in its attempts to establish accountability for violations such as assassinations and letter bombs directed against key individuals and associates in the liberation movements. The TRC Report states that 'it is this history with which we have had to come to terms. We could not pretend it did not happen. *Everyone agrees* that South Africans must deal with that history and its legacy' (TRC, 1 (1) 2 emphasis added).

The TRC decided not to date its investigations from the formal birth of apartheid, the election of the NP in 1948, and conceded that this placed limitations upon its own investigations by suggesting that the picture it portrays of violations is 'by no means complete' (TRC, 1 (2) 20). Whilst acknowledging the historical conditions and precedents of violations, the TRC limited its investigations to a time it characterizes as climactic of a 'deep conflict between a minority which reserved for itself all control over the political instruments of the state and a majority who sought to resist that domination'. This period saw an intensified level of conflict in which 'fundamental human rights became a major casualty', and 'the legitimacy of the law itself was deeply wounded' (TRC, 1 (2) 1). The 1960 Sharpeville Massacre, widely considered a pivotal moment in the history of resistance to apartheid, is taken by the TRC as the founding event of the intensification of conflict because *Umkhonto weSizwe*, the armed wing of the ANC, resorted to violent action at this point. However, the Report contends that Sharpeville was not a unique event, but 'simply the latest in a long line of similar killings of civilian protestors in South African history' (TRC, 1 (2) 8). This is striking, and somewhat in contradistinction to the mandate of the TRC because Sharpeville is given a special place in the mandate of the TRC, marking the significant date from which its investigations began, and the point at which the historical boundary demarcating a particular apartheid past, from a particular, and, the TRC argued, more violent apartheid present (the one deemed relevant to the transitional government), was drawn. However, the choice of 1960 as the date from which the TRC would conduct its investigations was conditioned by the political inception of the TRC itself: the terms of the amnesty agreement in which the NP had demanded that *all* parties to violence be subject to TRC enquiry. It was only from 1960 that the ANC had turned to violent opposition to the regime, and hence could be subject to investigation on the TRC's (and, importantly, the National Party's) terms.

From 1960 to 1990 the development of insurgency and counter-insurgency strategies intensified as a direct result of the ANC's call to violent opposition to the regime. The response of the government to the 'new threat' was twofold. It introduced tighter security laws, and embarked on what it described as an 'ethnic project' which entailed new repressive legislation. In particular, the 'Vorster' laws constrained the independence of the courts by suspending the principle of *habeas corpus* and limiting the right to bail, amongst other measures. In addition, a definition of 'sabotage' was introduced into legislation making almost all forms of dissent illegal. In his second testimony to the TRC, de Klerk maintained that this project was not without the idealist intention of creating a 'commonwealth of South African states' which were self-governing and independent. The Promotion of Bantu Self-Government Act in 1959 was justified by the regime as an attempt to counter what it perceived as the threat of a growing sense of African nationalist identity, with its aspirations to replace white minority hegemony with majority rule. It abolished indirect political representation of Africans in Parliament and provided for the later setting up of black 'homelands' or 'Bantustans' of Tranksei in 1976, Bophuthatswana in 1977, Venda in 1979 and Ciskei in 1981. These so-called 'homelands' were to be awarded independent status as a means of containing nationalist or insurrectionist claims against the state. Fragmented, over-populated and impoverished, these districts were declared 'independent' but failed to secure international recognition. This alleged 'idealism' has provided a struggle of re-interpretation for the TRC in establishing the truth about the past, and establishing accountability for violations.

More generally, the intensification of conflict during this period was informed on the NP side by the specter of black majority rule and sought broader legitimacy under the rhetoric of anti-communism. African political activity was suppressed by the government and the opposition parties, the ANC, SACP, and PAC were banned and forced into exile in 1960. However opposition continued, particularly in the expanding urban areas, and was also launched from the 'front line states' of Namibia, Mozambique and Angola. Added to the development of borderline hostilities was the transfer from white rule in Zimbabwe.[2] Violations perpetrated in these regions beyond state borders also form a substantial part of the TRC's investigations (a feature of its investigations that distinguishes it from other truth commissions that focus on a national pattern of violations).

The Report questions why the state continued to wage what became a thirteen-year war in Angola. The first interpretation positions Namibia as a threat to South African security because the South West African Peoples Organization (SWAPO) fought for Namibian independence from bases in Angola from the late 1970s. Secondly, the Report speculates that Angola became another frontier for the playing out of the Cold War, thus entailing a violent ideological confrontation with communism. Following independence from Portugal in 1975, the Marxist MPLA took power in Angola and the South African-backed UNITA movement waged a guerrilla campaign against the government. Consequently, the 'struggle to maintain white minority privilege was 'repackaged' as an effort to maintain the so-called western civilized values against the godless and evil forces of Communism' (TRC, 1 (2) 56). The discourse of struggle was henceforth re-articulated by the state along ideological rather than racial lines partly as a response to the strong alliance between the ANC and the SACP.

This shift constitutes an important locus of the TRC's investigations as amnesty was granted to those acts perpetrated with a *political objective.* For example, abuses perpetrated by security forces against what was perceived to as a 'communist threat' was legitimate within the remit of such 'political objectives'. In a testimony to the Commission, one ex-conscript alleged that during basic training in the 1980's, conscripts were told: 'this story that people tell you that there is a Communist behind every bush is nonsense. There are in fact two' (TRC, 1 (2) 56). However, the TRC conflicts with the ideological narrative of the state at the time, because it sustains a racial rather than an ideological narrative of struggle in its view of the past, arguing that 'it is. . . the view of the Commission that, at heart, the struggle for South and Southern Africa was a racial one and that notions of the "red peril" were manipulated to justify the perpetration of the gross human rights violations this Commission was charged to investigate' (TRC, 1 (2) 57). This narrative is, however, contradicted by the amnesty mechanism because it ensured that convincing amnesty application on the part of a former NP security agent could, under the rubric of the 'war against communism', secure a successful outcome. So, on the one hand, the TRC asserts a racial interpretation of the struggle but allows the solicitation of amnesty to proceed on the basis of an ideological interpretation which is not commensurate with the overall story that the TRC claims to be telling, at least at this narrative juncture.

The conflict was significantly conditioned in this period by a constellation of international forces. Firstly, the international dimension of the conflict was played out in the context of the Cold War in which South Africa sustained a shifting and uneasy relationship with Western powers. The state successfully managed for some time to portray itself as a bastion against communism, particularly during the wars against the liberation movements in the frontline states such as Angola and Mozambique. Secondly, domestic constituencies outside South Africa put pressure on respective governments through the international anti-apartheid movement, which saw a boycott against South Africa widely endorsed and enforced. Thirdly, international capital played a critical role, starting out by broadly supporting apartheid but becoming more critical until in 1986 the U.S. and E.C. banks called in their loans and threatened a complete investment boycott. Throughout the 1980's the government of P. W. Botha became more militaristic, and as a consequence saw foreign opposition to the regime's human rights abuses harden into economic sanctions.

As a result some of the features of apartheid were moderated, and there was an attempt by the government to reform the parliamentary system towards an elaborate form of power sharing through a tricameral system of representation. In 1984 a new constitution secured representation for the Indian and Colored communities who were given separate parliamentary assemblies. Botha agreed to negotiate a settlement of the counter-insurgency wars in Angola and Namibia in 1988 and in 1989 when F. W. de Klerk succeeded Botha as president he signaled further reforms which finally gave way to the CODESA multi-party negotiations. The TRC was finally agreed upon after the successful conclusion of the negotiations which had succeeded in establishing a 'human rights based democracy' for the first time in South Africa's history. The normative framework within which the TRC took place was thus well settled and based upon a significant consensus of opinion.

The Regional Narrative

The second time the TRC's narrative is iterated it seeks to narrate the social and political contexts within which violations took place, both within the state and within the Southern African region more generally (TRC, 2 (1)). This version constructs a *regional* rather than a national narrative, and is repeated within a different time frame from its first rendering: the time frame of the mandate of the TRC, 1960 to 1994, and concentrates upon the 'third historical phase' outlined in the first national history. The stated purpose of this narrative is to provide an 'overview of the context in which conflict developed and gross violations of human rights occurred' (TRC, 2 (1) 1). This context seeks to generate a political interpretation of the nature and extent of gross human rights violations, the 'major role-players', namely the South African state security forces and the liberation movements, and an account of authorization and accountability for the violations it identifies.[3] It renders a more agent-centered account of the violations than the first account and narrates 'patterns' and 'trends' in the gross violations reported, as well as 'patterns of behavior in groups and parties responsible for their perpetration' (TRC, 2 (1) 8).

This depiction takes in three main themes, entailing some repetition of the first narrative and thus compounds its political and disciplinary effects. The three themes comprise the social and political background to the conflict, the development of insurgency and counter-insurgency strategies from 1960 to 1990, and thirdly, and notably briefly, the transitional phase from 1990 onwards.

Social and political background
The 'social and political' narrative concentrates on the effects of race, decolonization and the Cold War as three constitutive aspects of the conflict. Race, it argues, was a 'powerful organizing framework' which conditioned, to varying degrees, the activities of all parties and was instrumental in the social construction of 'the other' and 'the enemy'. Further, the effects of decolonization 'served only to reinforce the tendency of whites to regard blacks as "the enemy"', whites being threatened by concomitant U.N. pressures to grant full civil and political rights to all citizens of South Africa (TRC, 2 (1) 22–23). The Cold War is also narrated as a key factor governing the actions of the South African state security forces during the 1960s under the rubric of 'anti-Communism'. The relationship between the ANC and the South African Communist Party (SACP) after 1960 further 'entrenched the National Party (NP) government's perception of a link between Communism and the struggle against white domination' and the Report notes that in the mandate period virtually all opposition was labeled 'Communist' (TRC, 2 (1) 24 and 26). It was this narrative of 'anti-Communism' that, as we have seen, framed many security force amnesty applications, and, if provided by the applicant in a compelling way, such as that provided by Benzien discussed previously, could secure amnesty for a deponent. Notably, whilst the story about decolonization and the Cold War have prominence here the TRC did nothing to investigate the role of international actors in creating the conditions under which violence was made possible. This was, in part, an effect of the po-

litical narrative of violence within the boundaries of the state that the TRC sought to render, which in turn was a function of its nation-building imperative.

Insurgency and counter-insurgency, 1960–1990

A second theme of the narrative takes up the development of insurgency and counter-insurgency strategies from 1960 to 1990 and details internal repression and the emergence and methods of armed opposition movements during this period. It begins by tying the 'history of resistance in South Africa' to 'the patterns and forms of gross violations of human rights'. Thus it makes explicit the trajectory of South African history as commensurate with, first, the violation of human rights, and second under the aegis of the TRC, the incorporation of human rights into the new political culture, which serves to elide, or rather subsumes, any other historical interpretation of political struggle—racial or ideological (TRC, 2 (1) 28). It argues that in response to the liberation movements' turn to armed struggle, the state intensified repression primarily through the use of detention of political activists and the use of torture. In addition, the development of 'counter-insurgency' thinking which emerged out of South Africa's wars in the former South West Africa and Rhodesia, impacted upon the methods of internal control and were used against the domestic civilian population. As a result, gross violations were increasingly attributed to units responsible for public order, including the riot police and South African Defense Force, and led to the development of covert units such as the *Vlakplaas*. From the mid-1980s 'this trend intensified. . . as the rationale of counter-revolutionary warfare took hold within dominant quarters of the security establishment' (TRC, 2 (1) 29). Countering these developments, the ANC developed insurrectionary modes of resistance which were shaped by the narrative of a 'people's war'. As a result, the TRC argues, violations were increasingly perpetrated not just by the ANC and its armed wing, but by their civilian supporters. The narrative concludes that 'violations associated with the liberation and mass democratic movements in the 1980s. . . tended to target those *perceived* to be collaborating with the policies and practices of the former government' (TRC, 2 (1) 30 emphasis added). This interpretation, by implication, widens a circle of possibly 'innocent victims' in particular and the numbers of victims in general.

The transitional phase

The final time period of this narrative, that of the transitional phase from February 1990 to 1994, was the period within which political negotiations began, an Interim Constitution agreed and the initial parameters of the TRC set out. During this period the TRC argued that a sea-change took place in 'the logic and the rules, written or unwritten, governing the contest for power in South Africa' (TRC, 2 (1) 166).

However, the poverty of this account, limited to just one paragraph, marks a decisive and controversial exclusion of some of the worst political violence in South Africa, and a period which the TRC failed to investigate with any real integrity of purpose. This violence took place mainly in the region of Kwa-Zulu Natal from 1990 to 1994, and was an intensive period of ANC-IFP rivalry which has often, and again controversially, been characterized as 'black-on-black' violence.[4] This was the period that was most under-researched and under-investigated by the TRC, and cannot be explained by a paucity of documentary evidence. As Adrian Guelke argues, 'it is evident that the violent power struggle that took place during the era of negotiations fits uncomfortably within the moral tale of the fall of apartheid that the TRC wishes to tell' (Guelke, 2000: 306). This morality tale was far more concerned with discrediting the old regime than with exposing the IFP's role in the violence that emerged out of transition. The failure to narrate violations occurring between the IFP and ANC was a result of these events not falling into the narrative of violence between predominant political protagonists—the NP and ANC. This point well illustrates the way in which the narration of the past is central to the contest for political legitimacy. This narrative failure also ignored other, since confirmed, suspicions that this ANC-IFP violence was initiated and perpetuated by a 'third force' promoted by the state.[5]

The Chronology

A third iteration of this national story appears in the form of a 'National Chronology' of these events. The chronology is prefaced by a statement which explicitly states that it selects 'significant events which helped shape the years 1960 to 1994' of 'national significance', and that 'in selecting these entries. . . an attempt is made to capture the unfolding drama of the South African conflict' (TRC, 3 (1), Appendix). This chronology, it seems, is deemed better able to dramatize the conflict, or at least emphasize the relevant (for the TRC) aspects of it. The Report notes further that the chronology is supplementary to the two previous historical narratives that deal with national and regional events respectively. The chronology appears much like a historical chronicle in tabular format which details first the date and then 'the conditioning' historical event of that year, as follows:[6]

National Chronology

From. . .

1899	The South African War between Britain and the Boer Republics ends with British victory in 1902.
1910	Union of South Africa comes into being.
1912	South African Native National Congress or SANNC (later African National Congress or ANC) is founded.
1913	The Natives' Land Act prescribes that no African person be allowed to own land outside designated reserves (approximately 7% of the land is allocated for African people, subsequently increased in 1936 to 13%).
1914	National Party is founded.

To...

1960	**Mandate period of Truth and Reconciliation Commission begins** On 21 March, sixty-nine people are killed and 186 wounded at Sharpeville when police open fire on marchers protesting against the pass laws. In Cape Town, two people are killed and 47 wounded in Langa when police open fire on a crowd of anti-pass protestors. At the end of March, a group of 30,000 people march from Langa to Cape Town in protest. A national state of emergency is declared on 24 March, lasting until 31 August. 11,503 people are detained. PAC leader Sobukwe is sentenced to three years for burning his pass. The ANC and the PAC are banned on April 8...
1961	The Indemnity Act indemnifies the government, its officers and all other persons acting under its authority and empowered to suppress internal disorder from civil or criminal proceedings. (The Act is made retrospective from 21 March 1960). Following South Africa's withdrawal from the Commonwealth, the first steps are taken to establish a military intelligence component in the South African Defence Force (SADF)...

And finally...

1994	One person is killed and several injured in an APLA attack on the Crazy Beat Disco in Newcastle, Natal on 14 February. PAC president Clarence Makwetu announces the suspension of the armed struggle... Nelson Mandela is inaugurated as President of South Africa on 10 May.

This tabular historical format functions in order to reinforce, in a visual, and in a linear temporal way, particular aspects of the more prosaic narrative descriptions elaborated in the first and second volumes. The effect of this listing of dates and corresponding events is to assemble and organize history in a categorical and indisputable way to achieve the appearance of an indisputable 'truth' of the events listed. This time, the events are not prosaically recorded as a narrative 'totality evolving in time', according to White's critique, but appear as boldly unequivocal historical 'facts'. Further, the chronology simultaneously conceals the selected nature of the events it records, the continuity it constructs between them, the contingent moment of its beginning in 1899 and closure in 1994 marked by the inauguration of Mandela as president. The clarity, indeed 'truth' of this dating, hinges upon the order of chronological reference which is, in fact, concordant with the *present* circumstances through which the events of the past are viewed, and in whose service a particular past is invoked. Further, as White notes, the production of stable and coherent chronologies 'are constitutive of putative "domains of history" that historians of a given age must confront as "problems" to be solved' (White, 1978: 56). As such, the TRC posits the events it highlights in its own chronology of South African history as the key 'problems to be solved' by its own investigations. All of the events presented are related to the development of apartheid, to its violent opposition, and to the transition from it marked by Mandela's inauguration as President.

Framing the Individual Testimonies

This official historical narrative was conjoined with the individual testimonies of victims and perpetrators through the statement-taking process of the TRC and the particular methodologies that were deployed in its service. Through this process, the governing narrative about political violence in South Africa disciplined and made intelligible individual submissions within the overall story the TRC sought to narrate.

Two of the three Committees of the TRC took statements: the Human Rights Violations Committee took testimonies from victims and the Amnesty Committee took testimonies from perpetrators with assistance from the TRC's Investigative Unit, the Research Unit and the Human Rights Committee. Information gathered by each of these bodies was fed back into and processed by the TRC's Information Management System or 'Infocomm'. Infocomm processed testimonies in several stages from the taking of individual statements to the production of 'national findings' based upon these statements (see Wilson, 2001: 38–41). An overview of these stages provides an insight into the methodological process through which individual accounts were synthesized as, and made to concur with, the national narrative.

Around three hundred statement-takers were located in the TRC's offices around the country. It was their job to register statements on the database, a process which demanded that each narrative was broken down into a number of particular violations and categorized in terms of one of forty-eight different violations types according to the coding frame of the TRC, discussed in chapter one. As discussed in detail in chapter two, the frame consisted of an elaborate taxonomy of violations which synthesized testimonies by dividing them into four main categories, 'killing', 'abduction', 'torture' and 'severe ill-treatment'.[7] Within these four categories, a complex of sub-categories was asserted such that the Commission formally taxonomized forty-eight distinct violation types, in addition to which it elaborated three different categories of agent, and four different types of truth. The agents were designated as victim, perpetrator, or witness. Truths included 'factual or forensic truth', 'personal or narrative truth', 'social truth' and 'healing and restorative truth'. The ostensible purpose of this definitional elaboration of truth was to allow different interpretations of the past to come to light and not to focus on the legalistic truths common to criminal trials. However, as Wilson argues, whilst 'narrative truth' appeared to be predominant early on in the TRC's work, a legalistic paradigm of truth dominated after the first year of its operations (Wilson, 2001: 37).

In order to make sure that 'as much *relevant* information as possible' (italics mine) was collated from the victim statements, this 'protocol' was developed in order that the victim statements could be structured and systematized (TRC, 1 (6) 9). At this stage in the process, the names of perpetrators, witnesses and victims were also recorded. Next, this data was 'captured' by a central database which was shared by the four main offices of the TRC. The next stage entailed the corroboration of the 'basic facts' of each case. Following on from this, regional 'pre-findings' were made by commissioners and committee members. During this process, testimonies could be rejected on the following grounds: if the events reported fell outside the mandate time frame, or they fell out of the mandate of the Act as perpetrated 'with a political objective' or they were considered to be false testimonials. Those accepted by the pre-findings process could be accepted on the basis of the given evidence, or on the 'balance of probability'. A sample of the regional pre-findings were then submitted to the National Findings Task Group which reviewed a sample of each region's findings.

However, this process represents the final stage of the development of the TRC's statement-taking methodology, and a review of the previous methods which allowed victim narratives to 'remain intact' is necessary in order to reflect upon the increased disciplinarity with which the TRC's statement taking process operated over time.

When the TRC began to take testimonies, it warranted that 'respect for deponents and victims involved treating statements with integrity, and keeping them intact to the limits of the available technology'. With respect to this it stated that 'narratives should not be fragmented, nor portions discarded through decisions of the Commission or inadequate representation' (TRC, 1 (6) 7b). However, as Wilson argues, the testimonies were in fact fragmented in order to make the data contained within them accessible to the data-management system (Wilson, 2001: chapter one). Wilson shows how the process of testimony collation changed from the early days of the TRC. At the beginning, groups of statement-takers were trained to preserve the victims' narrative whilst providing counseling and support where necessary. Inevitably, the questions asked by the statement-takers constrained the statements such that they were not entirely 'free' but there was, at this stage, a greater openness in what was recorded and 'captured' by the official process. In its early incarnation, the statement-taking methodology first involved the collator *listening* to the deponent without taking notes, sometimes for more than an hour. Only upon the second telling of the tale would an official record be made. The third part of the process involved the statement being read back to the victim and verified. The whole process took up to three hours per statement (Wilson, 2001: 42–43). This drew criticisms from

those higher in the TRC hierarchy who wished to promote a 'more corrobora-
tive' version of the past, and the TRC duly changed its processes:

> As the early statements were received and analyzed, it became clear that the initial
> protocol. . . was inadequate. This may be attributed to two factors. First, the struc-
> turing of information gathered from long and complex narrative statements im-
> posed some technical difficulties: narrative statements might contain information
> on gross violations of human rights which occurred on one or more occasions, at
> one or more places, to one or more victims and carried out by one or more perpe-
> trators. As different kinds of evidence of varying degrees of detail and complexity
> were gathered, it became clear that there was a need to adjust and fine-tune the
> structure of the protocol in order to ensure that all necessary information was cap-
> tured in a uniform manner (TRC, 1 (6) 11).

The emphasis here on 'uniformity' is telling. The earlier testimonies were too
'unstructured' because they relied more heavily upon an individual interpretation
which could not be captured by the data processing unit employed by the TRC,
nor framed within the taxonomy of violations which structured agents simply
into either 'witnesses', 'victims', or 'perpetrators'. As a result, a new form was
devised which meant that 'control was taken away from statement-takers as the
form became a checklist, not one requiring listening and an inter-subjective construction of a narrative' (Wilson, 2001: 43). The demands of the new form represented a shift in emphasis from the truths as seen by the victims to the production of an account commensurate with the TRC's overarching narrative of
violence within which accounts of gross violations of human rights were deemed
relevant. Throughout the work of the Commission, five versions of the statement
form or 'protocol' were used. Each of these was altered until in its final incarnation the protocol was a highly structured questionnaire that completely excluded
the first version's incorporation of an open section within which the victim could
present an open and free narrative interpretation of the events. This section had
in the past frequently comprised fifteen to twenty pages of testimony in the victim's own words and aimed to fulfill the TRC ideal of restorative justice which
stipulated that all victims should be allowed to relate their story in their own
words, and in return receive official recognition of their experiences. However,
by the time the final version of the protocol was in place it consisted of a short
questionnaire which directed the parameters of the testimony instead of allowing
a freer narrative to emerge.[8] By now, the statements were taking around thirty to
forty minutes to 'compose' instead of the original three hours or so.

Wilson documents the way in which the Infocomm system disciplined testimonies into a clear chronology which provided the organizing framework for
only the 'relevant information' to be solicited, and which constituted a linear,
narrative format from which statistics were generated and findings based. Chronology and linearity as organizing principles of the testimonial were thus epis-
temologically privileged by the TRC's information system. Further, information
was required only about the time period *immediately before* the violation being
documented, and *immediately afterwards*, and any wider historical or consequential details were deemed unnecessary and superfluous to the production of

statistical knowledge about gross violations of human rights. This was problematic because, first, the TRC stipulated that the *context* in which violations occurred necessitated a historical rather than an immediate context, and was important in order to understand the individual testimonial within the wider social and political context in which the event occurred.[9] But the methodology of solicitation prevented the fulfillment of this aim. Second, the methodology ran counter to the way in which victims related their accounts. In short, the Infocomm system forced the testimonies into a linear framework that was not adequately representative of what had been related. Wilson argues that victim testimonies were frequently characterized by the absence of a chronological framework which was essential to the 'factual' or 'forensic' truth-gathering system. He notes that 'instead, testimonials were jumbled, elliptical', that they were 'partial and fragmented, not magisterial. . .', and further that they were full of 'interpretation', which, sometimes, clashed with the interpretation that the TRC sought to render. Wilson characterizes the narrative 'sequence' of victim testimonials as follows, features that are not uncommon to trauma narratives which, typically, are characterized by disruption and disturbance than by 'pure' linearity and coherence:

> The narratives of victims and witnesses almost always began with the critical event itself—the phone call, the sound of an explosion. A survivor of the Seboking Night Vigil Massacre in 1991, Cecilia Ncuge, told of the sound of explosions and the screaming of neighbors. . . Trudy Shongwe of Soweto began with the moment when she was called from work to go to the hospital where her son lay dead. . . After the critical moment, testimonies go in one direction or the other—either into the aftermath and consequences of the event, or they detail at length the events preceding the event. Many testifying at TRC hearings showed no regard for chronology at all, jumping from one episode to another (Wilson, 2001: 49).

The failure of the system to capture this more elliptical mode of telling, and in turn imposing a chronology that was consistent with the story that the TRC wanted to tell, meant that the connections constructed within the victim testimony, it's individual associations, were lost. Infocomm decontextualized the testimonies from their location within wider social relationships and community networks, and recontextualized the events within the rationale of party-political allegiance which the TRC sought to secure. Violence which occurred outside of the narrative framework of a political context the TRC sought to narrate, was not accommodated.

Importantly, Infocomm frustrated the extant aims of restorative justice that the TRC purported to fulfill. The methodological process by which testimonies were solicited was ultimately entirely disjoined from the TRC's claim that a victim should be allowed to tell their story 'as he or she sees it' as part of the project of individual and social 'healing'. The result of this was that the TRC short-circuited the process of restorative justice it claimed to be absolutely crucial to its functioning. As such, 'victim justice' was sacrificed by the data-collection process of the TRC because the original system was considered to be unwieldy and too time-consuming to deal with the massive number, around twenty-two thousand, of testimonies made.

The effect of the changes in statement-taking methodology were to script the individual testimonies into the broader state drama produced by the TRC. In making commensurate the statements taken with the coding frame the Commission constrained victim testimonies by its own prior assumptions about what counted as *relevant* to its investigations and what was peripheral. That is to say, what was important to the national drama about the past, and hence the shape of the national future, and what was not. Consequently, the process of 'capturing' narratives and turning them into 'data' constituted an ineffectual channel for illuminating the experiential aspects of experiences of violence generally and torture in particular. Inscribed into the solicited victim narratives was the coding framework of violations established *prior* to the solicitation of the testimony. Individual truths were mediated by the process of data collection and selection in order to concord with official prior conceptualizations of what constituted the 'truth' about the past within the framing trope of 'reconciliation'. They were not considered as individual and valuable truth claims in their unique formulation. Wilson argues that many victims were frustrated at the way in which their stories did not fit into the model of information management articulated by Infocomm. As a consequence, 'their story was frozen in time, stripped to its "essential characteristics" and that which was outside the "controlled vocabulary" was discarded' (Wilson, 2001: 48).

The development of Infocomm was thus integral to the process by which individual stories made manifest the story-lines of the overall narrative which sought to endow meaning on South Africa's past by ordering the divergent stories of 'victims' and 'perpetrators' of gross human rights violations within the limits of the data management system which was framed by the given taxonomy of violations.

The amnesty solicitation process entailed a further constraint on perpetrator testimonies, and made material the appearance of the overall narrative within individual stories yielded to the Commission. Scott Veitch attributes this to the absence of legal reasoning on the part of the Amnesty Committee due to its retroactive nature (Veitch, 2001: 32–47). As Veitch notes, 'amnesty law starts in the present and looks back the way', which means that the law does not demand of its subjects that they 'ought to have done something or other'. Conversely, the amnesty law does not exist to prove one or another party guilty or innocent of a particular offence. Rather, the applicant is there 'to plead with the judicial committee to exercise its grace and to lift the sanction (or the possibility of sanction) from its attaching to the applicant' which represents an 'image in negative' of regular legal mechanisms' (Veitch in Christodoulidis and Veitch, 2001: 32–47).

The absence of regular legal reasoning meant that, as Veitch notes, the Amnesty Committee sought stronger recourse to the interpretation of 'facts'. It sought to locate them within a 'full' and 'coherent' narrative that fulfilled the demand of a 'full disclosure of the relevant facts' associated with 'a political objective'. As a result, the success of an amnesty application turned on the deponent's ability to narrate their account within the parameters of the mandate of the

Act which required that applicants understand and relate their actions as having occurred within the organizing rationale of a political objective. The necessity of this mode of narration was prior to the case being recognized by the TRC as co-herent within its own story, which then provided the foundation for amnesty be-ing granted. Without the perpetration of violations being related within the con-text of having occurred with a political objective, amnesty was withheld. As such, the success of an application turned on the ability of the applicant to as-similate the wider story within his or her own account, and to make the testi-mony accord with the 'moral parameters' of the TRC. Veitch compares the am-nesty decisions on two cases to illustrate this point. First, the decision not to grant amnesty to the police personnel responsible for the death of Steve Biko is attributed by the TRC to the failure of the applicants to make a 'full disclosure' of the events in question. This failure turned on the inability of those involved to narrate the precise moment of Biko's death. Biko, an ANC activist, underwent a lengthy and violent interrogation which resulted in his death in custody. The TRC wanted to know the precise moment at which he'd been killed. It wanted to know 'which was the blow that killed him, and who dealt it'. The four police officers involved were not able to yield this particular truth. Whilst the TRC ar-gued that the men had 'clearly conspired to conceal the truth of what led to the tragic death of Biko' it is not inconceivable that they did not know, or could not remember, this critical moment. This narrative 'failure' marked the failure of the amnesty application itself because it was not judged to be a 'full disclosure', nor coherent (or rather 'complete') narrative about the events under investigation. It resulted in the panel's decision that the violations were 'not political in nature but formed part of normal police duties' (Veitch, 2001:40). Veitch compares this case with the Benzien decision which was made on the basis of Benzien relating the torture of prisoners within the context of 'his duty as a policeman' which, for the TRC, amounted to there being 'no doubt that his action related to a political objective'. These examples demonstrate that in their reinterpretation of the past, amnesty applicants needed to re-narrate their actions within the frame of intelli-gibility provided by the TRC in general and the amnesty provision in particular, in order that their testimony be sympathetically judged. Further, the plausibility of the individual testimonies depended upon conventional methods for constitut-ing intelligible and coherent narratives which, ultimately, could be converted into a coherent master narrative.

Narrating Social Identity

Whilst the TRC placed material constraints on individual testimonies, it also worked to order and make sense of narratives in a less clearly coercive way than the example of the Infocomm system illustrates, and a discussion of how indi-vidual life stories get constructed by, speak to, and are embedded within broader social, political and historical narratives is necessary in order to understand the more subtle forms of constraint and production that go to shape micro-narratives. Individual narratives frequently respond to presiding fictions that are located in social and political contexts at both local and global levels, which function in order to include, exclude, validate or repudiate individual stories. Individual identities are partly constituted by governing narratives, or macronarratives, which sustain the legitimacy and mutual intelligibility of micro narratives (Sarbin and Scheibe, 1983). Individual narratives are guided and maintained by socially available narratives, even those which might be temporary and exceptional such as that that constructed by the TRC, which have a formulative stake in the construction of individual narratives and their location within the wider social community:

> Our micronarrratives are typically 'nested' within, and inseparable from, cultural macronarratives that shape their possible outcomes and meanings. Inevitably, a certain degree of social negotiation is required as individuals struggle to craft personal narratives that are consistent, believable, and flattering, both in their own eyes and those of others. To avoid 'ontological abandonment', individuals must work out strategies enabling their self-narratives to dovetail with those of others in their community (Hinchman and Hinchman eds., 1997: 121).

Individual and collective histories are largely governed by common narratives that facilitate a sense of community, which is mostly imagined to be in existence. Where 'new' narratives are in the process of being crafted, such as during a time of political transition, individuals may be obliged to abandon the premises upon which their former narrative identities were based or risk being excluded from the new public narratives such as that provided by the TRC. The TRC interpellated its subjects, victims and perpetrators, in a dialogic relation in which 'both recognize themselves to be operating within the same genre, the conventions of which neither of them unduly strains' (Dunne in Kearney, 1996: 150). That is to say, victims understand and play to the formal constraints of the victim testimonial as a particular mode of truth-telling designed to deliver a story about suffering and harm, and perpetrators, equally, understand the particular confessional terms upon which their own depositions should be written. These are constructed each in relation to the other, the remorseful confession a 'fitting' response to the anguish and torment rendered by the victim testimonial.

However, collective narratives are always subject to contestation and re-evaluation because individuals and sub-groups are not unwitting and powerless hostages to prevailing stories, but they can subvert, reorient or simply reinvent new storylines that are in conflict with powerful macro-narratives:

> Serious discordance, however, may press one party into the explicitness of telling and, indeed, it may be that the discordance is brought about in the first place by the quite explicit telling by the other party of a new story (or the recasting of patterns and events of the old story in a new way). . . telling, then, would arise in the face of anomaly or crisis. . . where the story perhaps cannot continue, without a major orientation (Dunne in Kearney, 1996: 150).

One of the most famous cases of repudiation of the TRC story was that of P.W. Botha who consistently evaded calls for him to testify at the Commission and still insists that apartheid, or 'separate development' was nothing more than 'good neighbourliness'. And F.W. de Klerk, joint architect of the transitional government, still claims that those responsible for torture and abuse were just 'rotten apples' acting of their own accord rather than operating within a systematic campaign of violence for which orders were issued and a clear line of command could be established. Eleventh hour contestations over what was to be included and excluded in the final Report by both de Klerk and ANC representatives meant that de Klerk managed to secure the deletion of allegations against him (TRC, 5 (6)). There was also early evidence to suggest that the majority of the white population had all but rejected the narrative framework of the Commission, many of whom asserted in a survey that past atrocities were perpetrated primarily by anti-apartheid activists, and to a lesser degree the security forces (Theissen, 1997). Many felt that their own stories were not pertinent to the TRC, or simply excluded by its mandate. Permission to narrate is not felt to be equally apportioned, nor is it granted to all:

> Narrative activity allows members of communities to represent and reflect upon events, thoughts and emotions, but this opportunity may be asymmetrically allocated, granting reflective rights to some more than to others. Crucial to the construction of a self, an other, and a society, co-narration crafts biographies and histories: yet the meaning of experience and existence—what is possible, actual, reasonable, desirable—tends to be defined by some more than others (Ochs in Van Dijk, 1997: 202).

The case of the Khulumani support group, discussed in detail in the conclusions to this book, is a case in point. Unhappy with the reparations provision offered by the TRC and its emphasis on symbolic reparations such as forgiveness, remorse and atonement, Khulumani took their claim for financial compensation to court in the U.S., attracting much criticism for their 'anti-reconciliatory' actions. Reconciliation, they were told, was 'not about money' but was embedded within a certain new national disposition towards the past, one that was conditioned by magnanimity (embodied by the figure of Nelson Mandela) towards past crimes, and hope for a future predicated on racial harmony, signified by the metaphor of the 'rainbow nation'.

The TRC itself presented a narrative discordant with South Africa's apartheid past. The transitional government of South Africa performed a rupture with the apartheid narrative. The TRC purported to 'remember in order to heal' and as such set about narrating the violent details of apartheid governance, compelling an 'obligation to remember' as the ethical foundation of the new nation. This process of transformation involved a separation of the past identity of the nation, or the question of 'who [we] were', from aspirations about 'who to become'. That is to say that although the TRC concentrated on abuses perpetrated during a specific period of the past, on a symbolic level it constructed a version of the past that was future-oriented, and was appropriate to, or rather meshed with, a new narrative of transformation and 'becoming'. In order to construct the possibility of a new national narrative, the TRC itself had to break with the presiding stories of the past.

Clearly, the political stakes in the construction of history are high, and the political uses of narrative reflect a struggle over the past which is 'not to achieve already constituted interests, but to constitute those interests in the first place' (Olick, 1998: 381). In this vein the TRC has been accused of bias in favor of granting amnesty to former ANC activists as against applicants from the former state security bodies, and this accusation has been largely responsible for the resistance to the Commissions' investigations demonstrated by former government ministers. Of the seventeen serving commissioners, not a single representative of either the National Party or the Inkhata Freedom Party participated in the organization of the procedures, compared with the Chilean commission which comprised of four commissioners from the previous military regime and four from the new government. As a consequence, Wynand Malan's withdrawal from the TRC was partly on the basis that 'various findings appear. . . to display, if not a lack of understanding of, then certainly a lack of empathy with certain groups living within traditional or nationalistic value systems who were party to the conflict' (TRC, 5 (9)).[10] In response to what he considers to be a partial, and politically animated, reconstruction of the past, Malan went further to criticize the very possibility of reconciliation in the future which, for him, could only have tenuous foundations. He argued that 'our understanding of history must accommodate all interpretations of the past. If we fail in this regard, we will fail to be a nation' (TRC, 5 (34)).

In sum, the presiding historical narrative articulated in detail in the Report broadly disciplined and subsumed the fragmentary and contingent details of related events rendered in testimonial 'evidence' within the explanatory matrix of its governing scheme. This historical framework fed into the information gathering system and constrained and marked the production of testimonial and confessional truths. The primary function of this process was to make individual accounts concord with the overall narrative generated by the TRC and to make commensurate divergent perspectives on the past in order to narrate the foundation of a future reconciliation. This entailed on the part of the TRC a sublimation of an account of violence that was informed by race and ideology to an account that was characterized as a series of 'gross violations of human rights.' This was an result of the attempt by the TRC, at the NP's insistence, to examine culpability and assign blame across all parties. One central (and deeply problematic) effect of this was—arguably, and against those critics who claimed the TRC to have a political bias—to obscure or make difficult any strong moral distinction between violence perpetrated by the apartheid state and its agents, and that perpetrated by parties who opposed the regime.

Notes

1. 1652 was the year that slaves were first imported, and 1834 when slavery was abolished.
2. The borders with these states saw frequent incursions into South Africa from insurrectionist groups within South Africa engaging in a number of counter-insurgency

wars, and in 1975 South Africa invaded Angola. In the same year, Namibia was illegally 'incorporated' into South Africa, and the South West African People's Organisation led resistance to this action. Supported by Cuban troops, insurgents from Angola launched a border war which finally led to independence from South Africa in 1990.

3. Namely, on the side of the State Security Forces the South African Police, the Bureau of State Security, Department of National Security, and the South African Defence Force. On the Liberation Movement side, the key protagonists in order of appearance are the African National Congress,including its executive and armed wings and the Pan Africanist Congress.Those holding authoritative roles in each of the organisations are named in the Report (see appendices 3 and 4 in TRC 2).

4. For disputes about this categorisation and the different ways in which the conflict was often interpreted along party political or ethnic divisions see Howarth and Norval (1998).

5. These suspicions were partly confirmed by the amnesty testimony of Ferdi Barnard, former member of a security force 'death squad'. Barnard linked the state's supply of arms to Zulus to killings perpetrated to destabilise the ANC during the political negotiations in the early 1990s. Thirty-nine people were killed in their homes in the most notorious incident, the Boipatong massacre in June 1992 in townships near Johannesburg (see McGreal, 2000).

6. The 'National Chronology' appears as an extended appendix to the third volume of the Report which catalogues and synthesises human rights violations within a series of geographical 'regional profiles' (see TRC 3 (1)). Note that the example given here is a selection of the dates and events rendered for illustrative purposes.

7. For details of the coding frame see TRC 5 (1). A fifth related category of 'associated violations' was added which allegedly facilitated the rendering of the *context* within which gross violations occurred, an enhancement of the overall picture of patterns of violations the TRC sought to establish.

8. As Wilson documents, one technician noted that 'the questionnaire distorted the whole story altogether. . . it destroyed the meaning' (Wilson, 2001: 45).

9. For further discussion of this point see chapter four of this book. The TRC's taxonomy of four different types of 'truth' were designed to accord with the Commission's aims of fulfilling restorative justice. To this aim, it was considered that 'social truth' reflected the wider circumstances within which violations occurred, and was a fundamental foundation of restorative justice.

Chapter Four
Narrating the Present: Confessional and Testimonial Truth-Telling

And ye shall know the truth and the truth shall set you free.

> St John 3:32. Frequently quoted at TRC hearings by Commissioners
> and deponents and at prayers opening the daily hearings. It became a
> maxim of the TRC's work.

Truth does not belong to the order of power, but shares an original affinity with freedom:
traditional themes in philosophy, which a 'political history of truth' would have to over-
turn by showing that truth is not by nature free. . . but that its production is thoroughly
imbued with relations of power. The confession is an example of this.

> Michel Foucault, *History of Sexuality: Volume 1* (London: Allen
> Lane, 1978).

The previous chapter discussed the ways in which the TRC reconstructed South
Africa's violent history. Part of this argument drew upon the discussion in chapter two that elucidated the way in which South Africa's past was constructed and
narrated around the, allegedly 'objective', notion of a human rights violation
rather than, for example, narrating a history that culminated in a successful just
war of opposition, or revolution, drawing the conclusion that, once translated
into the work of the TRC, human rights discourse had the effect of reducing
South Africa's violent history to a series of gross human rights violations that
was, partly, stripped of its broader context. Two problematic effects of the
TRC's casting of this history emerge. First, the TRC reduced the totality of
apartheid violence to a political contest from the 1960s onwards within which
gross violations of human rights were posited as the main objects of enquiry and

violations perpetrated with a 'political objective' the central moral problematic. Second, by evaluating violations perpetrated by all parties on the same grounds (by using a decontextualised taxonomy) the TRC, arguably, permitted a moral equation between those who perpetrated acts of violence in the name of apartheid, and those who perpetrated in opposition to the regime.

This chapter takes up the second part of the TRC narrative, moving on from its historical reconstruction of apartheid violence to its narration of the transitional present. The TRC narrated this present through the technology of the confessional, a process through which the nation was to be purged or cleansed of the 'sins' of its violent past in order to found a future reconciliation. The hearings, quasi-tribunal in nature, constituted the public site of this confessional and brought together the various narrative accounts or truths of the key protagonists of the reconciliation story. From 1996 to 1998, South Africans were exposed on a weekly and sometimes daily basis to public revelations about their violent past. The South African Broadcasting Corporation gave generous television and radio broadcast time to the TRC producing the 'Truth Commission Special Report'. This was televised regularly to a large audience and drew in more viewers than some of the most popular South African soap operas during the first few months of its transmission. More than one million listeners tuned in to Radio Zulu, which produced a weekly update on the TRC. Those who watched and listened were subjected to tales of extreme brutality: tales of routine and calculated killings and abductions carried out by agents of the state against its 'opponents' and 'ordinary citizens'; stories of corpses without hands, cut off to prevent identification; accounts of the necklacing of alleged informers in the townships in which a tyre filled with petrol was placed around the neck and set alight; and the haunting specter of the torturer's 'wet bag', a technique developed and perfected to extract confessions from captured anti-apartheid agents. Week after week, torturers, killers, and rapists 'confessed' their crimes and 'acknowledged' their guilt to the TRC, sometimes breaking down as they spoke. Some radio listeners complained that they did not like to mix 'blood with breakfast', but many were equally captivated by the ever-accumulating macabre revelations (Krog, 1999: 76).

The public ceremonial at which these stories were told interpellated and disciplined the new political subjects of South Africa, constituted 'truth' as the prime object of the confessional and conferred a moral authority upon these subjects and objects before a national audience. Within this public context, the confessional narrative, crucially, structured the testimonials within a *present morality tale* about South Africa's past which sought to instill repentance and remorse in the confessing subject, the perpetrator, as a necessary preliminary to the concluding narrative episode: reconciliation. This chapter takes on the task of exploring the workings of power in the confessional, and the subjects (victims and perpetrators), and object (truth), of the confessional discourse.

The Confessional

The legitimacy of the ceremonial of truth in South Africa was constructed in part through a series of official declaratory statements that served to establish and enforce the norms within which the TRC would come to operate. An important early example of this is Tutu's inaugural speech at the first meeting of the TRC on 16 December 1995, a date that now carries the annual memorial function of 'Reconciliation Day' in South Africa, and at which Tutu declared that the principal function of the TRC was to promote the 'healing of the nation'. He explained that healing could only begin once the disclosure of 'painful truths' about the past had taken place. Tutu sought to legitimize his statement, behind which lay the by now incontrovertible amnesty agreement, by invoking the diametric specters of the inquisition and the confessional in Christian history and tradition. Tutu stated that this truth-recovery process was not going to be a 'witch-hunt' and that it was not going to be an inquisitorial body 'hell-bent on bringing miscreants to book'. By contrast, Tutu argued, the TRC was going to constitute a sacramental ritual of 'contrition, confession, and forgiveness' which would contribute to a 'corporate nationwide process of healing' (Tutu, 1995).

By implication, within the TRC's discursive field and the parameters of the narrative it sought to tell, there were no 'evil miscreants' to be brought to account and duly punished. There were only potentially penitent souls who were willing to yield their truths at the behest of the TRC. By stating that the TRC would follow a confessional model, Tutu implied that the legitimacy of the TRC's work would not rest upon the forcible (legal?) extraction of truth, but only upon 'freely' produced truths. However, Tutu's declaration conceals the play of power entailed in the 'free' confessional truth as opposed to the 'forced' inquisitorial truth. A critique of this simple opposition is facilitated by a consideration of Foucault's work on the confessional, which argues persuasively that power is just as present, although less visible, in confessions that appear to be freely given, as in those that are violently extracted. He writes:

> One confesses—or is forced to confess. When it is not spontaneous or dictated by some internal imperative, the confession is wrung from a person by violence or threat; it is driven from its hiding place in the soul, or extracted from the body. Since the Middle Ages, torture has accompanied it like a shadow, and supported it when it could go not further: the dark twins (Foucault, 1978: 59).

Tutu's bifurcation of inquisition and confessional would not convince Foucault because his analysis, by contrast, suggests that the 'spontaneous' confessional is haunted by the historical relationship between torture and truth, an account of which lays bare the 'free' confessional as a model of power. The effect of an application of Foucault's argument is to militate against Tutu's assertion, and by implication the stated assumptions of the TRC: that a 'confessional' truth is freely rendered.

Spectacular Power

In *Discipline and Punish* Foucault charts the development of disciplinary society from the pre-Enlightenment 'great spectacle of physical punishment' which entailed drawn-out torture and execution. Foucault charts the ways in which the spectacle was gradually displaced by more systematic and bureaucratic methods of social control over individuals, and how discipline became manifest in modern penal practices such as prisons and penitentiaries that relied not upon the spectacle of sovereign power to compel submission, but upon the invisible workings of systems of surveillance and control.

To illustrate the trajectory of this shift, Foucault begins the book with a frequently cited gruesome anatomy of the public torture and execution of Damiens the regicide in Paris in the mid-eighteenth century. He notes that the stability of the sovereign truth—the truth to be produced at the public confession—was partly secured by the *prior private* interrogation of the subject during which the initial confession was extracted. By the time the subject reiterated the confession publicly, he or she had been *already* scripted violently into the sovereign truth *prior to* its spectacular reproduction. The public spectacle thus represented the site of *reiteration* of the 'confession' already solicited, and it constituted the subject as the living embodiment of an official discourse which had been reinforced and stabilized by its previous private 'rehearsal' which was then re-enacted in the public realm.

Foucault's description is directed towards the analysis of two functions of spectacular punishment. First, Foucault is keen to show how torture works to produce a confessional 'truth' from the site of the agonized body, and secondly and more importantly to this analysis, he endeavors to demonstrate the way in which torture inscribes sovereign authority directly onto the body of the subject, a practice that simultaneously constitutes the criminality of the subject. The body of the condemned constitutes the location of the exercise of sovereign power first, in its subjection to its punitive instruments, and secondly through yielding the 'confession'. The confession entails a further level of subjection in that the 'correct' or only acceptable confession merely reproduces the truth of the sovereign.

Foucault notes, however, that in spite of its tremendous force and horror, the torturous performance of power was not always seamlessly successful. The diary of Bouton, a witness of Damiens' execution, provides Foucault with a source of the various and grisly failures of this exercise of power which threaten the authority of the sovereign in whose name the spectacle is publicly delivered. Bouton's diary records how Damien's flesh failed to burn properly, and that his drawn and quartered body resisted its dislocation. Damien's body thus becomes a metaphor for the failure of sovereign authority. For Foucault, the body might provide the site of articulation of sovereign power, but it is also just as likely to become the site of resistance to it, a repudiation of its intended awe-inspiring and pedagogical exercise. Importantly, the occasional failure of torture to render total the subordination of the body also allowed for the transformation of criminals into heroes by spectators, their resistance speaking to and for those who might privately oppose sovereign authority (Foucault, 1977: 60–62).

For Foucault, the failure of the spectacle of punishment and its eventual transformation was attributable ultimately to its inability to deliver a secure and stable public lesson, a failure which is, I think, evident in Benzien's confession discussed in previous chapters and, as discussed later in this chapter, that of Winnie Mandela. On Foucault's account, the 'guilty' who managed to resist torture could be elevated to 'heroes' whilst others might 'confess' quickly in order to escape the excruciating treatment. As such, the veracity of the truth produced under duress was ambiguous rendering the subject of criminal discourse uncertain.[1] As Foucault documents, one of the prime consequences of this were that public punishment was subjected to a number of transformations towards the end of the eighteenth century during which time punishment became dependent upon the perceived necessity for a 'rational' calculation between the crime committed and the punishment apportioned. Thus the spectacle of excess, furnished by public executions, gave way to the principle of a rationally calculable punishment which purported to be proportionate to the crime committed. However the latter, crucially, retained the function of civic instruction in common with the spectacle through the moralizing principle of 'just deserts', which reflected the careful calibration of punishment in accordance with the crime. As such, the exercise of sovereign authority assumed a 'just' and 'rational' character and disposed of its overtly violent one, a shift that provided a new foundation for its legitimate execution which was now thoroughly predicated not upon torture, the 'art of unbearable sensations', but on the 'economy of suspended rights' (Foucault, 1977: 11).

Foucault captures the shift in punitive practices from the spectacle to modern systems of control, epitomized by the prison and penitentiary, by invoking Jeremy Bentham's panopticon as metaphor for the disciplinary society. The panopticon was a design for prisons in which inmates would be disciplined by the gaze of an invisible and anonymous administrator situated at the centre of the panoptic structure (Foucault, 1977: chapter three). Thus 'rational' social control came to be predicated upon constant surveillance and control rather than upon the sudden violent appearance of sovereign authority. This shift in punitive practices might be understood as an inversion of the logic of the public spectacle of punishment—this entailed a linear sequence of private interrogation followed by a public execution. By contrast, the modern ritual of truth inverts this relationship because it makes public the legal practice of interrogation (truth production), and makes private, or concealed from public view, the punishment of the 'guilty subject'. The search for truth and the final declaration of guilt or innocence thus displaces the historical spectacle of punishment which is now instead relegated to the private domain. Instead, the interrogation is now public and punishment private. Foucault makes a trenchant political point about this inversion because he argues that the now public character of the tribunal (the 'interrogation') makes a claim to legitimacy on the basis that it appears accountable to scrutiny by its audience (the 'general public'), in whose interests it claims to work.

The principle effects of this modern shift are twofold. First, it serves to constitute the regime as rational, deliberative, and considerate. And second, in the absence of violent spectacular power, the ceremonial of truth relies for its effectiveness upon individual discipline. What this means is that regimes of truth are profoundly pervasive, such that legal subjects and onlookers are internal to the discourses of power. As a result they reproduce the truth of the regime to the extent that they are self-regulating which, in turn, nullifies the necessity of a violent power display. Foucault's history marks this historical shift from practices of chastisement of the body to an emphasis on incarceration and reform which was designed to emphasize the restitution of the subject as its central function. This, Foucault argues, marked the 'entry of the soul on to the scene of penal justice' (Foucault, 1977: 24). Foucault's general purpose in marking this historical shift is to chart the development of disciplinary society in which individuals become largely self-regulatory to the extent to which they are constructed within and speak 'freely' to dominant social and political discourses or narratives.

Demonstrating Humanity

The self-regulating workings of disciplinary society and its relevance to the TRC are made apparent by a consideration of Foucault's account of the confessional, a historical procedure for the production of truth and through which the confessing subject was constructed as being in possession of a 'soul' (Foucault, 1978: 57).[2] Foucault correlates the rise of the confessional (as one of the primary rituals of truth production) with the decline of 'accusatory procedures in criminal justice', amongst which he lists the Inquisition (Foucault, 1978: 58). Foucault argues that concomitant with this rise was the evolution of the *avowal* in which individuals were no longer attested for by the references of others, but were beseeched to vouch for their own 'authenticity' through veracity of their declarations. As such, he or she was 'authenticated by the discourse of truth he was able or obliged to pronounce concerning himself', the result of which was that 'the truthful confession was inscribed at the heart of the procedures of individualization by power' (Foucault, 1978: 58–59). The confessional thus seeks to establish a fundamental relation to truth through the process of self-examination.

The confession, Foucault notes, is now located within Western discourse as a highly valued and meaningful strategy of truth production and has pervaded a variety of social formations from medicine to education, to the family and to intimate relations such that in general, 'western man has become a confessing animal'. The confessional imperative, both in political life and in popular culture, is arguably even more powerful today than it was at the time of Foucault's writing:

> The obligation to confess is now relayed through so many different points, is so deeply ingrained in us, that we no longer perceive it as the effect of a power that constrains us; on the contrary, it seems to us that truth, lodged in our most secret nature, 'demands' only to surface; that if it fails to do so, this is because a con-

straint holds it in place, the violence of a power weighs it down, and it can finally
be articulated only at the price of a kind of liberation (Foucault, 1978: 60).

With these lines, Foucault points us to the invisible workings of disciplinary
society, showing why we fail to see the locus of disciplinary articulation because
is has undergone such a profound shift and has become so internalized to our
everyday conduct and interactions. The command of the sovereign has become
deeply entrenched within the bodies, the habits, the customs and rituals of
those—all of us—subjected to the particular and invisible workings of power.

The confessing subject is made powerfully present by the ritual of the confessional, because it features the speaking subject as the subject of the truth disclosure. Simultaneously, the confession constructs a power relation between the
confessing subject and the other towards whom the confession is addressed. It is
dependent upon the presence, or virtual presence of another, an authority who
demands the confession, who either punishes, forgives, or reconciles in return,
and who represents the 'agency of domination' to which the confessing subject
is subordinate (Foucault, 1978: 62). The confession is a discursive ritual that is
an *outward* manifestation, or rather performance, that seeks to represent an *inner*
change on the part of the confessor where the act of producing the confession
itself 'exonerates, redeems, and purifies' the subject. It promises salvation (Foucault, 1978: 62).

In sum, and in contrast to Tutu's assertion that spectacular power (the
'witch hunt') and confessional truth do not bear comparison, Foucault shows us
that there is in fact a relationship between past spectacular power, through which
the presence of sovereign authority used to be manifest violently, and the present
practice of the confessional, which subsumes and hides the presence of authority,
the direct workings of power, but does not do away with it.

However, as with the spectacle of public torture, the confessional does not
always render complete the supplication of the perpetrator, as the testimonies of
Jeffrey Benzien to the TRC illustrate most powerfully. Benzien was adept at
aping the discourse of forgiveness and the posture of remorse, such that he sub-
verted the very story about remorse and repentance on behalf of the perpetrators
that the TRC was attempting to generate. Benzien stated in his public deposition
that he was grateful that certain victims named in one of his amnesty applications had agreed not to oppose him in his application for amnesty. He said 'we
are now all on the same side. . . it is now reconciliation, forgive and forget at its
best'. However, in giving his account of the 'wet bag' torture technique, for
which he was famous, Benzien reported, at odds with the style of the confessional and perhaps with some satisfaction, the 'efficiency' of his work. He stated
that his technique was so successful that victims usually 'broke' in under thirty
minutes. Benzien's account is subversive. In turns it wittingly deploys the language of forgiveness and reconciliation to frame his past actions—'life is pre-
cious, and based on today's political situation of reconciliation his (Ashley
Kriel's) death was unnecessary'—and at the same time certain slippages occur
where he professes to have been a patriot of the old South Africa, and, arguably,
displays a certain professional pride in his work as a torturer. Benzien even

claims victim status as his own: 'the African Youth League threatened to have demonstrations on my front lawn. . . I did terrible things to members of the ANC, but. . . I have also suffered. . . I have also been a victim.'[3]

Indeed, the amnesty provision itself provides any applicant with the justificatory discourse within which an application needs to be framed, and on a radical reading, one could argue that it provides the *justifications per se* for past violence, that Benzien utilized to such dramatic, and to some, appalling effect. The sincerity conditions of the confession are in fact undermined by the promise of amnesty offered in exchange for confession. Such an incentivized confession gives the lie to the possibility that there is genuine remorse animating its performance, and the confession is thus undermined by its unequivocal instrumentality.

The TRC as Confessional

For the first six months of the public hearings the Commission only heard the testimonies of the victims, but the longer these went on the need of the audience to hear the second narrative, that of the perpetrator, intensified. Krog, a journalist who followed and reported upon the hearings in detail wrote of the sense of expectation that she shared with other participants in the process, 'it had better be good' she states, it had 'better be powerful' and 'it had better display integrity. . . grief and bewilderment' (Krog, 1999: 56). Krog's account reproduces the general demand, generated by the TRC, that perpetrator confessions ought to be delivered with an appropriately remorseful attitude in order to fulfill the conditions, indeed expectations, of reconciliation. In order to meet the requirements of the confessional the deponent had to accept a charge in a suitably regretful manner, display subordination to the authority of the confessor and judge, the TRC, and ask for forgiveness from the named victim or victims. Any disturbance of these confessional presuppositions threatened the plausibility of the public confession.

Sometimes, Krog avers, the second narrative *did* sound good, such as Eugene de Kock pleading that he had just been following orders and that his orders 'came right from the top. . . from the President' during his time in command of the infamous Vlakplaas death squad. He ended his testimony with an apology. But frequently, perpetrator narratives completely failed the confessional imperative. They were not delivered in an appropriately remorseful tone. The condescending confession of General Deon Mortimer was a good example. Mortimer gave evidence about the security force assault on ANC facilities in Matola, launched in retaliation for ANC car bomb attacks on Air Force Headquarters in Pretoria in 1983.[4] Krog records the contempt with which he used the word 'terrorist', and the 'relish with which he pronounces the words "ban" and "unbanning"' (Krog, 1999: 57). Mortimer's account provoked the Commissioner, Reverend Khoza Mgojo, to respond as follows:

> In this presentation I see self-righteousness and self-justification . . . There is

nothing as a sign of confession as I said before. We need to use an approach of confession and sorry. . . this to me is depressing because if you are writing history bringing reconciliation we need to be honest so that we can be sure of what we have done. So I need to say that I am very disappointed about that and again what has disappointed me most is that in this chronology of operations there is nothing said more, I see statistics when this is dealing with other organizations such and such thing happened, so many people, etc. but when you come to for instance the raids of Lesotho and Mozambique is not only the, it is very. . . ANC operation de-stabilized. People died there. There are tombs, funerals there and people are cry-ing they miss their loved ones who are buried there.[5]

Mortimer refused in his account to be conditioned by the reconciliatory truth the TRC wanted to tell. He refused to adopt the lexicon of remorse as the narrative framework of his own account of past violations.

Sometimes the confession was equivocal, it was more complex than either a simple fulfillment or repudiation of the confessional. Krog reported that Win-nie Mandikizela-Mandela consistently responded to the TRC's accusations of her own culpability with cries of 'ludicrous' and 'ridiculous' (Krog, 1999: 391). Tutu finally made a lengthy entreaty in which he appealed to Mandikizela-Mandela's 'greatness' and begged her to ask forgiveness for her past actions:

> I speak to you as someone who loves you very deeply. Who loves your family very deeply. I would have said to you, let us have a public meeting. And at that public meeting for you to stand up and say there are things that went wrong. . . There are people out there who want to embrace you. . . I beg you, I beg you, I beg you please. . . You are a great person and you don't know how your greatness would be enhanced if you were to say sorry, things went wrong, forgive me. I beg you.[6]

Winnie Mandela finally suggested that it was just possible that the Mandela United Football Club had taken its authority too far, with violent consequences: 'things went horribly wrong and we were aware that there were factors that led to that. For that I am deeply sorry'. However, her confession was, generally, not considered to be heartfelt. Whilst her actual words fulfilled the condition of the confession, Mandikizela-Mandela's attitude did not, much to the outrage of the onlookers, and in particular the victims. Krog protested 'she didn't mean it! She simply aped the words Tutu put in her mouth—she aped it for the benefit of in-ternational media coverage!' (Krog, 1999: 392). However, as Veitch has argued, 'aping' the words of the TRC was much more likely to secure amnesty, and those perpetrators adept at this, like Benzien, were more likely to be successful in their applications (Veitch, 2001).

These examples of conformity to, and disturbance of, the confessional model of power point to a further level of constraint that is imposed by the inter-nal narrative structure of the confession. The processes intrinsic to the confes-sional are linked in a linear and causal way, starting with the 'recognition' of a concealed or repressed 'truth' and ending with a regretful admission of account-ability. An audience feels deprived, as in the case of Mandikizela-Mandela, if the confession fails to fulfill the expected narrative trajectory because this, accom-

panied by the correct attitude, represents the outward sign that the inner transformation of the soul has taken place.

The TRC constituted an extraordinary public model of confessional power.
As a political procedure it utilized the confessional as a means of producing the
truth about the past, and through which the confessing subject—the perpetrator—was constructed as being human being in possession of a soul. It also
sought to establish a fundamental relation to truth through the process of soul-
searching and revelation, but it simultaneously concealed the powerful source of
the truth reproduced because the structure of the confessional is predicated upon,
indeed relies for its veracity, upon rendering the impression that the confession is
freely and spontaneously produced. However, it is striking that whilst the TRC
conformed strongly to Foucault's confessional paradigm in which the direct
workings of power are invisible and subjects appear to be self-regulating, it also
retained some features of spectacular power. Notably, the stability of the truth
produced at the hearings was partly secured by the prior private process of testimony solicitation by the TRC, which organized and synthesized testimonies
through its Infocomm system, as previously discussed. By the time the selected
confession was re-articulated in the public domain, it had been thoroughly conditioned by the truth regime of the TRC, which had been imprinted during 'private
rehearsal'—the testimony solicitation process—prior to its spectacular reproduction. The public spectacle served to reiterate and reinforce the truth of the Commission, constituting the perpetrator as the living embodiment of the official
discourse, thus doubling the voice of the regime. In addition, the public spectacle
was used in order to perform and compel the truth of the regime, of which the
visual semiotics of the hearings is evidence. During the victim hearings for example, seating was arranged to make sure that the victim was positioned at the
same level as the panel of Commissioners by way of deconstructing the usual
hierarchies of the court in order to reflect the privileged position that the TRC
accorded to victims, and to serve the therapeutic function for victims of 'being
listened to', rather than being instrumental to, the proceedings.

In spite of some similarities with spectacular power, it is important to emphasize here that at the TRC it was the soul rather than the body that constituted
the site through which truth was articulated, and subjection to the sovereign narrative of reconciliation actualized. The public character of the TRC concealed
the extant workings of power in that the TRC was made to appear accountable
to examination by those whom it purported to serve. The effect of this was to
constitute the TRC as perspicacious, judicious and considerate. The confessional
conceals the more direct and forceful workings of power as it appears to spring
from an inner impulse on the part of the supplicant, rather than being imposed
from without. The confessional presents itself as 'the infinite task of extracting
from the depths of oneself, in between the words, a truth which the very form of
the confession holds out like a shimmering mirage' (Foucault, 1978: 59).

The doubt with which Winnie Mandela's confession was met seems to
point to the failure of this working of power, because at this moment power was
made transparent, and for the confessional to appear spontaneous the workings
of power must remain invisible. Tutu's entreaty thus seemed to make visible the

truth regime of the TRC. Whilst it would have been politically unwise for Mandela to repudiate Tutu's appeal, her positive response cynically reproduced the truth of the Commission and revealed her own replication, as a hollow imitation, of the TRC's truth claims. However, what is interesting here is that this failure was perceived, by spectators such as Krog, as being Mandela's failure rather than that of the Commission. That Winnie Mandela failed properly to confess, to show sufficient regret, to wholeheartedly enter into the reconciliatory process did not reflect negatively upon the TRC but upon her own disposition and character.

The truth regime of the TRC scripted not only its direct subjects into the state narrative, but also those who participated in the various audiences, either at the public hearings or the many televised and radio broadcast bulletins. Immediate subjects and onlookers were made internal to the discourse of power by virtue of their participation in the production of confessional, either as confessors or as adjudicators of the 'authenticity' of the confession. However, the confessional constituted the principal technology through which the subject positions of victim and perpetrator were publicly interpellated, sustained, and compelled, and it is to this issue that I now turn.

'A Victim is a Victim is a Victim'[7]

Whilst the confessional constituted the public site of the performance of South Africa's new political and national subjects, there were also other technologies which reinforced and compelled them. The TRC enforced certain modes of identification whilst excluding others by interpellating, for example, 'victims' rather than 'survivors', and 'perpetrators' rather than 'war criminals'.[8] The TRC's confessional narrative constituted and compelled the new political subjects of South Africa as victim and perpetrator, a strategy that circumvented the old racialized identity divisions of apartheid and party-political expressions of difference and opposition, in an attempt to reformulate the political subjects of apartheid and reconstruct national identity as inclusive. A new discursive mode of social division, and of social understanding, was thus instituted and which Tutu claimed to be 'politically, socially, and racially neutral'.

The pre-eminence of the TRC's discourse was sustained by a combination of processes. These included the symbolic, such as the confessional, and material, such as the amnesty and reparations processes. But these different sites of articulation of identity forge consent and require collusion on the part of the subject(s) towards whom it is directly addressed. However, as Norval argues in her discussion of the apartheid regime, 'while the forging of consent and the exercise of domination may differ in degree, they do not differ in kind. That is to say, even where subjects are interpellated into a discourse and where they may be argued to have "consented" in some sense, force is not absent' (Norval, 1996: 4). Force takes different forms. The force of discourse and the inclusions and exclusions that it entails is but one aspect. Norval applies this analysis to the maintenance of discourses and subjectivities that were integral to the apartheid regime; my contention here is that the same operation of force that was common to apartheid is *also* present in the construction of the post-apartheid political field. The TRC enforced the subjects of its narrative via its legal mechanisms. For example, alleged perpetrators were commanded to make an appeal to the TRC through the use of subpoena, the first time that a truth commission had been endowed with more powerful legal mechanisms.

The new political order abolished the old apartheid subject positions—'whites', 'coloreds', 'Indians' and 'blacks'—and the TRC replaced these with what it claimed to be racially cross-cutting categories of victim and perpetrator, thus instituting a new mode of national identification.[9] Tutu's assertion cited above—'a victim is a victim is a victim'—represented an attempt to be more inclusive on the part of the TRC, to represent all victims of violence in the past, to construct a democracy of victimhood that aimed to undermine and reorganize former apartheid subject positions.

The putative aim of recognizing *all* victims of the political violence regardless of their racial designation is resonant with the key themes of the ANC's program of nation-building, which promoted a civic rather than a racial view of African nationalism as a way of fostering a common national identity.[10] These principles of non-racialism have long been central to the ANC, a party constituted by a coalition of different racial, ethnic, ideological, and religious elements, and this is a principle now enshrined in the new Constitution (Constitution of the Republic of South Africa, 1996: 1:1). But it is clear that different views of nationhood and legitimacy are persistent sources of contestation today and vary from the ANC's 'one nation' project, which propounded an inclusive, civic nationalism, to the more exclusivist modes of identification underpinning the politics of, for example, the IFP and Afrikaner nationalism. In discursively constituting an inclusive polity in South Africa, the TRC appeared to be motivated more obviously by ANC ideals, and has consequently come up against criticism from those with different claims to nationhood, particularly Afrikaners, many of whom felt not simply excluded by the TRC process but vilified by it. Indeed, Norval in her speculations on a 'new political imaginary' for post-apartheid South Africa states that the mythical and symbolic renderings of unity and of social division articulated by the new National Party, the IFP and the far right all share some characteristics and present alternative modes of ordering to the ANC. Writing in 1996, Norval's comments upon South African prospects for constructing an inclusive national discourse that transcended the divisions inaugurated and compelled by the apartheid regime note that 'the discourse of non-racialism, clearly dominant in the construction of a post-apartheid order, will have to contend with and take account of these alternative myths if a successful transition to democracy is to be instituted' (Norval, 1996: 275). It can be argued that this has now been borne out by resistance to some of the findings of the TRC, and to its casting of post-apartheid South African subjects as victims and perpetrators.

Inevitably perhaps, the putative neutrality of the TRC's identity categories were thrown into question by its practical workings. Tutu claimed that:

There is no distinction between someone who is a victim of human rights violations, perpetrated by, say, the liberation movements, or one who is a victim of violations perpetrated by the apartheid dispensation. Once someone comes before the
Commission and we say yes, a gross human rights violation has happened, we
don't ask what is your political affiliation. In the matter of amnesty, no moral distinction is going to be made between acts perpetrated by the liberation movements
and acts perpetrated by the apartheid dispensation. We can make that distinction,
as most human beings would, but the act itself makes that moral distinction superfluous (Tutu, 1996: 43).

However, contrary to Tutu's statement, it was necessary to enquire into the 'political affiliation' of the amnesty applicant because this was a *prior* condition of
amnesty, as it was granted *only* for violations found to have been perpetrated
with a *political objective*. Party political violence provided both the narrative
context within which the violation(s) took place, and constituted the organizing
rationale of the amnesty application, for which party political affiliation would
be integral to an acceptable justification for the perpetration of a gross violation.
For that 'political objective' to be made apparent, it was necessary for the applicant to reveal his or her political affiliation at the outset.

This procedural point apart, the Commission contradicts the position taken
by Tutu here on another count. On the question of making 'evenhanded' judgments, the Report states that great care was taken to ensure that 'victims' were
dealt with equally but that that *moral judgment* was not suspended (TRC, 1 (1)
52–56). Indeed, it was fiercely argued during the TRC's investigations that the
Commission would fail if it refused to make a moral judgment *against* the agents
of apartheid and *in favor* of those who resisted state violence. This argument was
elaborated by Kader Asmal, Louise Asmal and Ronald Suresh Roberts in their
book *Reconciliation Through Truth* which was published during the TRC hearings (Asmal et al, 1996). The authors argued that if the TRC failed to make a
clear moral distinction between the architects and defenders of apartheid and
those who fought against it, then its attempt to construct a new moral order
would miscarry. A moral narrative had to make judgments about right and
wrong, about the agents of good and the agents of evil. It could not simply sus-
pend this judgment and simultaneously claim to lay new moral foundations for
the nation. The authors are keen to point out that the founding legislation of the
TRC, The Promotion of National Unity and Reconciliation Act did not make
provision for the elaboration of a clear moral judgment because it did not make
any distinction between the perpetrators and the victims on the various sides of
the conflict. The mandate of the TRC is here thus at odds with what these critics,
and many others, considered to be the vital task of the TRC.

Tutu's comments on moral distinctions (or lack thereof) was at odds with
the balance of testimony that was aired at the public hearings, which stands in
contrast to the overall attempt to allocate blame 'proportionately' across the parties. The voice of the victim was overwhelmingly black, and many were women.
By contrast, the voice of the perpetrator at the amnesty hearings resonated most
strongly with the voice of the National Party which was represented overwhelmingly by white male security agents of the old regime. The hearings thus had the

effect of assigning, broadly, perpetrator identities to agents of the apartheid state, and victim identity to liberation agents.

Importantly, it is not only the hearings but the findings based upon the investigated cases which were instrumental to assigning political subjectivity to parties to the conflict within the broader narrative about past violence that the TRC sought to relate. Anthea Jeffery makes a detailed analysis of the findings emerging out of the amnesty hearings and argues that the TRC made a series of errors and omissions, which carried particular political consequences (Jeffery, 1999). Jeffery argues that the TRC made an insufficiently systematic attempt to enquire into the role of liberation movements in initiating and sustaining 'people's wars' and that disproportionate blame was allocated to the South African Police and IFP and not enough to the ANC, with particular reference to the violence in KwaZulu-Natal and other instances. This resulted in a disproportionate number of non-state perpetrators being assigned to parties other than the ANC. Jeffery also notes that some of the TRC's findings were at variance with former judicial rulings on particular cases. For example, the TRC at least doubles the number of fatalities at the hands of the police in its investigations of the Sebokeng shootings in March 1990. This, she argues, was one effect of poor methodology and selective investigations, relying upon the 'balance of probabilities' rather than upon proof beyond reasonable doubt. This, according to Jeffery, meant that 'disproportionate' blame was allocated to former state security agents and the IFP, and the culpability of the ANC was minimized in the TRC's findings. However, I would argue that Jeffrey reduces the truth produced by the Commission to a highly legalized and positivistic truth. She focuses on what she sees as the paucity of the truth recovery process because it did not require corroboration or cross-examination of witnesses, and misses a key objective of the Commission which lay in its attempt to illuminate a truth that exceeded these narrow legal parameters. The deliberate refusal to cross-examine was justified by the TRC because it argued that victims had suffered enough. Cross-examinations would only add to 'the harrowing experience of victims' and subject them to the further 'indignity' of doubt. As a result, in cases that had already received attention, the TRC relied upon 'the basic facts about what had happened' which it claimed were 'already well known' (TRC, 1 (5) 45). In addition, by the time the TRC produced the first, incomplete, version of the Report—upon which Jeffrey relies—most of the amnesty evidence had been heard from security force applicants and relatively little from ANC, UDF and PAC applicants. Jeffrey's criticism, however, highlights a general and critical tension running through the work of the TRC between its quasi-legalistic processes and the moral-political narrative it was trying to generate.

The narrative of the Report is an additional site of the bifurcation of identity into victim and perpetrator, in that it lists the names of all of those found to be victims of gross violations, although it defends its decision to 'establish a finite list of victims' (TRC, 1 (4) 133). The finitude of this list performs an act of closure on the past with the aim of precluding the possibility of any further future petitions for reparations and preventing the re-opening of past wounds. It states that 'it became increasingly clear that there would be no value in simply handing the government a list which included a broad category of unidentified persons for consideration as victims deserving of reparations'. The Report asserted that it would be 'unrealistic to give the government what would, in effect, have been an open-ended list and, on this basis, to expect the state to make a commitment to paying reparations' (TRC, 1 (4) 134). A limit was placed on the politics of restitution, which would ultimately have to materialize as financial reparations, and concomitantly, a narrative cut-off point was designated.[11]

The politics of naming cuts two ways. It was designed to perform both the 'restoration of human dignity' of victims and the 'shaming' of perpetrators. The accomplishment of 'visibility' and 'public recognition' is a constitutive feature of naming. In the early stages of discussion about the means of dealing with the past, the TRC defended its decision not to conduct a criminal tribunal because this ran the risk of fetishizing perpetrators and their truths, which would have the effect of ontologically privileging perpetrator narratives about the past (TRC, 1 (1) 20–32). In the process, according to the Commission, this would have risked the truth recovery process which instead was greatly facilitated by the amnesty provision because amnesty provided a huge incentive for perpetrators to approach the TRC with their accounts. Criminal trials, the TRC argued, would also have required the cross-examination of victims resulting in new ordeals, potentially retraumatizing, rather than providing the catharsis and recognition promised by the TRC. A cathartic and restorative function was also assigned to perpetrator's testimonies which, in the context of the public confessional, were assumed to instill a 'new moral sensibility' into the confessor:

> For many the testimonies before the TRC—from victims and perpetrators, such as Benzien, Cronje, Hechter, Mentz, Van Vuuren, and De Kock—provided much more than cold objective and factual information. These testimonies encouraged moments of truth, where people were converted to an understanding of what injustice is, while at the same time becoming aware of a new notion of justice. Confronted by the stories, the face of evil became visible to these people, giving birth to a feeling of shame and to a notion of justice. The latter is of particular importance, for through this feeling of shame, a moral responsibility for what went wrong in the past may also be acknowledged. In other words, in the confrontation with the past a dialectical tension often develops. Within the context of this tension we begin to see things in a different light and experience a new moral consciousness (Esterhuyse, 2000: 152).

The TRC suggested that the practice of naming was integral to the process of the confessional, the first act of self-recognition, and then of public revelation facilitating a formal naming and the identification and attachment of a person to a particular violation. The Act stated that those found eligible for amnesty should be named in the Government Gazette as they had, by implication, already identified themselves as perpetrators by applying for amnesty in the first place. As such, perpetrators were implicated in their own subjection by going to the Amnesty Committee to make their submissions, an act which predetermined the parameters of their testimony to the TRC. Before naming was carried out, the TRC sent notice to the perpetrator warning that they were about to be named.

Naming was usually a result of the alleged perpetrator appearing in a number of testimonies and where a witness had confirmed their identity. A reasonably 'high level of corroboration' was required.[12] Although the TRC justified naming, it recognized the tension between the public interest in the exposure of wrongdoing and the need to ensure fair treatment of individuals in what was not a court of law. Given the investigative nature of the Commission and the limited legal impact of naming, the Commission made its findings on the 'balance of probability' rather than on 'proof beyond reasonable doubt'. This required a lower burden of proof than that demanded by the conventional criminal justice system, and it meant that, 'when confronted with different versions of events, the Commission had to decide which version was the more probable, reasonable, or likely after taking all the available evidence into account' (TRC, 1 (4) 155). Naming consequently took place after enough evidence had been made available to make a finding on a balance of probability, although this was *not* a finding of legal guilt but of *responsibility* for the commission of gross human rights violations for which amnesty may or may not have been granted.

The TRC constructed as a privilege assigned to its participants, and in particular, to those it interpellated as victims of gross human rights violations who were constructed as the new constitutive pillar of society. In spite of this, perpetrators have frequently been seen as the greater beneficiaries of the Commission in that a 'guilty' finding did not carry the consequences of the criminal justice system if the crime was found to have been politically motivated. There was thus a perceived tension between the work of two of the Committees, the Committee on Amnesty, and the Committee on Human Rights Violations, and the different truths each generated. The Committee on Amnesty dealt primarily with perpetrator testimonies, and the Committee on Human Rights Violations dealt with victim depositions. The main task of the Committee on Human Rights Violations was to record, acknowledge and make public the experiences of victims as part of its restorative judicial remit. The Report states that the establishment of a full picture of past violations had to be coupled with a 'public, official acknowledgement of the "untold suffering" which resulted from those injustices' (TRC, 1 (5) 2). But the pursuits of these two aims were seen by some to deepen injustices already experienced by victims. The Committee on Amnesty had the power to implement an amnesty ruling with *immediate effect* whereas reparations for victims were subject to a much more lengthy and considered investigation with no immediate award of reparations. Perpetrators, then, benefited almost immediately from their confessions as amnesty was implemented with immediate effect whereas victims were subjected to further reviews over a lengthy period of time in order to clarify the precise reparations award. It is important to take into consideration such procedural constraints on the discursive construction and privileging of particular subjectivities, of victims over perpetrators. Whilst victims appeared, publicly, to be privileged by the TRC's discourse of reconciliation, they were also undermined by the bureaucratic and lengthy procedures which determined reparative measures, but also by the foundations of the TRC which were thoroughly grounded in and conditioned by the amnesty agreement. Reparations were, in effect, an afterthought. In addition, victim testimonies constituted evidence which could be used in support of amnesty claims leading to freedom from prosecution and in some cases prison, on the basis of 'full disclosure' by the amnesty applicant. Where, some wanted to know, was the justice in this? Whose truth, then, did the process privilege? In order to get closer to these issues a consideration of the nature of truth mediated by the Commission is necessary.

Truth: Four Types of Ambiguity

The TRC posited truth as the foundation of national reconciliation and towards which the political subjects of the confessional were oriented. The Commission stated that it 'sought to uncover the truth about past abuses' as part of the 'struggle of memory against forgetting', an aim which explicitly sought to 'recover' aspects of past violence that had been concealed by the previous regime. This represented an explicit endeavor to 'overcome the temptation to remember in a partisan, selective way; to recognize that the narrow memories of past conflicts can too easily provide the basis for mobilization towards further conflicts' (TRC, 1 (5) 51). Cognizant of the role of memory in conflict, the TRC suggested that a more 'inclusive' official memory of the past which allowed different parties to represent their perspectives in an official forum was more likely to prevent the resurgence of violence in the future. This recognition was constitutive of the pragmatism of the TRC. By contrast with the former regime which sought to represent and violently enforce only the truth of Afrikaaner nationalism, the TRC claimed to bring together a multitude of truths about the past in order to reflect the different experiences of the various parties engaged in the conflict. Further, and more importantly, the TRC sought coherence between these accounts by organizing the plethora of truths solicited at its behest within the overall teleological framework of reconciliation. Reconciliation as political process aimed to go further than to 'simply' mark the end of violent conflict, but was directed towards a more complex and abstruse process of coming to terms with the past. The Commission justified its search for a more 'replete' historical record and articulated the relationship of truth to reconciliation by stating that 'lies, half-truths and denial are not a desirable foundation on which to build the new South Africa' and that 'there can be no genuine, lasting reconciliation without truth' (TRC, 5 (8) 5). As such, truth was clearly established as the necessary and causal precondition of reconciliation, without which it was assumed that reconciliation would be an impossible objective.

In order to maximize the recovery of truth about the past and militate against a narrow memory of the conflict, the TRC elaborated a complex definition of truth within which victim and perpetrator narratives came to be framed (TRC, 1 (5) 29–45). Importantly, this complexified truth sought to maximize commensurability between the various accounts in order to facilitate the reconciliation process. This taxonomy was partly designed to expand the idea of truth beyond that of a legal or forensic truth, which would facilitate the emergence of only a 'narrow' parameter of truth. The TRC wanted to grasp the *full complexity* of the past, and to construct a layered discourse of truth that both victims and perpetrators might deploy—in their justifications of past violence, and in rendering accounts of suffering—in their accounts of the past. To this effect, and after much debate, four different categories of truth were constructed: The categories that were established by the TRC were 'factual or forensic truth', 'personal and narrative truth', 'social truth', and 'healing and restorative truth'.

Factual or forensic truth

This category refers to the 'familiar legal or scientific notion of bringing to light factual, corroborated evidence, and of obtaining accurate information through reliable ('impartial and objective') procedures' (TRC, 1 (5) 30). The pursuit of this type of truth sought to engage two main aspects. The first of these related to the precise details of individual findings: establishing what happened to whom, where, when, and how, and involving whom. The second aspect attempted to establish the contexts, causes, and patterns of violations.

Personal and narrative truth

This category refers to the individual truths of victims and perpetrators alike, and emphasized the value of all truths to the TRC, and the 'healing potential' of truth revelation. On the subject of narrative truth, Tutu stated during the public hearings that the Commission would 'listen to everyone'. He argued that it was crucial that 'everyone should be given a chance to say his or her truth as he or she sees it' in order to give 'meaning to the multi-layered experiences of the South African story', and to provide 'unique insights into the pain of South Africa's past' (TRC, 1 (5) 35). This dimension of truth-telling, Tutu argued, had particular resonance in the South African context which continues to attach importance to the 'oral tradition'. Tutu thus claims this to be a culturally authentic mode of reproduction of the past which had a specific resonance, function, and power, within its social context.

For the TRC, personal and narrative truth recognizes the individual contingency of truth, and emphasizes the role of interpretation and of divergent interpretations of particular events. It seeks to contextualize the actions and interpretations of social agents within broader narratives of race, ethnicity, political ideology, and nationalism. Without an appreciation of the wider discourses shaping human action, for example, the way in which the discourse of Afrikaaner nationalism led to the emergence of 'separate development', it is impossible to understand the context in which violations took place and the development of individual subjectivity and political identity formation, the TRC argued.

This category of truth sought recourse, for its legitimacy, to the *Promotion of Unity and National Reconciliation Act* which inaugurated the TRC. The Act provided a prior iteration of the assertion that storytelling has a 'healing potential' by linking the 'restoration of human and civil dignity' of victims to the importance of granting official validation of those stories in a public context. The official authorization of previously denied or silenced individual accounts, namely victim testimonies, was considered on the one hand an important function of restorative justice, but on the other crucial to the process by which those participants might offer 'history lessons' to the nation (TRC, 1 (5) 37).

Social truth
Social truth is, in the words of Judge Albie Sachs, the 'truth of experience that is established through interaction, discussion and debate' (TRC, 1 (5) 39). It is under the sign of social truth that the Commission came closest to acknowledging its own role in truth production, stating that 'it was in its search for social truth that the closest connection between the Commission's process and its goal was to be found'. However, the TRC explicitly upheld a notion of social truth that is itself revealed or liberated by a dialogic encounter whose norms are presented as being self-evidently legitimate and therefore beyond contestation. The Commission argued that 'participation' and 'transparency' were the fundamental properties of a dialogic social truth, and suggested that the TRC itself provided the main forum for the exposure of a variety of situated perspectives on the past, from those of the faith communities, to NGOs and the medical professions. The Report states that:

> The process whereby the truth was reached was itself important because it was through this process that the essential norms of social relations between people were reflected. It was, furthermore, through dialogue and respect that a means of promoting transparency, democracy, and participation in society was suggested as a basis for affirming human dignity and integrity (TRC, 1 (5) 42).

However, the 'essential norms' of the TRC rather than those of 'objective' social relations between people were the norms reflected by the dialogic encounters between victims, perpetrators and the Commission itself. The space for encounters constituted by the Commission certainly made such a dialogue possible but the norms it purveyed were not *reflected* but *constituted* by the TRC.

Healing and restorative truth
The fourth and final category of truth considers the nature of 'healing truth', through which the TRC sought to place 'facts and what they mean within the context of human relationships—both amongst citizens and between the state and its citizens' (TRC, 1 (5) 43). This category stresses the importance of 'acknowledgement' to the establishment of truth, and its 'healing properties'. 'Acknowledgement' requires that official history is re-written, that newly-revealed truths are placed on public record and due recognition given to individual suffering. Further, 'acknowledgement is an affirmation that a person's pain is real and worthy of attention' (TRC, 1 (5) 45). This category of truth is directed towards three things: it seeks to narrate individual truths within a national context, officially acknowledges victim experiences as a function of restorative justice, and is directed towards preventing future violence. Healing and restorative truth seeks to expand the limits of factual truth because, the TRC argues, 'it is not enough simply to determine what had happened' (TRC, 1 (5) 44).

The real value of truth recovery, according to the TRC, was to help *victims* become 'more visible and valuable citizens through the public recognition and official acknowledgement of their experiences', and at least three of the four types of truth are designed to address this issue (TRC, 1 (5) 27). Personal and narrative truth provides insights into painful experiences in the past, social truth seeks to integrate and authorize these stories within a social context and healing truth asserts the palliative effect of the testimonial and of official recognition. An interesting omission to this category is that of 'confessional truth' by which perpetrators seek to 'restore their humanity' and re-enter society as reformed souls. This function of truth was not spelled out in the official documentation, although, as discussed, the confessional was the powerful discursive paradigm through which perpetrators were afforded the opportunity of demonstrating their humanity.

These four categories of truth were constructed by the TRC in order to reflect the relationship between truth and reconciliation, and the relationship between individual, social and national truths. To this end, forensic truth aims to establish the minutiae of what happened, when and how. Personal truth adds individual interpretation to the forensic picture, and social truth places that individual truth within a broader context, making plain the way in which certain truths are generated by the interests and actions of a group, political or otherwise. The TRC as arbiter of social truth aims to weave these various group perspectives together through an open and public process of negotiation, with the aim of generating a healing truth explicitly directed towards the process of national reconciliation.

Of these four types of truth, three are most obviously victim truths as they are specifically directed towards the recognition, rehabilitation, and restoration of the 'visibility' and 'dignity' of victims. The effect of this is to constitute victims as the ontologically privileged subjects of the TRC's narrative, making the 'victim's status as victim the constitutive pillar of a new political order' (Steiner, 1997: 31).

However, the TRC did not make entirely clear how the different aspects of truth are made to relate to one another, and the Report fails to elaborate the connection between each category of truth. Additionally, the TRC did not provide the forum for victims and perpetrators to speak directly to one another, to negotiate in a dialogic fashion their various perspectives on the past. Indeed, they were very much separated by the structure of the TRC because victims and perpetrators approached different committees with their depositions. A further separation was constructed by the temporal organization of the hearings. Victim testimonies were aired during the first six months of the hearings, and perpetrator accounts were publicly rendered *after* the victims had been heard.

Wilson notes that only two of the categories were compelled with any force: forensic truth and narrative truth (Wilson, 2001: 37). Wilson argues that forensic and narrative truths were regularly set in opposition to one another, and that each was dominant at different times in the life of the Commission. Consequently, narrative truth presided over the early life of the Commission and the forensic paradigm came in to force subsequently. These truths were alternately hegemonic because the first stages of the TRC were devoted to hearing victim testimonies, upon which the importance of 'narrative truth' turned, and the later hearings concentrated on amnesty cases to which the establishment of 'forensic truth' was critical. However, against Wilson I would argue that narrative truth was as much crucial to the amnesty hearings as was forensic truth. Amnesty was conditional as much upon depositions being framed within the organizing framework of a political objective—requiring that the applicant articulate their past actions as having been carried out within, and as part of, a political conflict—as it was upon full disclosure, that is, rendering the factual details surrounding every violation with which an applicant might have been associated.

An expanded truth paradigm emerged out of the idea that forensic truth was limited because it did not adequately serve the reconciliatory process. And yet one of the key achievements of the TRC, as Michael Ignatieff has argued, was that it reduced the number of 'permissible lies' that circulated unchallenged in public discourse, which rest, arguably and primarily upon the forensic model (Ignatieff, 1996: 111). This was because the TRC was able to establish a considerable amount factual evidence regarding violent security force tactics against political opponents, details which had until its work been rumored but not established. The work of the TRC made it impossible to state, for example, that the practice of torture by state agents was not systematic and widespread. It was no longer possible to sustain the claim, as did many from the former regime, that only a few individuals acting on their own initiative were responsible for gross violations, that it was due to just a 'few rotten apples'. And the Commission gathered sufficient evidence to prove that missing political activists were systematically interrogated, tortured, killed and buried on farms all over the country. At the beginning of the TRC's investigations, there was a paucity of information about this issue in particular, but as time went on, evidence that such farms existed in the old Natal, the Transval, the Orange Free State, and the Eastern Cape emerged. The evidence amassed filled out the TRC's narrative about the far reach of the state's operations against its opponents. However, some of the triumphs of truth claimed by the TRC had already been established by the ANC's earlier investigations into abuses in its own camps. The Commission was able to make very detailed presentations of the abuse of human rights in relation to the treatment of detainees, among other issues, in the military camps of the ANC precisely because the ANC had conducted its own internal commissions of enquiry, the Stuart report, and the Skweyiya and Motsuenyane Commissions (1992 and 1993 respectively). The TRC drew upon these reports and enquiries to present evidence of ANC violations. Many of the truths the TRC generated were clearly not new, although the TRC enabled these details to enter the public domain much more effectively than these previous enquiries had managed to do.

In spite of the necessity of the production of a legally authoritative forensic truth, the expanded truth paradigm developed in part out of a critique of it. The TRC was compelled in the first place to point up the limitations of forensic truth because the amnesty process was mandated by the Act to rationalize accounts of violations within the wider *context* of a political motivation. As such, the narrative component of truth was already stipulated by the legal parameters. This feature already represented a departure from the forensic truth paradigm upon which 'regular' court investigations are based, which on the whole do not seek to establish the legitimate context of the 'crime' *prior to* the beginning of the trial. It is this feature, I argue, added to the decision against retribution, that led to the development of an expanded truth paradigm which, in my view, was a compensatory gesture towards victims for the fact that retribution was not a possibility. As a result, the four truths appear, ostensibly, to favor victim truths, giving substance to the TRC's claim that the victims of past violence would have a public forum through which they could exorcise their suffering and find some kind of cathartic release from the torments of the past. However, I would argue that this compounds victim subjection to the TRC process because none of the types of truth conflict with a reconciliatory outcome and all appear to be subsumed to it. There is no alternative type of truth through which victims might voice their opposition to the current order: each truth is directed towards reconciliation. Indeed, as Verdoolaege has demonstrated, victim testimonies were oriented towards reconciliatory outcomes in the exchanges between commissioners and victims during the public hearings, and victims were often explicitly asked by the Commissioner at the end of a testimony whether or not they would consider forgiving a perpetrator (Verdoolaege, 2006). The case of Ms Seatlholo who made a testimony about the random killing of her husband in Soweto in 1976 is a case in point.[13] Yasmin Sooka, TRC Commissioner, said to her 'we have heard many young women of your age who have had an experience of losing their loved ones' and goes on to ask how might someone like Seatlholo 'begin to heal and understand the idea of reconciliation'. Seatlholo replies 'I want to forgive those people who killed my husband' but states that she cannot until they come forward to confess publicly their crimes.

Yet some victims *did*, occasionally, depart from the reconciliatory script. Bettina Mdlalose refused to forgive those who had killed her son after being asked by the Commissioner, Mr Dlamini, if she would reconcile with the killers:

> Commissioner: But one other thing that's an objective of this Commission is that after we have ventilated about the atrocities that were committed to us, is that we should reconcile as the community of South Africa at large. The perpetrators, those who committed those atrocities to you, killed your son, according to our records haven't come forth for amnesty. . . But one question I would like to ask is that, if today those perpetrators would come forth and say, 'Commission, because you exist today, we would like to go and meet Mrs Mdlalose to ask for forgiveness', would you be prepared to meet with the perpetrators? I know they haven't come forward, they have not even admitted an application for amnesty, but still we would like to ask from you, to get a view from you that if they come to you and ask for forgiveness would you be prepared to sit down with them, shake hands with them, and reconcile with them. Would you be prepared to talk to them? (TRC hearing cited in Verdoolaege, 2006: 67–68).[14]

Mrs Mdlasose responds that she would not authorize a meeting, and is told by the Commissioner not to 'feel bad' for this refusal, and promises that when the perpetrator gets in touch with the Commission, the Commission will contact her to let her know. Not only is her refusal made to seem discordant with the expectations of the Commission and the principles of the reconciliation process, but in this case the perpetrators had *not, in fact, come forward with a confession in the first place*, the condition upon which forgiveness might in fact be forthcoming.

Conclusions

The TRC's narrative of the present turned upon two aspects. The first of these was the public spectacle of the hearings. The second comprised the technique of the confessional through which the dramatic and 'cathartic' revelation of truth was played out, the subjects of its narrative constituted and compelled and truth (as confessional and testimonial) as the foundational property of national reconciliation performed.

As a discursive ritual, the narrative of confession has an internal logic which constrains the actions and words of the supplicant and the confessor, its end point already pre-ordained before the confessing subject begins. The effect of this narrative structuration is to enact the moralizing force of its closure, which centers on the 'reform' of the confessing soul. The teleology of confession functions in order to admonish rather than punish the confessing subject.

However, and problematically, the moral demands of the confessional were incommensurate with the mandate of the TRC, which outlined the conditions under which amnesty would be granted. There was no formal stipulation for the truth disclosure to be delivered in the style of a confessional. This resulted in a tension during the hearings because the public narrative, charged with conveying moral lessons to the nation, privileged the confessional model of truth because it required remorse and regret to be articulated. The confession played into the narrative of reconciliation in a way that a simple articulation of the 'facts' could not because it performed the 'healing' of the perpetrator by signaling the 'restitution of the soul' that the confession attempts to constitute.

In addition, whilst the TRC's truth taxonomy widened the parameters of truth, it also constrained what could be said, or called for, in its name. Perpetrator and victim stories were both disciplined and constrained by this taxonomy. Perpetrators had to narrate their actions within the context of a political struggle in order to secure amnesty. Without this framing rationale, the TRC rejected the application. Victims appeared to be given more narrative freedom due to the fact that a particular outcome or ruling was not contingent upon the story given. However, victims could not simply relate their accounts 'as they saw them'. They could not demand justice for what they had endured. One woman related a horrifying account of her torture by the South African Police and ended her testimony with the plea that her torturers be brought to justice. To this plea, one of the commissioners responded simply 'thank you for contributing your story to the national process of reconciliation' (Chidester, 1999: 135). Yet another 'victim' argued that if 'perpetrators' were truly remorseful they would subject themselves to punishment rather than amnesty (Krog, 1999: 38). Victim narratives were thus compelled by, insofar as they are called for and subordinate to, the organizing teleological framework of reconciliation *even when they called for retribution*. Victims, in short, had to be reconciled to reconciliation.

Notes

1.   Foucault notes that the transformation of punitive practices was attributable to 'logical' rather than 'humanitarian' analyses by Beccaria and other Enlightenment reformers, who objected to the likely 'quality' of the truth produced under duress and suggested practical reforms on that basis.

2.   Foucault's work on the confessional is focused primarily on the production of the 'truth of sex' but his account is easily applicable to the confessional as a technology of truth production more generally.

3.   TRC, *Amnesty Hearing: Jeffery T. Benzien,* Cape Town, July 14, 1997.

4.   TRC, *Armed Forces Hearings: Maj. Gen. B. Mortimer, Submission IRO The Former SADF: SA Defence Force Involvement in the Internal Security Situation in the Republic of South Africa.*

5.   TRC, *Armed Forces Hearings,* Cape Town, 7–10 October 1997.

6.   TRC, *Mandela United Football Club Hearings,* Johannesburg, 24 November–4 December 1997 and Johannesburg, 28–29 January 1998.

7.   Phrase coined by Desmond Tutu (1996).

8.   The Commission 'for the sake of consistency' and 'in keeping with the language of the Act' continued, despite some protests, to use the word 'victim'. The TRC does however acknowledge the contested nature of the term, stating that some might prefer "survivor" and notes that 'many played so crucial a role in the struggle for democracy that even the term "survivor" might seem an inadequate description' (TRC, 1 (4) 39).

9.   See definitions of victims and perpetrators in the TRC's discussion of its terminology (TRC, 1 (4) 37).

10. For example, see then deputy president Mbeki's speech during the adoption of the new constitution in May 1996: 'I have seen what happens when one person has superiority of force over another, when the stronger appropriate to themselves the prerogative even to annul the injunction that God created all men and women equal in his image. . . We are assembled here today to mark their victory in acquiring and exercising their right to formulate their own definition of what it means to be African. The constitution whose adoption we celebrate constitutes an unequivocal statement that we refuse to accept our Africanness will be defined by our race, colour, agenda, or historical origins. . . It gives concrete expression to the sentiment we share as Africans. . . that the people shall govern' (Mbeki, 1996).

11. Volume 7 of the TRC Report lists names of victims along with descriptions of violations in each case. The Commission confined the victims eligible for reparations to three main categories; those who personally made statements to the commission; those victims named in a statement made by a relative or other interested person, for example a colleague, friend, or neighbour; and finally, those victims who were identified through the amnesty process.

12. A 'low level of corroboration' meant that the witnesses had to confirm an event but were not required to confirm the identity of the person involved. There was no naming where the identities of individuals were unclear, and where the TRC had insufficient evidence to send out section 30 notices to those implicated in violations.

13. TRC, *Human Rights Violations Submissions: Dorothy Seatlholo,* Soweto, July 22, 1996.

14. Full transcript at TRC, *Human Rights Violations Submissions: Bettina Mdlalose,* Vryheid, April 16, 1997.

Chapter Five
Narrating the Future: Theology and Therapy in Reconciliation

Mrs Mandela. . . I long for our reconciliation. . . I have had to struggle to come to some place of learning, to forgive, even if you do not want forgiveness or even think that I deserve to offer that to you. I struggle to find a way in which we can be reconciled for the sake of this nation and for the people that I believe God loves so deeply.

> Bishop Paul Verryn, speaking during the TRC's special investigations into the Mandela United Football Club.

This final chapter completes the three key chapters of this book in which the central argument is set out. Chapter three reflected upon the ways in which the TRC narrated a *past* conditioned by violence, and chapter four upon the spectacular confessional by which the *present* transitional moment was narrated. This final chapter turns to a discussion of the TRC's goals in terms of the *future* condition of reconciliation to which the narration of past violence and present confessional were directed. The central argument advanced here is that the subjects of the reconciliation narrative—victim and perpetrator—were narrated by the TRC as if they were emerging out of a violent rupture, caused by the event of apartheid, to a previously harmonious relationship. The language of reconciliation in the TRC was underpinned powerfully by two central theological and therapeutic discourses, namely, forgiveness and healing, which worked to address this alleged rupture and to 'recover' a 'lost harmony' between victim and perpetrator, a harmony that would, the TRC hoped, in turn map onto and simultaneously restore the unity of the nation.

In the documents founding the TRC, to the public hearings, the final Report, and in various public declarations within South Africa and abroad made by the TRC's officials, the discourse of forgiveness was expressed as a critical lynchpin of the TRC's work. The TRC argued that 'the key concepts of confession, forgiveness and reconciliation are central to the message' of the TRC (TRC, 1998: 1(1) 65), whilst Tutu commented upon the 'astonishing magnanimity and willingness to forgive' on the part of victim participants (TRC, 1998: 1 (1) 71). The TRC stated that 'the expressions of remorse and seeking for forgiveness' on the part of perpetrators was 'encouraging' (TRC, 1998: 5 (8) 9), and victims echoed the TRC line that perpetrators must 'expunge their guilt by telling the truth and seeking forgiveness from their victims' (TRC, 1998: 5 (9) 37). Indeed, long sections of the TRC Report are devoted to 'exemplary' accounts of seeking for and granting forgiveness by both perpetrators and victims.

In tandem with this theological framing, the purported effects of the TRC's work were also articulated in broadly therapeutic terms. Prior to the start of the TRC's investigations, the Interim Constitution had already suggested that a national reconciliation process would facilitate individual healing. It stated that 'the pursuit of national unity, the well-being of all South African citizens. . . require reconciliation' (Interim Constitution of South Africa Act no. 200 of 1993, postamble). The Interim Constitution represented the first formal site in which this assumption was articulated, and the TRC's assumptions later came to be continuous with, and a further elaboration of, those suggested in this document. The TRC deployed popular psychotherapeutic metaphors to describe the effects of its processes, joining together in a linear and causal relationship the concepts and processes of 'disclosure' (truth) and 'closure' (reconciliation). It suggested powerfully that the 'Commission's disclosure of truth. . . helped people to reach 'closure' and thus achieve psychological well-being' (TRC, 1998: 1 (5) 14), and that the 'process of reconciliation and healing', which are here expressed as coterminous, would take place through a 'disclosure of the past' (TRC, 1998: 5 (6) 105).

Thus theology and therapy, forgiveness and healing, became conjoined in the work of the TRC both at the level of its formal declarations and in the individual depositions made to the Commission. Over time, during the period of the public hearings, participants began to suggest that forgiveness was also necessary for healing, arguing that if perpetrators wanted forgiveness 'they should come and expose themselves so that they can also get the healing that victims are getting' (TRC, 1998: 5 (9) 46). These two discourses, and the assumptions they contained, provided the crucial, complex, and powerfully suggestive underpinnings of reconciliation in South Africa. Without these, Judge Richard Goldstone had argued, the TRC would have been an 'empty legal vessel which would do a great deal of harm and achieve nothing' (Goldstone in Boraine and Levy 1995: 120).

This chapter investigates the production and implications of these discourses. It has, however, a more speculative quality than the preceding chapters because it attempts to broaden out the discussion from the *specific* institutional mechanisms and practices of the TRC in order to evaluate its *intended* effects upon the social whole and upon the national culture and psychology of post-apartheid South Africa. As such, this chapter explores the ways in which the

TRC implied that reconciliation, forgiveness and healing were, as a result of its work, to take place not just in the psyches of these who took part in the process, in the psyches of those victims who told their stories and those perpetrators who applied for amnesty, but that they were also to take place within the *national* psyche as a whole. This chapter investigates the claims made by the TRC that it was to be the particular mechanism by which South Africa became a forgiving and forgiven, a healing and healed and ultimately, a reconciled nation.

Reconciliation and the Prelapsarian State

The TRC acknowledged from the outset that reconciliation was a 'highly contested' idea and that there was 'no simple definition of reconciliation' (TRC, 1998: 1 (5) 10). It described reconciliation as 'both a goal *and* a process', one that entailed a conciliatory journey towards a reconciled outcome (TRC, 1998: 1 (5) 11–12, emphasis added). The TRC located four different arenas in which reconciliation needed to occur: first, reconciliation at the individual level—victims being reconciled with a painful past and perpetrators coming to terms with guilt and shame; second, reconciliation between victims and perpetrators, which might require forgiveness; third, reconciliation within and between community members; and fourth, national unity and reconciliation. This, it suggested, might entail expressions of forgiveness and apologies at the elite level because these would constitute 'gestures important in the public life of a nation attempting to 'transcend the divisions and strife of the past' and would help the national process of leaving behind a 'legacy of hatred, fear, guilt and revenge' (TRC, 1998: 1 (5) 11–23). This fusion of theological principle and political process generated debate and contestation about what reconciliation might mean, and produced conflicting versions of reconciliation ranging from the theological to the political, to non-racial ideologies of reconciliation, all of which were put forward by political parties and civil society actors, amongst others (Hamber and Van der Merwe, 1998).

The TRC's version of reconciliation implied and demanded a complex combination of processes that crossed different levels of relationships, happened in different locations and fora, and over different periods of time. Reconciliation, in the words of one commentator was not to be 'an event', a single act of unification, rather reconciliation was to be a subtle process that could only emerge over time (TRC, 1998: 5 (9) 130). Indeed, reconciliation is not readily identifiable as a concrete practice because it was not engineered by the TRC within a precise institutional context. Unlike the practices of truth telling and amnesty, which had a specific institutional performance rooted in the Human Rights Violations and Amnesty Committees respectively, reconciliation was instead invoked by the TRC as an *imaginary future horizon* against which its reflection upon past violence and the present confessional, concretized by truth-telling and amnesty, made sense. Without truth-telling and amnesty, the TRC argued, there could be no reconciliation because it was through these processes that victims and perpetrators were invited to reflect upon, testify to, account and take responsibility for apartheid violence, and, ideally, to reach a point of mutual understanding. Conversely, and most importantly, amnesty would not have been acceptable *without* reconciliation as an overall objective, since reconciliation was the central moral discourse that was used to justify the amnesty agreement. Amnesty rather than punishment, the TRC suggested, was more likely to lead to reconciliation because it offered the forum by perpetrators were called upon to account and atone for their actions, to be 'rehumanized' by the process of confession and to signal their readiness to belong to the post-apartheid national community. However, reconciliation was not, could not, be attached to a single and specific process like amnesty. It was instead understood by the TRC to the culmination of an aggregation of diverse and interrelated processes and practices—quasi-legal, symbolic, spiritual and therapeutic—such as truth-telling, amnesty, reparations, official acknowledgement, forgiveness and catharsis—but was also not reducible to any one or another of these and at the same time superseded all of them.

The TRC's grounding of reconciliation within a Judeo-Christian framework presented some of its most problematic implications. On the one hand, as I will show, reconciliation as theology opened up the idea of what constituted a just response to past violence in South Africa by providing alternatives to the regular, or retributive model. However, and on the other hand, the theological interpretation of reconciliation put forward by the TRC, which was accompanied by the concept of *ubuntu*, was problematic because it seemed to *require* forgiveness rather than punishment thus making it incumbent upon victims to forgive. An effect of this was to *exclude* the possibility that punishment might indeed contribute to reconciliation and as such the theological framework provided a crucial justificatory discourse of the amnesty decision.

Early in the TRC's proceedings, Desmond Tutu invoked reconciliation in the following way:

> Having looked the beast of the past in the eye, having asked and received forgiveness and having made amends, let us shut the door on the past—not in order to forget it but in order not to allow it to imprison us. Let us move into the glorious future of a new kind of society where people count not because of biological irrelevancies or other extraneous attributes, but because they are persons of infinite worth created in the image of God (TRC, 1998: 1 (1) 91).

Tutu's words called upon the Edenic, or prelapsarian human condition, and hailed a return to a condition of harmony and unity that preceded The Fall. It is this notion that forms the core of reconciliation in Tutu's invocation, and it works to subject South Africa to a seamless continuity of representation that stretches back to the beginning of human time. Reconciliation, on this reading, seeks to cohere divergent narratives about the past by evoking the idea of 'return', a return to an originary, unified, harmonious social and political formation which, it assumes, preceded the 'breakdown' that the TRC seeks to address and to provide redress for. Reconciliation performs in order to suggest that a condition of national harmony and accord in South Africa actually *did* exist prior to its alleged 'rupture'. All this, as Krog notes, in the context of South Africa's 'stark circumstances' in which there is 'nothing to go back to, no previous state or rela-

tionship one would wish to restore' (Krog, 1999: 108). Krog notes that 'reconciliation does not even seem like the right word' and suggests as an alternative
'conciliation', an concept much more suited to South Africa's political circumstances, stripped of the problematic theological connotations carried by reconciliation but also of the idea of a former harmonious national community.

The idea of reconciliation in South Africa was haunted, overwhelmingly,
by this idea of the 'return', as evidenced by its various dictionary definitions. To
reconcile is to 'restore a person to friendly relations with oneself or another after
an estrangement', to 'restore to concord or harmony', to 'reunite', to 'bring a
person (back to) peace, favor, etc,' to 'cleanse, purify, reconsecrate', to 'absolve'
or to 'bring into acquiescence with, acceptance of, or submissions to a thing,
condition, or situation'. The condition of reconciliation has been described vari-
ously as 'the action or act of reconciling a person to oneself or another, or es-
tranged parties to one another', or 'harmony, concord', and, in Christian theology, 'the condition of humanity's being reconciled with God'.[1] In order to
investigate how the effect of 'return' is produced, it is necessary to enquire into
the performance of reconciliation as both narrative *and* metaphor, an enquiry
which reveals reconciliation to perform in different and contradictory ways.[2]

The idea of the 'return' underwrites the *narrative* performance of reconciliation because 're' denotes a move *backwards* in the sense that it implies a
return to an earlier state of harmonious union. Reconciliation is a story told in a
single word. It tells a tale of prior harmony, a rupture (a wrong perpetrated) and
a subsequent reunion, predicated here on the confessional and forgiveness. Reconciliation relates these implied events in a causal and linear fashion—harmony,
rupture, reunion—and prefigures narrative closure as reconciliation, the end
point of the story. Reconciliation bears a reverse trajectory in time. It looks back
the way, despite being oriented towards change and closure in the future.

However, if we read reconciliation as a metaphor, we find a more 'open'
and plural account. Metaphors carry both a descriptive *and* a prescriptive force
and 'describe the enigma and promise of the human situation and prescribe certain remedies for that situation' (Tracy, 1979: 89). Metaphors combine two or
more domains of meaning which give rise to multiple possible interpretations of
their meaning. For example, to take a rather prosaic and over-used metaphor as
an example, when we say that 'love is a battlefield' we are suggesting an equivalence between 'love' and 'battlefield,' and we propose a transferable similarity
between the two. That is to say that there are elements of the battlefield in the
experience of love. In juxtaposing two terms, conventionally constructed metaphors such as this comprise meanings related to the two concepts or ideas it
unites. At the same time, the metaphor generates a third dimension of meaning
which arises out of the conjoining of the two elements, a meaning which is not
reducible to either one of the constitutive elements and is a the same time surplus
to both.

However, as Paul Ricoeur argues, metaphor does not have to comprise two
distinct elements, but 'takes the *word* as its unit of reference' (Ricoeur, 1986: 3).
The range of 'transferences' of meaning are not simply generated by the constituent elements—'love' and 'battlefield'—but are also generated by the social

or political site of utterance. On Ricoeur's account, which contextualizes any utterance of the metaphor and suggests that the context is as much evocative as are the metaphor's constituent concepts, we could understand reconciliation as metaphor. The TRC invoked reconciliation as a theological concept within a political context, and as such the Commission constituted the institutional nexus between different domains of meaning, the theological and political, and was the site through which the transference of the properties of the Christian range of interpretations of reconciliation to the realm of the political was facilitated and took place. An important effect of this was that the Christian connotations of reconciliation worked to extend its meaning *beyond* the idea of a pragmatic settlement or agreement, with the effect of representing human actions 'as higher than they actually are', of elevating human conduct and experience (Ricoeur, 1974: 109). Thus the deployment of reconciliation as a theological principle endowed the TRC and its agents with a transcendent moral authority that went beyond that endorsed by the state and the political settlement out of which it was born.

Reading reconciliation as narrative and metaphor renders a double interpretation of reconciliation possible. Reading reconciliation as narrative suggests that reconciliation closes off plurality, contestation and debate because a narrative account of reconciliation shows how it seeks to cohere and unify divergent perspectives on the past. But on the other hand, if reconciliation works as a metaphor then it would also be suggestive of a plurality of competing interpretations as to what it might mean. When understood in this way, reconciliation demands not, as Aletta Norval notes, 'a simple restoration of a community with itself and to itself', but 'a difficult, restless and unceasing negotiation' which materializes in political debate and contestation and is fundamental to democratic process (Norval, 1999: 510).

The political animation of religious metaphors and narratives might provide the occasion for a different way of doing justice, such as that required by the post-apartheid political order, because they appear to interrupt the regime of retributive justice, which, founded upon vengeance and arbitrated by the state, seems fated to reproduce the very conditions it aims to redress. This, it is argued, threatens to further rather than stem cycles of violence.[3] On this theme, Michael Dillon excoriates the sovereign limits of the 'normal model of justice', arguing that this legal paradigm issues from vengeance and from a system of analogous exchanges that can only serve to sustain the conditions it seeks to absolve (Dillon, 1999). However, for Dillon, the possibility of 'another justice' haunts the given order and, refusing to accept the 'normal model' as necessary and inevitable, he offers a critical proposition that is 'neither a supposedly habitual tradition' nor a 'contractual negotiation' (Dillon, 1999: 172). Dillon echoes Derrida's reflections on justice, friendship and democracy in this spectral evocation, and appeals to the *unwritten* character of justice, that element that resides beyond the textual codifications and disciplinary practices that are state endorsed and enforced by the rule of law (Derrida, 1994 and 1997). This spectral justice, he argues, is instead an 'irruptive and inventive practice called up by specific historical circumstances' (Dillon, 1999: 172). This, I would suggest, might be where the power of the reconciliatory discourse, and the restorative mode of justice it entails, lies. It is, perhaps best and necessarily to be regarded as an *exceptional* response to past violence which carries the potential to transform violence by granting a second chance to perpetrators. Regular practices of condemnation and punishment do not carry this possibility. As such, reconciliation appears as both an irruption and a pragmatic response to the impossibility of adjudication and judgment in the post-apartheid moment that Dillon suggests is symptomatic of the 'ineradicable' plethos of the self, and the acceptance that there can be no sovereign point of departure from which to cast judgment (Dillon, 1999: 157). Reconciliatory gestures issue not just from the state, but from plural and diffuse subjects such as apologies by members of the political elite and declarations of forgiveness by victims, and consequently promises a different way of doing justice that carries the hope of discontinuing the system of equivalent exchanges and the cycle of vengeance that stands at the heart of the retributive ethos. This is the promise of reconciliation, a promise that the TRC suggests but does not quite deliver. On closer inspection, as I shall argue in the following part of my argument on the subject of forgiveness, the TRC reveals itself to be based on the contractual negotiations that Dillon eschews because forgiveness in the TRC is based upon a system of obligation and reciprocity.

Whilst I would argue that it is important to be open to the ways in which Christian metaphors and narratives may answer to the 'call of another justice', may indeed answer to the failings of the retributive order and perhaps help to institute an mode of justice that is responsive to the demands of an exceptional transitional politics, I would suggest that it is equally important to remain attentive to the way in which they also operate as a refutation of that call. Theological narratives, instead, work *against* the possibility of constituting different political configurations and allegiances. They perform, once incorporated into political process, in order to reify the national boundaries of community and the contractual relations adjudicated by the state, and to re-establish the boundaries of the existing legal order. They are, perhaps, ultimately resistant to plural interpretation as they carry the trace of a founding moment that is formulaic and cannot be refigured in response to the particular circumstances in which they are invoked. Indeed, the effects of the TRC's discursive strategy was in fact to legitimize the decision against holding criminal trials. Reconciliation underpinned the TRC's emphasis on restorative rather than retributive justice and the promise that no criminal trials would be brought against those who applied for amnesty. This decision was also constituted by the trope of 'original sin' whereby the burden of guilt is carried by all, which problematizes and makes highly complex the question of judgment. In addition, the emphasis on restorative rather than retributive measures proved to be an expedient measure. The costs in terms of time, money, and stability should all perpetrators be dealt with in accordance with a retributive model of justice were considered by the transitional government to be too great to bear. Amnesty, in effect, was cheap.

Before moving on to consider the role of forgiveness in the reconciliation process, I want to take a moment to defend the particular mode of interpretation being advanced here against an important criticism of etymological surveys. Amongst these critics, Gadamer has argued that:

> I do not hold etymologies to be of such great importance. Neither Heidegger nor Derrida has yet succeeded in convincing me that an etymology can tell us something important if what is uncovered does not somehow continue to speak to us in the living language of today (Gadamer, 1998: 201).

However, in the case of the TRC, an etymology of reconciliation is valuable precisely because the transferences of meaning from the religious have a strong purchase on the political in the 'living language' of the particular political moment within which reconciliation is mobilised. It is impossible to understand the range of ways in which reconciliation can and is being interpreted without conducting such a survey.

Forgiveness: A Political 'Gift'

Any discussion of forgiveness in South Africa must begin with the empirical fact of amnesty. The amnesty agreement meant that the state had already forgiven, in a legal manner, the perpetrators of past violations *before* the TRC staged its public confessional. So, amnesty was a formal type of forgiveness that had already taken place between the state and those designated as perpetrators of past violations. However, forgiveness was supposed, on the TRC's account, to take place between victims and perpetrators *as a result* of the TRC's work and as part of the process of reconciliation, although in fact it was *entirely superfluous* to an amnesty decision. To receive amnesty, perpetrators had to submit the details 'in full' of their involvements in gross violations. They did not have to deliver these details in a remorseful or conciliatory manner, the condition, surely, of forgiveness. They simply had to provide the bare details, the 'forensic truth'. Forgiveness was, however, integral to how the TRC saw its work. It applauded those who demonstrated 'a willingness to forgive' and where, as a result the 'rebuilding of relationships was initiated' (TRC, 1998: 5 (9) 3). Whilst victims were not obviously coerced into offering forgiveness they were not afforded the choice of a criminal trial of the perpetrator, and their public testimonies were often directed towards forgiving outcomes by strategic interventions on behalf of the Commissions, as demonstrated in the previous chapter.

The language of forgiveness that dominated the public hearings of the TRC gave the impression that South Africans were willing to forgive in such a way as to make the earlier amnesty agreement appear to be representative of the broader social mood. The ground for this 'mood', had, however, already been laid by the Interim Constitution, various public declarations by Commission officials, and ultimately by the work of the Commission itself and in particular the public hearings. Forgiveness worked retrospectively to legitimize the amnesty decision but was made to appear as if it had somehow been generated by popular will. It operated to fill out the moral dimension of amnesty where one might be seen, with some serious plausibility, to be lacking. In what follows, I discuss on more theoretical terms what the incorporation of forgiveness into politics attempts to constitute, how it might more plausibly operate, and suggest an understanding of forgiveness, contra Derrida, that might provide a more constructive response to past atrocity because seeks to constructs new relations of obligation between the forgiven and the forgiver.

My first thoughts on forgiveness were provoked by a conversation I had with a theologian at a conference in 1998. Charles Villa-Vicencio, one of the commissioners on the TRC, related to me a discussion he had with Derrida who was visiting South Africa at the time that the TRC was beginning its work. The story went that whilst the two of them were discussing forgiveness over dinner Derrida claimed that forgiveness should not be incorporated into politics because as a 'freely given gift', forgiveness is radically at odds with politics. Villa-Vicencio, the pragmatist replied, 'well, if that's what you think, then you're more of a theologian than I am!' In our conversation, Villa-Vicencio, later asserted that he thought that reconciliation was too high a demand and that what should be expected in post-apartheid South Africa was no more than peaceful co-existence. Derrida's provocation merits investigation because the metaphor of the gift offers a telling insight into the nature of *political* forgiveness, which, as Derrida argues, is 'anything but pure and disinterested' but is grounded in the contractual relations of the state (Derrida, 2001: 31).

The TRC was keen to assert that 'confession, forgiveness, and reconciliation in the lives of nations are not just airy-fairy religious and spiritual things, nebulous and unrealistic' but are 'the stuff of practical politics', thus tying the political necessities of South Africa's transition to the broader moral-theological framework within which it was cast (TRC, 1998: 5 (9) 4). But criticisms of this stance came from those, like Malan, keen to highlight the difficulty of understanding the *national* meaning of unity and reconciliation and the 'potentially dangerous' use of a religious interpretation of reconciliation that was more typically applied to interpersonal, rather than social and political, relationships. It was argued that religious interpretations should be clearly demarcated from a limited and political notion of reconciliation that might be applied within the context of democratization. However, the TRC argued against accepting a narrow understanding of reconciliation and stated that symbolic gestures such a, for example, apologies made by individuals, representatives of institutions, and political leaders were gestures that were 'important in the public life of a nation attempting to transcend the divisions and strife of the past' (TRC, 1998: 1 (5) 16–21).

The issue I find particularly intriguing here is *not* the question of whether Christian principles like forgiveness should or should not animate politics. I am not particularly concerned with providing a taxonomy of political forgiveness, nor with arguing for forgiveness as a way of cancelling 'moral debts' incurred in the past (see Digeser, 1998; Müeller-Fahrenhoz, 1997; Ricoeur, 1996; Shriver, 1995). Of far more interest to me here is the way in which the moral parameters of the new South Africa were constructed by the open co-presence of religious and political discourse, and the political ramifications of that construction. One of the consequences of this was that reconciliation was interpreted as having a significance extending beyond the idea of a pragmatic settlement, enhancing it and giving it a far-reaching and profound resonance, because without the incorporation of Christian principles, as Goldstone had argued, the TRC would have been little more than a mechanistic legal operation and would have failed to induct a new moral order.

But before considering the implications of Derrida's critique it is necessary to enquire first into what the 'regular formula' of forgiveness comprises. Forgiveness is commonly understood as an individual gesture of clemency towards a 'wrongdoer' and is directed towards the reconciliation of those it engages. Broadly speaking, in Christian theology, reconciliation assumes a rupture in a previously harmonious relationship, a rupture that might be repaired by confession and a display of remorse on the part of a 'perpetrator' which could be met, in turn, by forgiveness on the part of the 'victim'. For forgiveness to be possible, it must be situated within a recognition, or pre-comprehension of its meaning, and comprise a face-to-face encounter which, as Derrida argues, is 'required by the very essence of forgiveness' (Derrida, 2001: 48). The immediacy of this performance—the confession, an expression of remorse and a declaration of forgiveness—sanctions the transaction and lends force to its application. The direct exchange of forgiveness as an intimate encounter is a necessary constituent of reconciliation since, as Arendt notes, 'forgiving. . . enacted in solitude or isolation remain[s] without reality and can signify no more than a role played before one's self' (Arendt, 1953: 237). Arendt deems forgiveness to be a personal and individual process, and claims that 'forgiving and the relationship it establishes is always an eminently personal affair in which *what* was done is forgiven for the sake of *who* did it' (Arendt, 1953: 241).

The offer of forgiveness, and hence the possibility of reconciliation, demands that the perpetrator acknowledge responsibility for the deed, a responsibility which must be made manifest in a sincere and outward show of remorse, a public performance of that remorse, which in turn evinces an alteration of an inner attitude. It is upon this outward display—which of course is no guarantee— that forgiveness, necessarily, is contingent and in which it has faith:

> The formulae of forgiveness. . . are. . . outward signs of alterations to situations which are essentially inward, so that the mere public utterance of them does not of itself guarantee that the alteration has occurred. . . We demand that the penitent be sincerely remorseful and that the formulae of forgiveness are more than lip service. Since public utterances provide no cast iron warrant that the sincerity-conditions have been met, forgiveness is not something we can expect to happen as if it were an entitlement flowing from a contract, but only something for which we may hope (Holliday, 1999: 45).

Once these 'sincerity-conditions' are believed to be met, the offender is released from the moral debt incurred by the wrong through the act of forgiveness, which attempts to restore the relationship to a prior condition of harmony, of reconciliation. The offender is thus not only absolved of the transgression but is also taken into favor again by the victim by virtue of a display of penitence. The

victim identifies with the wrongdoer through this remorseful attitude and together they enter upon a new relationship which contains and perhaps to some
degree retains, although now in a more transformed, perhaps even positive manner, the memory of the wrong committed. Central to this transaction is the puri-
fication from sin of the wrongdoer and the reconstitution of the disrupted unity
and harmony of the relationship between the two parties. Forgiveness works to
restore both victim and perpetrator by creating the possibility of conversion of
the perpetrator, restitution or reparation of the victim, and recognition of the
harm done and of the humanity of the perpetrator, which can then followed by a
reconciliation between the two. I must emphasize that this depiction, as I have
said, is a description of the *regular* formula and assumptions of forgiveness.

A declaration of remorse is not, of course, a guarantee of 'authentic' repentance, nor is it a guarantee of its acceptance by the victim. Forgiveness cannot be
expected, Holliday argues, 'as if it were an entitlement flowing from a contract',
but is a gift which may be only be hoped for (Holliday, 1999: 45). Forgiveness
must remain 'freely given' and unconstrained by the demands and expectations
of a contractual engagement. This interpretation of forgiveness concurs with
Ricoeur's argument in which he argues that 'forgiveness. . . far exceeds political
categories'. For Ricoeur forgiveness belongs 'to an order—the order of charity—
which goes even beyond the order of morality' and 'falls within the scope of an
economy of the gift whose logic of superabundance exceeds the logic of reciprocity' (Ricoeur, 1996: 10). Like Derrida, Ricoeur deploys the gift metaphor in
order to demonstrate the transformational capacity of forgiveness. Through his
appeal to the realm of 'charity' he invokes the theological, implying that forgiveness, besides being in excess of politics, 'goes beyond' morality, and has a
'logic of superabundance' that defies that of reciprocity and as such carries the
potential for transformation, for 'overcoming' past conflict.

According to Derrida, forgiveness loses its 'pure and disinterested' character once incorporated into political processes. Once it is institutionalized and
arbitrated by the state, forgiveness loses its necessarily spontaneous and contingent nature, and seeks recourse to the economic logic of reciprocity central to
political process and to retributive justice: the principle of the *lex talionis*, 'an
eye for an eye'. 'One could never' remarks Derrida, 'in the ordinary sense of the
words, found a politics or law on forgiveness. . . because it [politics and/or law]
always has to do with negotiations. . . with calculated transactions, with conditions. . .' (Derrida, 2001: 39). A closer look at the TRC reveals that yes, once
subsumed into the political, forgiveness does take on a contractual character that
might obviate its transformational capacity. Because the TRC (and not victims)
offered amnesty in return for 'full confessions' it disturbed the interpersonal and
spontaneous economy of forgiveness. As Nuttall points out, the political, incentivized, and public confessional makes it far less likely that the confession is
freely and remorsefully offered, or it makes it more difficult to determine
whether or not the confession fulfils the sincerity conditions of the private and
free exchange:

> Confession typically presupposes a constellation of notions about the private self
> tormented by guilt and the private conscience exposed to self-criticism. However,
> the fact that people confess to their crimes does not necessarily imply a compul-
> sion to confess as an escape from a burden of guilt. . . the conscience of memory
> may be less at stake that the fear of exposure before the TRC in the present. Con-
> fessions. . . are constructed and not discovered (Nuttall, 1999: 87).

The confessional mode presupposes a knowing, self-consciously acting and
hence fully responsible agent, an agent with the capacity to reflect and reform.
However, the private process of self-reflection and questioning is replaced here
by the public spectacle of interrogation by the TRC. Thus the TRC presents itself
as the 'conscience of the nation' in holding up the mirror to the 'guilty' and
'tormented' face of the 'perpetrator' who capitulates to its greater authority and
confesses his or her 'sins'. Any incumbent show of remorse is consequently not
to be trusted as an outward articulation of internal change as it is not freely produced but incentivized by the 'reward' of amnesty.

To return to Derrida's point, if forgiveness is to be kept out of the realm of
politics because it is 'freely given' then what does this tell us about the economy
of the political? Must forgiveness remain beyond the realm of the political or,
once subsumed within it, can it take on a reciprocal or contractual character that
might work to fuel relations of obligation and thus underpin reconciliation more
effectively? Here I take 'the political' to mean the process that is about the constitution of the political community, and argue that forgiveness perhaps *should*
on the character of the social contract once it is animated as part of a discourse
that attempts to reckon with past atrocity. As such, within the context of the
TRC, forgiveness might actually work to perform new contractual relations of
obligation between perpetrators and victims as follows: the articulation of 'I forgive you' is a speech act which is situated within the institutional framework of
the TRC, which itself authorizes certain individuals to enact that declaration and
simultaneously commands others to recognize the gesture. Furthermore, the
speech act of forgiveness in this context functions as part of a discursive economy that is contractual. This contractual agreement might be characterized like
this: in forgiving, victims agree to give up the right to perpetuate old grievances,
and in being forgiven and in showing remorse, perpetrators are bound not to repeat violations. Forgiveness thus performatively attempts to constitute relations
of obligation and reciprocation between victims and perpetrators in the absence
of retributive forms of justice, and is directed towards the 'restoration of human
dignity' which designates a 'basic level of humanity' to victims and perpetrators
alike.[4]

However, this formula is problematic for several reasons. First, it depends
upon a clarity of distinction between victims and perpetrators, a distinction that
was not always evident, as the TRC notes:

> A further problem of perspective is the thorny question of whether perpetrators
> may also be viewed as victims. Although one may wish to have a clear-cut posi-
> tion on perpetrators it is possible that there are grey areas. Perpetrators may be
> seen as acting under orders, as subjects of indoctrination, as subjected to threats,

as outcomes of earlier doctrinaire education. In the most pernicious situation, *askaris* (former ANC cadres who were 'turned' frequently through torture, threats and brutality, into state agents) are themselves transformed into killers and torturers. Military conscripts could view themselves in part as victims of a state system. . . it is important to recognize that perpetrators may in part be victims.' (TRC, 1998: 5 (7) 53–54).

This is a question not simply of distinct and distinctive subjectivity but also one of power. For example, who is to be accorded the status of forgiver, and who the forgiven? In the case of the TRC the status of each is pre-given as it is constituted by its founding legislation and processes of investigation. The TRC decided who the victims were, first, and then conferred upon them the 'right' or power to forgive, and thus subordinated the forgiven to the forgiver. Subcommandante Marcos, the leader of the Zapatista rebellion in Chiapas, Mexico, illuminates here something of the power constellation inherent in this ordination in his response to a formal pardon issued by the Mexican government to the Zapatistas:

> For what do we have to ask pardon? For what are they going to pardon us? For not dying of hunger? For not keeping quiet about our misery? For not humbly accepting the enormous historical weights of contempt and abandonment? . . . Who has to ask for pardon and who can give it? (cited in Digeser, 1998: 89–90).[5]

Second, the TRC formula of forgiveness produced confusion about the role of the TRC and the place of forgiveness within it, given that amnesty was a separate process and one that could only be formally granted. Indeed, forgiveness may even have been withheld, but amnesty could still be forthcoming.

Third, forgiveness places too much emphasis on the victim to be able to relate their story in a public context and to make amends. Forgiveness requires the public narration of the event, the acknowledgement that a 'wrong' has been done, and a display of remorse. However, giving public space to air personal grievances may be problematic where trauma does not give way to articulation. Indeed, Elaine Scarry, who has explored the relationship of pain and narration through the examination of the use of torture in a political context has claimed that the 'traumatized body' does not always yield to a verbal articulation of its experience, a claim that is corroborated by some of those who testified before the Commission (Scarry, 1985). The testimony of Greta Appelgren is one such example. She was arrested in June 1986, tortured and placed in solitary confinement for her alleged involvement in the planting of an ANC bomb in a Durban bar. Appelgren gave a sparse account of her ordeal of solitary confinement claiming that 'I don't even want to describe psychologically what I had to do to survive down there. I will write it one day, but I could never tell you' (Tutu, 1999: 106–107). Thus an insistence on *relating* traumatic experiences is problematic in that attempting to speak, to narrative past trauma, might instead promote rather than assuage psychological and emotional difficulties.

A reading of Mauss's anthropological classic, *The Gift*, facilitates an interpretation of the forgiveness that gives weight to this economic interpretation of the TRC because Mauss interprets the gift as being incorporated within, rather than being excessive to, a 'general economy' of exchange, with important effects (Mauss, 1990). Mauss asserted, in opposition to Malinowski (who attempted to separate the activities of commerce from gift giving) that the obligation to reciprocate the gift sets up a perpetual cycle of exchange. In his view, gifts are not separate from, but constitute a part of this general system of exchange which includes the commercial, and works similarly to incur a debt on behalf of the recipient. For Mauss, the 'free' gift is a nonsense because it is based on a 'misunderstanding' which exempts the donor from return gifts from the recipient and is thus challenging of one of the key functions of the gift: the constitution of social relations. A free gift, as Mary Douglas notes in her foreword to Mauss's book, 'does nothing to enhance solidarity' and is therefore a 'contradiction' (Douglas, 1990: vii). According to Douglas the 'refusal of requital' that the free gift institutes puts the act of giving outside the constitution of mutual and social ties. On this account, forgiveness as a free gift would remove it, on this account, from the service of political reconciliation which would also be nonsensical.

Mauss has been criticized for constructing an overly synthetic account of 'human solidarity' in which 'the whole society can be described by the catalogue of transfers that map all the obligations between its members' (Douglas, 1990: ix). However, I think that this need not necessarily diminish the argument here. In making the leap from the material to the discursive institution of the gift, I propose that the performance of the gift represents an *attempted*, rather than an *actual* engagement of people in 'permanent commitments' that both articulate and reflect dominant institutions.

Against Mauss, Derrida suggests that the transformational properties of the gift are obviated if it is subsumed under the general economy of exchange and reciprocation. He regards the act of giving as necessarily *outside* the cycle of exchange, and by implication, beyond the construction of mutual ties. Derrida's rejection of any reciprocal relation in the gift is due to what he considers 'an immoral binding of free subjects' (O'Neill, 1999: 131). He describes Mauss's linking of gift and exchange as a nonsense, for gifts *should not* be instigated with the intention of being reciprocated. Derrida proposes the impossible—a gift that is neither consciously given, nor consciously received. For Derrida, only such a gift can shake itself free from the constitution of relations of obligation and reciprocity that an economic interpretation enforces.[6] The 'miraculous', or the transformational, can only be performed by the offering of a gift that, by its nature, supersedes, or is surplus to that of the closed cycle of transactions. If, and this is a very big 'if', the gift of forgiveness could present a rupture to the exchange cycle, it might performatively constitute the break with the past that is repeatedly cited by the TRC as a desirable outcome of its investigations.

We are left with a paradoxical and perhaps incommensurable view of the possibilities of forgiveness, but a fairly unequivocal view of the nature of its political animation, a view that confirms Derrida's suspicion. Forgiveness promises, on Derrida's account, to transform conflict, to move beyond the cycle of equivalent exchanges and institute a new order. And yet an economic interpretation necessitates a reconciliation founded upon, as the TRC states, 'an altered sense of responsibility' in *return* for wrongs committed (TRC, 1998: 1 (5) 111). This, I argue, if possible to inculcate, might provide a more fruitful and pragmatic foundation upon which a future reconciliation might in fact rest.

Healing Past Violence

As I argued at the beginning of this chapter, reconciliation was also filled out or underpinned by a therapeutic discourse entailing metaphors of sickness and health, which endeavored to express individual and national well-being and unity. This final section is dedicated to an evaluation of the therapeutic assumptions of the TRC and the particular features, and political effects of the therapeutic ethos.

Deponents to the TRC spoke of 'the real extent of the sickness that . . . afflicted our beloved motherland' and asked for 'the right diagnosis' and 'the correct medicine' in order that this might be addressed (TRC, 1998: 1 (1) 66). These comments reflect the way in which the narrative of individual and national sickness and healing was central to the work of the TRC, and its 'healing work' was very much expressed by recourse to psychotherapeutic platitudes and assumptions. The TRC constantly rendered the assumption that the 'truth about the past' was fundamental to political change and in order that a nation 'made sick by lies' could be healed by revealing what had previously been suppressed (Ignatieff, 1996: 110). Crucially, the TRC sought to 'restore the human and civil dignity of victims by granting them an opportunity to relate their own accounts of the violations of which they are the victims' (Promotion of National Unity and Reconciliation Act, no. 34 of 1995: 3c). The importance of narrating, of testifying to past violence, was connected by the TRC to the restoration of the human dignity of victims. Victim testimonials constituted the means by which official acknowledgment of experiences of past violence might be conferred, acknowledgement being pivotal to the restoration of dignity, and to healing the psychological legacy of past violence.

In addition, a therapeutic assumption was embedded within the TRC's brand of restorative justice because it put forward the view that the practice of giving testimony contained a 'healing power' which was essential to the recovery of victims. One victim stated 'I feel that what has been making me sick all the time is the fact that I couldn't tell my story. But now it feels like I got my sight back by coming here and telling you the story' (TRC, 1998: 5 (9) 9). Crucial to the belief in this 'talking cure' is the structure of narrative which seeks to organize past events in a serial order of time, and to institute a boundary between past and present. On this interpretation, the past may be 'closed off' from the present in order to prevent the trauma of the past from 'disturbing the present'. The process of 'healing' the 'wounds' of the past is, in these two ways, explicitly related by the TRC to the power of testimony and to the necessity of truthtelling.

Therapeutic platitudes were not knowingly instituted by the TRC *as* psychoanalytic discourse, although given the numbers of psychologists working on the Commission assisting testimony solicitation, counseling victims and so forth, it is unsurprising that psychoanalytic tropes entered the TRC's wider rubric of social healing. Rather, the incorporation of therapeutic truths bears testimony to the way in which scientific and other discourses, already normalized as part of everyday speech and understanding, were incorporated into the processes of the TRC.

Throughout the public hearings, the many public declarations by officials of the TRC and the narrative of the TRC Report, the metaphor of the wound and the language of healing were repeatedly iterated to evoke the legacy of apartheid violence. Justice Minister, Dullah Omar, spoke of 'ANC wounds. . . PAC wounds' and 'the wounds of our people'. He argued that 'people are in need of healing, and we need to heal our country if we are to build a nation which will guarantee peace and stability' (Omar, 1998). Tutu spoke of the need for 'national healing', eschewing the party political subjects central to Omar's appeal in favor of South Africa's new subject category of victim. He stated that 'victims and survivors who bore the brunt of the apartheid system need healing' (Tutu, 1996: 8). The TRC implored that 'the wounds of the past must not be allowed to fester'. They must 'be opened', they must be 'cleansed' and 'balm must be poured on them so they can heal' (TRC, 1998: 1 (1) 27). Commentators on the TRC reflected and reinforced this discourse by reproducing popular therapeutic platitudes about denial and mental health. These included the axioms that recalling buried memories or truths about past trauma can help to alleviate anxiety and emotional suffering, and prevent the unsettling and disruptive 'return' of the past:

> The Truth and Reconciliation Commission. . . can contribute to rehabilitation by breaking the culture of silence. *We all know* that concealing, suppressing or repressing painful memories commonly brings in its wake psychological symptoms: stress, anxiety, and depression. *We also know* that speaking about upsetting things in a supportive and affirming setting makes people feel better (Dowdall, 1996: 34, emphasis added).

According to this view, testifying sets trauma to rest, closes the door on the past and allows a new orientation to the future.

During the work of the TRC wounded victims became ciphers of the nation, and particular individuals were constituted as the key bearers of the nation's wounds such as Father Michael Lapsley and Constitutional Court Judge Albie Sachs, both former ANC activists. Lapsley, former ANC chaplain, lost both hands in a letter bomb attack in 1990 whilst living in exile in Zimbabwe. Where once his hands were, now are two metal hooks, which Lapsley describes as his '"entrée" into the Black community' (Scheper-Hughes, 1998: 121). Sachs lost his arm in a car bomb attack in 1998 whilst working as a civil rights lawyer in exile in Mozambique, a story which he recounts in his autobiography, *The Soft Vengeance of a Freedom Fighter* (Sachs, 1990). Scheper-Hughes commented that the narratives of their wounding contain 'in microcosm, the history of the anti-apartheid struggle, the courage of the comrades, their certainty in the moral goodness and rightness of their cause, their willingness to suffer the consequences of "putting one's body on the line"'. This was a narrative repeatedly iterated by the TRC in which accounts of individual suffering were conflated with national suffering, and individual healing with national healing, unity and reconciliation, such that individual healing became commensurate with national reconciliation. Therapeutic assumptions about individual processes of coming to terms with the past were transposed onto the nation. Each victim testimonial and every perpetrator confessional constituted a specific site of national healing where every wounded body and every story of suffering acted as a morality tale by which the national reconciliation process was guided and played out.

As discussed in the previous chapter, two technologies governed the process by which the Commission produced the truth of suffering: the testimonial and the confessional. These techniques constructed and compelled the key subject positions of the TRC as victim and perpetrator. Victim testimonies were rendered in private statements and at public hearings where, as part of the healing mandate of the Commission, victims were encouraged to relate their experiences 'in their own words'. The TRC assumed that the act of testifying functioned as a talking cure, a cathartic process by which memories of past violence might be purged. It understood the testimonial to be integral to the recovery of victims, who, in return for their stories received 'official acknowledgement' of their experiences as reparation. The power, indeed veracity of testimonial truth was predicated on the spectacle of victim suffering at the public hearings at which were communicated not just the forensic details of a violation, but the personal pain emanating from the act, or perhaps the unrelenting anguish of not knowing, for example, whether a relative might be dead or alive or where their remains might have been buried, secretly.

By contrast, the power of a confessional truth lay in its potential to redeem, to demonstrate the humanity of a perpetrator, to which a public display of emotion, of remorse, or perhaps even an apology, was crucial. The public confessional attempted to lift the burden of responsibility insofar as the confession signified a statement of personal virtue and of repentance. Tutu argued, in a precarious conflation of victim and perpetrator, that 'perpetrators are victims too' and that they were 'victims of the apartheid system and they, too, need healing' (Tutu, 1996: 8).

The therapeutic culture that infused the post-apartheid political order was manifest, primarily, as a general ethos or orientation through which was constructed a particular understanding of the apartheid past. It provided a set of reference points and symbolic practices around which a new understanding of apartheid violence was negotiated, one which served to make victims symbolic of the new political order, and in which perpetrators were also to be understood as victims of the apartheid past. This therapeutic regime provided the language through which suffering was acknowledged and reparations administered. It demanded the public exposure of pain and open contrition for past wrongs. The therapeutic assumptions upon which the TRC was based reproduced some of the givens of popular psychology, and inscribed them as a system of moral understanding which ordered and made meaningful to the reconciliation process divergent victim and perpetrator experiences of past violence. The grammar of

suffering and healing thus became the template upon which divergent testimonials at the public hearings, victim and perpetrator, were scripted, and through
which was performed a suffering solidarity in which victim and perpetrator were
identified by their respective wounds. The therapeutic ethos thus transformed the
moral crisis about South Africa's apartheid past into an emotional or psychological one.

Features of the Therapeutic Ethos

Therapy as a moral frame of reference displays distinctive features that produce
particular political effects, as James Nolan has argued (Nolan, 1998). The therapeutic ethos, unlike traditional moral orders, is essentially self-referential and
looks to the self rather than to natural law or divine reason in order to provide
the moral boundaries of society and the 'tools for its navigation' (Nolan, 1998:
3). As such, the TRC required perpetrators to hold up their inner selves for public scrutiny and judgment, and to express remorse as an outward sign of an inner
regeneration. The public belief in the confessional is predicated on a general
conception of the self that bears an inclination to the good, and is capable of reform and transformation.

Second, central to therapy culture is an 'emotivist ethic' that privileges
open displays of emotion (Nolan, 1998: 5–7). At the TRC, the public display of
emotions was intimately linked to the production of truth where truth was perceived to be accessible through an open expression of sentiment rather than
through rational judgment and deliberation (Nolan, 1998: 6). Truth revelation as
emotional performance is also related by the TRC to the process of healing,
where catharsis and 'relief' were weighed in proportion to an open communica-
tion of feelings, and a failure to emote signified a failure or refusal on the part of
the deponent to transform the wound inflicted by past violence. Conversely, an
inability to emote was linked by the TRC to 'denial' and a refusal to come to
terms with the past. Debra Kaminer et al argue in their study of the relationship
of psychiatric health to forgiveness in survivors of human rights abuses that a
lack of forgiveness in victims is related to 'poor psychiatric adjustment'. . .
where 'being unforgiving, although an understandable moral response to being
violated, also carries an increased risk of psychiatric morbidity' (Kaminer et al,
2001: 375). Their study concludes that a lack of forgiveness and understanding
'may be an important predictor of psychiatric risk in the population'. Such findings lend scientific credence to therapeutic assumptions that the psychological
health of victims is jeopardized by a failure to forgive, and that displays of anger
and calls for revenge only threaten to perpetuate the cycles of violence that reconciliation seeks to stem. In line with this assumption the TRC conflated retributive justice with revenge, arguing that feelings of revenge would militate against
the possibility of reconciliation. It deployed therapy as a legitimizing strategy in
order to make palatable the political decision to grant amnesty to perpetrators,
and in order to govern victim expectations of, and reactions to, a reconciliation
process to which amnesty was central. But, as Derek Summerfield has argued,

'one man's revenge is another's social justice', and feelings for revenge 'carry a moral interrogative that points to social and individual wounds and to shared ideas about justice, accountability, and punishment that hold a social fabric together' (Summerfield, 2002: 1105).

A third feature of the therapeutic perspective is that it pathologizes human actions and represents particular forms of human behavior as if they were diseases needing proper diagnosis and treatment. Such a pathological approach to human behavior concentrates on causal factors, symptoms and development of a condition, and upon the necessary professional interventions required to ameliorate disease. Pathological approaches to wartime atrocities have a particular historical lineage, from the treatment of shell shock during the First World War to the invention of Post-Traumatic Stress Disorder (PTSD) in the wake of the Vietnam War, a crucial constitutive moment in the development of psychiatric responses to war trauma (Shepherd, 2000). The incorporation of PTSD into the lexicon of psychiatric diagnostic categories in 1980 brought with it a shift in interpretation of soldiers' agency in war since a diagnosis took into account the conditions under which war was fought rather than concentrating upon the 'intrinsic' psychological dispositions of individuals.[7] War trauma, or PTSD, came to be understood in terms of the structural and functional 'changes' produced by the experience of a 'psychologically traumatic event that is generally outside the range of usual human experience.' (American Psychiatric Association, 1980: 236).

Such pathological perspectives on, and approaches to, war trauma have particular implications for conceptions of human accountability for atrocities perpetrated during war. Summerfield notes that the invention of PTSD 'was a powerful and essentially political transformation: Vietnam veterans were to be seen not as perpetrators or offenders but as people traumatized by roles thrust on them by the US military' which 'legitimized their "victimhood" and gave them "moral exculpation"' (Summerfield, 2001). Medical professionals treating returning Vietnam soldiers were alert to these implications at the time, one of whom remarked upon the '"potentially explosive impact" of stress related diagnoses on "societal approaches to responsibility and accountability"' (Shalev, 1997). Therapeutic perspectives thus sometimes feed into and legitimize self-understanding as victimization.

Political Effects of the Therapeutic Ethos

Therapy constructed the moral boundaries of reconciliation with the effect of organizing and converging diverse experiences and testimonies about past violence. It replaced other moral codes that we might expect to play an important role in dealing with past atrocities. Specifically, it displaces the moral order represented by a retributive response to gross violations, one which emphasizes punishment as the correct response to wrongs committed. It operates *in place of* retribution, compelling self-reform without punishment. Therapeutic responses to the effects of atrocity were crucial to the work of the TRC because it was empowered to grant amnesty but not to prosecute. Therapy thus acted upon amnesty to legitimize it and to *discredit and disallow calls for retributive justice*, by grounding moral authority in self-reflection, remorse, repentance and internal change rather than in punishment. This, however, was problematic because therapy militates against popular understandings of right responses to violence that are predicated upon the notion of just deserts. For example, as Wilson has documented, the TRC's restorative approach to justice was in conflict with popular interpretations and practices of 'local justice' in the townships that were thoroughly grounded in retributive responses to wrongdoing (Wilson, 2001: chapter 7).

In addition, therapy is, problematically here, a very agent-centered discourse. Due to the fact that the TRC was empowered to grant amnesty to individuals on the basis of claims about violations being perpetrated within a political rationale, the TRC acted upon the effects of transacted violence rather than with the *structures* within which violence was made possible.[8] As such, therapy excluded a proper accounting of the structural effects of apartheid regime, of the race, education and pass laws, of which many thousands more people were victims. Because therapy emphasizes the psycho-social effects of conflict emerging out of individual acts of violence, it fails to acknowledge the material deprivations that were concomitant with past atrocity and as a consequence, it works to *discredit claims for material compensation* which more frequently ensue from claims relating to structural inequalities. Therapy sidesteps redress of the deep structural and economic inequalities within which gross violations of human rights are made possible, concentrating instead on changing people's behavior through altering their self-perception. Simultaneously, therapy precludes an investigation into the *beneficiaries* of apartheid violence, as the subjects of reconciliation, those requiring healing, are only the victims and perpetrators of party political violence alone. It does not address those who profited but did not, at least directly, perpetrate.

The more political implications of making victims central to the new post-apartheid order are astutely observed by Michael Humphreys who notes that the TRC staged the 'spectacle of victim pain and suffering in order to publicly project the power of the state' (Humphrey, 2003: 171). In other words, the TRC inverted the logic of apartheid power thus: where the power of the former regime was founded on the state's capacity for terror, the power and legitimacy of the new order was grounded in the public performance of the state's power to restore, heal and reconcile. However, it is arguable that the possibility of founding reconciliation on a therapeutic order is uncertain, since 'the therapeutic emphasis on the victimized and emotive concerns of the self are tendentiously anticommunal', thus presenting a fragile basis for reconciliation (Nolan, 1998: 301).

Overall, however, whilst therapy seemed to provide a compelling narrative through which to relate the harms of the past, the therapeutic performance of the TRC failed on several counts. It failed because the mandate of the TRC required victims to tell their stories 'in their own words', but the Commission decided quite early on in its work that allowing victims to record their full testimony was too time consuming and inefficient. In addition, the work of the TRC attracted enormous interest from international researchers who reproduced testimonials in a wide variety of academic fora. In response, some victims expressed anger at the way in which their testimonies were reproduced, unacknowledged, by writers, researchers and commentators on the Commission's work, and complained that they ultimately lacked control over representation of their experiences (Ross, 2003: 334–335).

The therapeutic ethos seemed, symbolically, to make victims the central subjects of the new post-apartheid political order but it is arguable, however, that perpetrators rather than victims were privileged by the process because amnesty was accorded with immediate effect, whereas victims had to wait for reparations to be decided. In addition, many victims placed a premium on financial compensation rather than acknowledgement and healing, a claim that was obscured by the TRC's broader therapeutic discourse that placed greater emphasis on symbolic reparations. These encompassed a range of practices, the significance of which lay to a significant degree in their therapeutic intent of restoring the dignity of victims and survivors. For example, public truth telling and official acknowledgement of victim stories, many of which had met previously with various forms of official denial from, for example, state security operatives or the refusal of doctors to treat seriously the effects of torture, were indispensable to the TRC's attempt to produce a new historical record. Other gestures aimed to recognize and rehabilitate individuals—such as legal measures like granting death certificates in the case of disappearances, expunging criminal records for those individuals sentenced for politically related offences, and accelerating outstanding legal matters, and rituals of exhumation, memorial and reburial—to gestures directed towards the reinscription of memories of apartheid violence such as renaming streets and public facilities, erecting memorials and monuments, and declaring a national day of remembrance (TRC, 1998: 6 (2) 13–15). Community rehabilitation programs were also set up to 'promote healing and recovery of individuals and communities affected by human rights violations'. These entailed interventions at both community and national levels including demilitarization programs, mental health and trauma counseling, and programs aimed at rehabilitating and reintegrating perpetrators into 'normal community life' (TRC, 1998: 6 (2) 16).

Overall, there was an important *disjuncture* between the *symbolic order* instituted by the therapy culture and the expectations it generated, and the *material processes* by which applications for reparations and amnesty were administered by the TRC. The therapeutic script sought to forge unity around the experience of violence and suffering by privileging symbolic over financial reparations. But instead the TRC *displaced* the site of struggle and produced new conflicts around other issues, especially around the question of financial reparations to victims, perhaps the most serious contestatory narrative to the story the TRC sought to tell about its transition, and a story to which I attend more fully in the conclusions of this book.

Conclusions

Notably, the TRC failed to provide the platform for encounters between victims and perpetrators so it failed, in effect, to perform the forgiving foundations of the reconciliation it sought to establish. Victims and perpetrators spoke to the nation in turn, but did not, could not, turn towards one another. Whilst Tutu frequently enjoined victims to forgive, there was no formal mechanism through which this might have been enacted. As such, forgiveness remains a rather disembodied narrative which, nevertheless, shaped the discursive imaginary of the TRC because it was often repeated throughout the public hearings. Acts of forgiveness were forthcoming, although sometimes not from the direct subjects interpellated into the TRC's narrative. Krog notes that during the second week of the Human Rights Violations hearings at which victims gave their stories, Tutu read an anonymous letter in Afrikaans pleading for forgiveness. This letter was sent to the TRC and was clearly promoted by the spectacle of the hearings at which victims revealed their terrible and tragic stories:

> Then I cry over what has happened, even though I cannot change anything. Then I look inside myself to understand how it is possible that no one knew, how it is possible that so few did something about it, how it is possible that often I also just looked on. Then I wonder how it is possible to live with this inner guilt and shame. . . I don't know what to say, I don't know what to do, I ask you to forgive me for this—I am sorry about all the pain and the heartache. It isn't easy to say this. I say it with a heart that is broken and tears in my eyes (Krog, 1999: 70).

That forgiveness was not facilitated by direct encounters between victims and perpetrators also points to a failure of reconciliation, as the structure of the TRC kept them apart through the work of its separate committees, each dealing with victims and perpetrators in isolation from one another. However, the TRC attempted to materialize reconciliation through various formal processes, namely the amnesty provision for perpetrators and the reparations process for victims. Reconciliation and healing conditioned the process by which testimonies were solicited to the point that 'statement-takers. . . were selected for their ability. . . to listen with empathy and respect, so that the interview itself became part of the therapeutic and healing work of the Commission' (TRC, 1998: 5 (1) 19). It is in this disciplinary framework that the workings of the reconciliation narrative are made palpable in its framing of the individual accounts.

So, whilst reconciliation performed as the unifying trope through which all the testimonies and divergent narratives were assumed to be synthesized, reconciliation was envisaged as a future, rather than a present condition. Consequently, its workings were most powerfully manifest through its retrospective structuration of the individual testimonies where victims were largely compelled to speak in terms of reconciliation rather than revenge, and seek restorative justice which sought to endow them with a recognition of their suffering. Similarly, perpetrators had to relate a particular account of violations that worked within the overall teleology of the reconciliation narrative.

In sum, as I have argued, the discourse of reconciliation in South Africa was underpinned by a number of theological and therapeutic discourses which produced different and sometimes contradictory effects. One the one hand, reconciliation seemed to reify a historically continuous national subjectivity, but on the other it seemed to provide the possibility of breaking with such continuities by putting forward a different version of justice which might just transform the polity. This contradiction, as I see it, arises in part out of a tension between the *homogenizing* discourse of national unity and reconciliation and the pluralizing processes of the TRC, which included the solicitation and public performance of *divergent* testimonies. These offered different perspectives on the past because there was a tension between a) the TRC's attempt to produce an authentic and unitary version of the past, a version which attempted to produce the presumed securities of a continuous national community (that was albeit marked by the 'traumatic' event of apartheid), and b) the complex and different truths about South Africa's past that were illuminated in the statement taking process. The key tension here is between the *rhetoric* of political reconciliation and the *processes* by which by the TRC assumed this was to be achieved. However, the TRC sought to bring together and unify these divergent testimonies, making them converge to produce the nation as a cogent and stable sign of identification through the notion of reconciliation, the key trope that mobilized the national healing process. The language of reconciliation constituted a common horizon of understanding, or the attempt to harmonize 'incommensurable world views' in order to make 'differences stand at least within a single universe of comprehensibility' (Asmal et al, 1997: 46). To some extent the TRC was successful in doing this. Its theological discourse, as I have shown, went some way towards sustaining common understanding throughout the transitional period, and provided an important source of legitimacy of the new regime.

The religious and secular tropes sustaining the idea of reconciliation might also be seen to be in tension with one another, and responsible for creating some of the confusion around, and multiplying the meanings of, reconciliation itself. Where theological discourse appeals to an external moral order, therapeutic tropes, by contrast, look inwards and emphasize self-reflexivity. This conflict, I would argue, is not a simple failing of reconciliation but a perennial feature of any discursive formation which, as a central feature of any social, moral and political order, can never be synthetic, unified and uncontested. However, there might be more continuities between the theological and therapeutic perspectives than is initially apparent, and any inconsistency perhaps not as marked as it first appears. As Nolan argues:

> . . . the therapeutic code of moral understanding is uniquely suited to assuage the tensions of modern pluralism. It is both a derivative of the modern "scientific" discipline of psychology and quasi-religious in nature. . . Yet the language, organization, and personal nature of the therapeutic ethos are also reflective of religious sentiments, usefully absent of their sometimes divisive and sectarian qualities. Thus this ethic transcends the modern chasm between science and religion and offers to those from culturally diverse faith and non-faith communities a religion-like system of collective meaning (Nolan, 1998: 19).

The TRC drew upon the prevailing sacred and secular discourses in society that would resonate with the task of post-apartheid nation building, and shore up political legitimacy. The language of healing and therapy operates as a discourse of commonality in the face of diversity, but common to both religious and secular discourses are the principles of 'catharsis' and 'healing'. The subject positions of 'victim', 'perpetrator' and 'nation' are also shared by both discursive modes, to the language of forgiveness, reconciliation, therapy, and healing and as such what seem to be two apparently divergent perspectives have, on closer inspection, some important overlaps and continuities.

Notes

1.   All definitions taken from *The New Shorter Oxford English Dictionary* (1993).

2.   Reconciliation can be described as a coupling of narrative form and metaphorical process. For a detailed discussion of this point see Ricoeur (1975): 107–145.

3.   The assumption that retribution is founded upon vengeance is deeply problematic but one forcefully advanced by the TRC in its repudiation of the retributive paradigm. For a discussion of the problematic conflation of retribution with vengeance see Crocker (2000).

4.   The 'restoration of human dignity' is one of the aims of the TRC and is explored fully in volume five of the Report, and specifically in relation to forgiveness.

5.   Whether this type of gesture can be regarded as forgiveness at all is another matter for discussion. Attempts to taxonomize forgiveness have been made by Digeser (1998) and Shriver (1995), in which formal pardons are separated from amnesty and from individual acts of forgiveness.

6.   O'Neill criticises Derrida for his aneconomic interpretation, and decontextualization of the gift, claiming that 'there is no society whose members do not understand the language games of economic exchange and gift exchange that obtain in kin and non-kin relations' (O'Neill, 1999: 133).

7.   See the incorporation of PTSD into the formal trauma lexicon by the American Psychiatric Association's *Diagnostic and Statistical Manual of Mental Disorders,* Third Edition, in 1980, commonly referred to as 'DSM III'. This incorporation marked the birth of PTSD as a formal diagnostic category.

8.   The term 'transacted violence' is used by both Humphrey (2003) and Feldman (1999). For both authors 'transacted violence' designates, within the TRC's logic, individual violent actions of state security and party political agents giving rise to 'gross violations of human rights' as defined by the TRC mandate. Transacted violence is counterposed by both authors to structural apartheid violence such as the pass and education laws. However, it would be to misconstrue the point if the two were seen to be distinct and separable, as the conditions within which transacted violence took place were rendered by the particular history and structures of white power and privilege that gave rise to 'separate development' and the policies that implemented and enforced it. The TRC did make an attempt to sketch out the structural conditions—the institutions and business interests—that kept apartheid alive. However, the TRC was not empowered to act upon any findings it made in this regard and these investigations were less fundamental to its public authority than were findings against particular individuals.

Conclusions
A Book of Confessions

Moral imperatives are a phenomena of their times and locations.

Wynand Malan, ex-TRC Commissioner.

The TRC attempted to found a new politico-moral order in South Africa by narrating apartheid *violence* and *resistance* to it as the single salient truth of South Africa's history. This narration resulted in the TRC's chief indictment: that apartheid, as a form of systematic racial discrimination and separation, was a 'crime against humanity' (TRC, 1998: 5 (6) 71). In its final reckoning, the TRC endorsed the position that the liberation movements, and in particular the ANC and PAC parties, were engaged in a 'just war' of opposition to the apartheid regime. The TRC's final position was informed and bolstered by international humanitarian law and in particular the Geneva Conventions and their adumbrations of what constitutes just war. Further, the Commission argued that the strategies by which the opposition parties executed their campaign were not comparable, morally, to those deployed by the state because the state comprised of 'powers, resources, obligations, responsibilities and privileges that are much greater than those of any group within that state'. The TRC argued that the state 'must therefore be held to a higher standard of moral and political conduct' (TRC, 1998: 5 (6) 72). This unequivocal finding stands in contradistinction to the frequent impression generated during the public hearings, an impression to which the ANC was keenly attuned, that the TRC appeared to grant a rough moral equivalence to all violations perpetrated and to apportion culpability equally across all parties, regardless of their political positioning in the conflict.[1]

At the same time as producing a direct indictment of the old order in its final documentation the TRC recognized that its appeal to international laws and conventions both legitimized and strengthened its own findings, but also simultaneously provided the potential to destabilize the TRC narrative and proceedings because it opened up the possibility of, and indeed bolstered the rationale for, prosecutions. The international legal order relevant here deems prosecution the only just response to a crime against humanity, which was the TRC's finding regarding apartheid. However, the TRC attempted to foreclose the possibility of future prosecutions because, as it saw it, prosecutions threatened to undermine the reconciliatory political order it sought to establish. The TRC stated that 'the definition of apartheid as a crime against humanity has given rise to a concern that persons. . . might become liable to international prosecutions', and sought to counteract this claim by requesting that 'international recognition' should be given to the fact that the TRC has 'sought to deal appropriately with the matter of responsibility' (TRC, 1998: 5 (8) 114). With these words, the TRC suggests that the sovereign political process should take precedence in this case over the international legal order. Part of the reason for this is contained in key paragraphs of the report in which reconciliation is described as a 'never-ending' and 'painful' process, which, by implication, would only be disturbed by an internationally led punitive process (TRC, 1998: 5 (8) 115). As such, in its concluding remarks the TRC squarely privileges national order *over* international justice.

The entirety of the TRC's work is not, of course, reducible to a single finding. Eight years in the writing, the final TRC Report completed in 2003 represents a cathartic 'book of confessions' for the nation, in which is narrated the traumatic legacy of apartheid rule and South Africa's harrowing transition from it. This document provided an important paradigm for the truth commission report and established it as a specific genre of human rights literature, a genre that is marked by a patchwork of different styles of documentation, containing a range of data and supporting material including statistics about gross violations of human rights on the one hand, and individual testimonies of suffering on the other, which are situation and synthesized within a broad social, political and historical narrative. The TRC Report also reiterated the new set of creeds, catechisms and doctrinal statements that pithily encapsulated the basis of the new political order: truth, reconciliation, *ubuntu*, and healing. Taken together, these tenets constituted the official mandate of the post-apartheid regime, but also, and importantly, generated the moral foundations upon which not only the new South Africa was to be based, but which were subsequently taken up and applied in a number of other transitional processes in different geo-political contexts.

These doctrines have been, and are now, in the process of reproduction and institutional consolidation on two key fronts: first, at the global level in numerous transitional contexts where new truth commissions have been set up and have taken the South African model as their basis, as discussed in the early parts of this book; and second, and intriguingly, in the emergence of a new 'right to truth' currently in the making, and indebted in no small measure to the influential work of the TRC. However, and simultaneously with the proliferation of these norms, a third and important front of *contestation* has opened up in South Africa, involving two central issues: reparations for victims and retroactive prosecution for apartheid crimes. First, since the TRC finished its work the political compromise upon which reconciliation was built has led to an important challenge to its promise of financial reparations to victims, a promise which was not properly fulfilled by the TRC. This has led to victim groups pursuing compensation against multinationals through courts in the United States, which, whilst unsuccessful to date, have provided a strong criticism of one of the central ideologies of the TRC—that of 'victimology'—one that has not yet been properly answered to. Secondly and most recently, a lawsuit issued against one of apartheid's key ministers for law and order Adriaan Vlok, resulted in him receiving a ten-year suspended sentence in August 2007 for giving orders to the security police to kill, in 1989, the Reverend Frank Chikane, a leading anti-apartheid activist. The case implicated the former police commissioner, Johan van der Merwe, and three other former high-ranking police officers and under the terms of the plea bargain, Vlok is obliged to assist in any future prosecutions over crimes that he has information about. These two cases demonstrate that far from closing off its apartheid past, South Africa's reconciliation story in fact produced, and continues to produce, new conflicts around its meaning.

I will turn by way of conclusion, to these three scenes, two of proliferation and one of contestation, by first demonstrating the power and hegemony of reconciliation as a narrative of transition, and second, by pointing to its limitations. By far the greater portion of this book has attended, deliberately, to the hegemonic force of reconciliation, its construction and maintenance, and for this reason I shall dedicate more space here in the concluding pages to the third scene, that of its contestation by the Khulumani victim support group.

The Global Proliferation of Reconciliation

As I argued in the introduction to this book, the South African experience has secured reconciliation, its attendant principles and mechanisms, as a central political ideology of transition today. I have shown that since the TRC began its work the number of truth commissions has more than doubled, and subsequent commissions have referred to and built upon the South African experience. Since South Africa, many new commissions have been inaugurated in diverse social and political contexts such as in Sierra Leone, Peru, Ghana and Liberia to name but a few. Evidence of the proliferation of South Africa's reconciliatory tenets and practices is abundant. At the start of the public hearings in Sierra Leone in 2002, President Kabbah spoke of the 'traumatic experience' of the country and stated that its Truth and Reconciliation Commission—named directly after its significant predecessor—was to be 'one of the most significant pillars of peace, justice and reconciliation ever created', and that its key function would lie in its 'therapeutic contribution to the entire peace process and to the search for lasting reconciliation' (Kabbah, 2003). The Peruvian Commission, set up in 2000, also took its name directly from South Africa, *Comisión de la Verdad y Reconciliación*, and deployed public hearings. This was a feature that had been absent from pre-South Africa Latin American commissions, which had been distinguished from their African counterparts by closed-door investigations carried out away from the public eye. Peru was directly and explicitly informed in principle and in practice by South Africa. The Peruvian TRC's President, Salomon Lerner, also reproduced publicly the discourse of healing and reconciliation so central to the South African experience. At a press conference for the first public hearings, Lerner spoke of the necessity of giving voice publicly to victims as a way of healing and of restoring dignity. The mandate of Ghana's National Reconciliation Commission set up in 2000 notes that the Commission was charged with providing 'healing to victims and perpetrators', and links explicitly healing, forgiveness, and reconciliation as related and necessary principles underpinning the process.[2] And the Truth and Reconciliation Act of Liberia passed in June 2005, speaks of the need to establish a truth commission in order to 'promote national peace, unity, security, reconciliation and contribute to the cause of human rights by . . . providing an opportunity for victims and perpetrators of human rights violations to share their experiences, in order to create a record of the past and facilitate genuine healing and reconciliation', and to make recommendations 'for the rehabilitation of victims. . . in the spirit of national reconciliation and healing' (Truth and Reconciliation Act of Liberia, 2005).

The second site of proliferation of reconciliatory principles has developed in direct response to the truth-seeking model and its moral justifications. The 'right to truth' on behalf of victims and their families is now in the process of emergence and adumbration as a new and distinctive human right, and one that is very clearly located within the history of transitional justice, reconciliation and truth telling. Two key moments in its development are worthy of note here. First, in April 2005, the UN Commission on Human Rights adopted a new Human Rights Resolution on the Right to Truth (UNHCR Resolution 2005/69). In so doing, it invoked the canon of international law relating to human rights—the UN Charter, the Universal Declaration of Human Rights, the International Covenant on Civil and Political Rights and the Geneva Conventions. In particular it drew attention to the various articles and resolutions that were directed towards the following: a) establishing the rights of families to know the fate of their relatives; b) identifying victims of massive or systematic violations of human rights; c) establishing such details to combat impunity including the identification of perpetrators of violations; d) establishing the relationship between a right to the truth, access to justice, and the right to remedy and reparation; and e) the duty of the state to acknowledge its role in the perpetration of violations. These principles, resident in existing international legal standards, are, the UN argues, constitutive of an already existing, perhaps latent, right to truth that needs to be articulated more clearly as a specific right in and of itself. In order to make material this right, the resolution encourages the deployment of judicial mechanisms, such as the ad-hoc tribunals for Rwanda and the former-Yugoslavia, and, more pertinently, non-judicial mechanisms such as truth commissions. In the words of the resolution, truth commissions 'compliment the justice system' in the pursuit and protection of this right to truth.

Second, in June 2006 the Organization of American States (OAS) adopted a resolution on 'the right to the truth' which, it argued, would contribute to 'ending impunity and protecting human rights'. The OAS first began to articulate this right as the right of families to know the fate of their relatives, a right that stems from the American Convention on Human Rights, the Inter-American Convention to Prevent and Punish Torture, and the Inter-American Convention on the Forced Disappearance of Persons to provide victims and next of kin legal recourse for violations of fundamental rights. In making this argument, the OAS cites Articles 25, 8, 13, and 1.1 of the American Convention on Human Rights, which relate respectively to the right to judicial protection, the right to due process and judicial guarantees, the right to freedom of expression, and the duty of states to respect and guarantee human rights, and also the provisions of the Universal Declaration of Human Rights, the International Covenant on Civil and Political Rights, the Convention against Torture and Other Cruel, Inhuman or Degrading Treatment or Punishment, the Geneva Conventions of 1949 and the 1977 Additional Protocols, and other relevant instruments of international human rights law and international humanitarian law, as well as the Vienna Declaration and Programme of Action. Importantly for our story here, the OAS invokes the UNHCR resolution 2005/66 on the right to the truth as its significant precursor. In addition, the OAS cites the Inter-American Commission on Human Rights and the Inter-American Court of Human Rights as having recognised the right to the truth in their respective recommendations and judgements in various individual cases of human rights violations in the Americas. The OAS explicitly recommends the establishment of truth commissions to facilitate the realization of this right—thereby recommending the truth commission as *the main institution through which the right to truth might be pursued and secured*, thus supporting its proliferation. The OAS encourages the Inter-American Commission on Human Rights to provide states with the necessary and appropriate assistance in order to realise the right to the truth, through technical cooperation and information exchange on national administrative, legislative, and judicial measures that might be taken, as well as experiences and best practices geared toward the protection, promotion, and implementation of this right. It also encourages all states to 'take appropriate measures to establish mechanisms or institutions for disclosing information on human rights violations, and to ensure that citizens have appropriate access to said information, in order to further the exercise of the right to the truth, prevent future human rights violations, and establish accountability in this area' (OAS, AG/RES 2175 (XXXVIO/O6).

It is hard to overestimate the role of the TRC in the generation and proliferation of truth mechanisms and principles on the one hand, and in the construction of the 'right to truth' on the other. The founding documents and declarations of truth commissions following South Africa echo intimately its mandate, principles, and practices, as I have shown. And although the OAS statement draws upon many of the Latin American experiences, the most notable of which were Argentina in 1983 and Chile in 1991, it is significant that its statement on the right to truth is issued only in the wake of the South African experience, which elaborated complex and distinctive notions of truth, victimhood and reparations which are all intrinsic to this right.

Contestations of Reconciliation: *Khulumani vs Barclays et al*

When South Africa embarked upon its reconciliatory project in 1995, one might have predicted that the amnesty provision that both preceded and precipitated the TRC's work would eventually prove reconciliation's undoing. However, not amnesty for perpetrators but reparations for victims have come, at least in the immediate aftermath of the TRC's work, to represent the critical site of contestation of reconciliation. This is because the TRC privileged symbolic reparations, embedded in the discourses of therapy and theology, over material reparations in such a way as to leave severe material inequalities unaddressed by reconciliation. The Khulumani contestation challenges a key tenet of reconciliation: the centrality of the victim and victim experiences to the new moral order. This tenet was expressed through the main discourses of the TRC which constructed, symbolically, victims as the new constitutive pillar of society. However I have argued that, contrary to the TRC's claims it was *not* victims but perpetrators who were privileged by the process. This was because amnesty was accorded with immediate effect, whereas victims had to wait for reparations to be decided. In addition, many victims themselves placed a premium on *financial* compensation, a claim that was obscured by the TRC's broader discourse that placed greater emphasis on symbolic reparations. These encompassed a range of practices, the significance of which lay to a large degree in their therapeutic intent of restoring the dignity of victims and survivors. For example, public truth-telling and official acknowledgement of victim stories, many of which had met previously with various forms of official denial from, for example, state security operatives or the refusal of doctors to treat seriously the effects of torture, were indispensable to the TRC's attempt to produce a new historical record. Other gestures aimed to recognize and rehabilitate individuals—such as legal measures like granting death certificates in the case of disappearances, expunging criminal records for those individuals sentenced for politically related offences, and accelerating outstanding legal matters, and rituals of exhumation, memorial and reburial—to gestures directed towards the recasting memories of apartheid violence such as renaming streets and public facilities, erecting memorials and monuments, and declaring a national day of remembrance (TRC, 2003: 6 (2) 13–15). Community rehabilitation programmes were also set up to 'promote healing and recovery of individuals and communities affected by human rights violations'. These entailed interventions at both community and national levels including demilitarization programmes, mental health and trauma counseling, and programmes aimed at rehabilitating and reintegrating perpetrators into 'normal community life' (TRC, 2003: 6 (2) 16).

In tandem with symbolic reparations, victims were also promised material compensation. But, the final financial settlement on reparations was made *over seven years* after the TRC began its work and more than four years after the TRC submitted its initial reparations recommendations to the government. In April 2003, Thabo Mbeki announced that victims who had testified before the TRC would be eligible for a single one-off payment of R30,000 ($4,500), and that a total of $85 million would be paid to just over 19,000 victims.[3] The total amount allocated was much less than that initially recommended by the TRC, which stated that the government should pay the equivalent of $474 million in reparations to all who testified. As Michael Humphrey has argued, victimhood was arguably 'short-changed' by symbolic reparations (Humphrey, 2003: 184).

In response, victim support groups in South Africa, dissatisfied with the reconciliation process, started the process of claiming financial compensation from multinationals for apartheid crimes, a claim that was predicated upon an alternative story about South Africa's apartheid past that was marginalized by the TRC narrative.

'Unfinished Business': Compensating Apartheid

In *Khulumani et al v. Barclays et al*, filed in November 2002 in New York, Khulumani ('Speak Out') represented some thirty-three thousand South African victims and brought the case for reparations against a number of U.S., U.K., German, Swiss and Dutch multinationals from the oil, armament, banking, transportation and information technology industries—including British Petroleum, Shell Oil, Barclays, Credit Suisse, Deutsche Bank, Ford Motors, IBM and Rio Tinto—all alleged to have profited from their business associations with South Africa (*Khulumani, et. al. v. Barclays National Bank, et. al.* Case No. 02-CV5952 (S.D.N.Y. 2002)).[4] The Khulumani group has a special relationship with the TRC because it was originally established by survivors of political violence in order to provide support for victims testifying to the TRC. It helped victims to register their TRC testimonies, fill out applications for reparations and appeals, and provided individual and group counseling throughout the process.[5] Khulumani also organized meetings with TRC officials and represented victim interests to the government, helping to give victims an active voice throughout the work of the TRC.

However, since 2001 Khulumani has concentrated on addressing the 'unfinished business' of the TRC and argues that the TRC had underestimated the importance of financial compensation to reconciliation. In addition, Khulumani argued that the majority of victims of apartheid were excluded by the TRC's mandate as they were not victims of party political violence but of the systemic effects of apartheid, such as the pass laws, labor practices and forced migration, in which a number of multinationals are alleged by the group to be complicit. Khulumani argued that nothing in the Promotion of National Unity and Reconciliation Act that established the TRC prevented individual business personnel from making disclosures about complicity with the apartheid regime, and yet not one foreign business agent approached the TRC to apply for amnesty.[6] As a result, Khulumani announced its intention to sue the government of South Africa in July 2002 for failing to consult victims on the reparations policy prior to submission of the TRC Report.[7]

This lawsuit petitions for compensation on an individual basis in relation to the experiences of racially structured violence. This includes specific acts of violence to which victims were subject in addition to their lived experience under apartheid during which they were subject to the pass laws, forced removals, job and housing restrictions, poor living conditions and education provision and other direct forms of repression, in all of which the defendants are claimed to be complicit. The case claims accountability for corporate violations under a host of international rulings on crimes against humanity, genocide, extrajudicial killings, torture, unlawful detention and cruel, inhuman and degrading treatment. It argues that apartheid is a *jus cogens* violation of international law equivalent to slavery, drawing upon Article I of the International Convention on the Suppression and Punishment of the Crime of Apartheid and the Rome Statute of the International Criminal Court. Both of these classify apartheid as a 'crime against humanity' with reference to the existing Convention.[8] In addition, the case invokes the third party liability precedent set by Nuremberg, which ensured that the bankers financing the Third Reich were held liable for crimes against humanity.

The lawsuit seeks to prove two types of liability: third party liability for 'aiding and abetting' the apartheid regime, and criminal enterprise liability imposed by customary international law and domestic law.[9] The case puts it that 'during the relevant period, global industrialists and financiers knew or should have known of the danger to the black South African population' as the UN had 'put the world on notice' during the 1970s and an international boycott that included embargoes on arms, oil and technology was well under way by the 1980s. In spite of this, the defendants 'acted in conscious disregard of or with deliberate indifference to these dangers by providing substantial assistance or encouragement to the apartheid regime', with some corporations continuing to assist the regime throughout this period and, sometimes, concealing fraudulently their cooperation by establishing offshore trusts to obscure their transactions (*Khulumani et al v. Barclays et al*, 2002: 165). The case argues that the defendants were 'active participants and initiators in constructing a political and economic system which, in the end, was classified in international law as a crime against humanity' adding that in fact 'the period of extreme repression, from 1960 onwards, was intended to save the system that protected privilege based on race, thereby continuing to guarantee business its exclusive place in the South African economy and society' (*Khulumani et al v. Barclays et al*, 2002: 75–80).

The case cites numerous examples of companies aiding and abetting apartheid including IBM and Fujitsu ICL who provided the computers that enabled South Africa to create the pass book system that facilitated control of the black population. The case argues that pass books made possible organized forced labor and gross violations of human rights such as murder, torture and massacre. Car manufacturers provided armored vehicles used to patrol the townships, oil companies and arms manufacturers violated embargoes on sales to South Africa, and banks funded the expansion of the police and security apparatus. Some of the companies are charged with defrauding (mainly) black employees who deposited their money into pension, health, life, unemployment, and retirement funds but received nothing in return.

Importantly for the analysis here, the lawsuit transforms the TRC's symbolic reparations programme (based on therapy and theology) into the realm of legal disputation, and is notable for two reasons. First, it is a move that is consistent with increasing pursuits of financial reparations for past injustices that have become a conspicuous and contentious feature of contemporary human rights claims. This case promises to be an important moment in their reinforcement.[10] And second, it rearticulates therapeutic reparations as financial compensation, communicating differently from the TRC the subjects, objects and practices central to reconciliation in South Africa. In contrast to the TRC's therapeutic regime, the lawsuit considers victims of *structural* rather than political violence, and enquires into the *beneficiaries* of apartheid. It considers not the gross human rights violations emanating from party political violence, but the 'everyday violence' of apartheid that shaped and constrained the lives of those who were subject to its insidious and all pervasive regulations. Further, it seeks financial compensation *in furtherance of reconciliation* from the corporations who benefited from apartheid. The complaint mentions the need to 'broaden the victim's personal reconciliation processes beyond the scope of the TRC' (*Khulumani et al v. Barclays et al*, 2002: 8). It does not once mention the need for, or aim of, forgiveness or healing.

The Lawsuit and its Relationship to the TRC

The lawsuit shifts the focus from individual perpetrators to a systemic analysis of violations and makes a strong case for charging the beneficiaries of the system with moral responsibility for apartheid thus providing an alternative account to that narrated by the TRC of South Africa's past. Interestingly, the campaign draws heavily upon evidence produced by the TRC's own enquiry into the role of the business community in sustaining the regime. The TRC generated a subordinate, and potentially destabilizing narrative strand (which in fact feeds the lawsuit), about the economic underpinnings of apartheid. The lawsuit takes up and foregrounds this story in a way that threatens to displace the morality tale about party political violence and individual gross violations of human rights emanating from it, given centre stage by the TRC.

The TRC found that although some business sectors bore more responsibility than others, business in general was culpable because it benefited from operating in a racially structured environment. In response to these findings, the TRC recommended that wealth taxes be imposed on business as appropriate restitution but it lacked any legal power to enforce these recommendations. The lawsuit draws upon statements from the TRC on the complicity of the business community and finds, importantly, its legal and moral underpinning in the TRC finding that:

Business was central to the economy that sustained the South African state during the apartheid years. Certain businesses, especially the mining industry, were involved in helping to design and implement apartheid policies. Other businesses benefited from co-operating with the security structure of the former state. Most businesses benefited from operating in a racially structured context (TRC, 1998: 4 (2) 161).

The lawsuit plays into long standing debates in South Africa about the relationship between apartheid and capital, an argument that has a critical bearing on the question of corporate accountability for apartheid violence.[11] This debate is usually pitched as one between 'liberals' and 'radicals', along with all the normative assumptions that those terms imply, and it shaped the business submissions to the TRC and responses to them.[12] In brief, liberal arguments claim that apartheid was in conflict with free market capitalism since it entailed far-reaching state intervention into the labor market and other sectors of the economy which affected profit negatively by undermining productivity growth (Moll, 1991). By contrast, a radical perspective claims that apartheid was a system of racial capitalism in which segregation minimized the cost of black labor in order to maximize white corporate profitability (Lipton, 1985). The radical position is the concordant basis for any claim to financial reparations since it recognizes the enduring effects of apartheid ideology and practice on the economy, and upon the majority of the population subject to its deleterious material effects.

The liberal-radical debate was manifest in the various submissions to the TRC during its investigations into the business communities and in which the TRC set out the relationship between business and the power of regime, and articulated the continuing legacy of this alliance. Different interpretations of this relationship turned on the extent to which apartheid was considered to have facilitated or impeded business interests, and upon the responsibility of businesses for shaping apartheid legislation. Had business been involved in the commission of human rights violations, the TRC wanted to know. And did business benefit from apartheid or had it acted to hasten its demise?

In order to grasp the relationship between business and apartheid the TRC enquired into the culpability, collaboration and involvement in apartheid of different sectors of the economy including white business, black business, employers' representatives and trades unions in which the mining, defense and banking sectors emerged as sectors central to the apartheid order. The TRC distinguished between first, second and third orders of business involvement with apartheid. A *first order* finding required *direct collaboration* in the design and implementation of apartheid policies, for which the mining industry was held directly accountable (TRC, 1998: 4 (2) 23). Mining capital played a major historical role from the early days of the Boer Republics in driving cheap labor policies and was instrumental in influencing legislation that forced black workers into a wage system in which pay was capped and brutal repression of black workers and trade union action was endemic. The exploitation of black labor was key to the relationship between business and apartheid, and in its submission to the TRC, the Congress of South African Trade Unions, COSATU, argued that the heart of apartheid was to be found in the radicalized cheap labor system promoted and enforced by a mining industry that saw black wages in 1969 below the wage levels of those in 1896. The mining industry was opposed to all industrial action directed towards raising the cost of black and white labor, although it accepted the enhanced position of white employees over time, whilst black worker power was progressively eroded by the mining industry. There were few admissions of accountability by the mining business community, and in fact the relationship between mining and apartheid was described by the TRC as 'complex and contradictory' since the protection of white labor, an effect of apartheid, was claimed by the corporations concerned to increase costs to business. Many submissions by the mining magnates to the TRC on the costs of white job reservation testify to what was perceived by mining business to be a 'major apartheid-related thorn in the side of the industry' (TRC, 1998: 4 (2) 69). The TRC asserted that gross violations of human rights were perpetrated as a result of negligence of health and safety issues by covering up the dangers of asbestos, and the large numbers of accidents and deaths that were a consequence of working in the mines under poor conditions.

The TRC maintained a distinction between those businesses that profited by direct engagement with state repression and those who could not have expected their business dealings to have contributed directly or subsequently to repression. *Second order* culpability was contingent upon business *knowing* that products or services would be used for morally questionable purposes, an important example being the military-industrial complex in which the defense industry became 'willing collaborators in the creation of the apartheid war machine which was responsible for many deaths and violations of human rights' and out of which defense profited (TRC, 1998: 4 (2) 73). The imposition of an arms embargo against South Africa in the 1960s led to the development of a localized arms industry that provided the means for the maintenance and defense of the apartheid regime, and that for profit manufactured goods that it knew to be used in the perpetration of human rights violations both inside and outside South Africa. Armscor, the state-owned Armaments Development and Production Corporation, was largely responsible for the development of a local arms industry which provided the 'material means for the maintenance and defense of apartheid' and was declared by the TRC as 'guilty of directly and indirectly perpetuating the political conflict and associated human rights abuses' (TRC, 1998: 4 (2) 74). By the end of the 1970s, Armscor was central to a new military-industrial complex that contracted out much of its production and research to the private sector, including the majority of South Africa's private companies as well as some important multinationals such as Shell and IBM. As such, many private sector companies were made responsible by the state for protecting essential state installations and for developing nuclear weapons. Armscor claimed to be doing 'normal work' in contributing to the defense of the state, a position questioned by the TRC by highlighting the domestic site of Armscor's security operations. Armscor could not have ignored the fact that the government was using military means for internal oppression, the TRC alleged.

Banks, particularly international creditors, were also found to play a second order role in supporting and sustaining apartheid. Swiss Banks in particular profited from sanctions stepping in when other lenders, notably Chase Manhattan, reduced their services to the regime. According to the TRC, banks worked with government agencies, and were 'knowingly or unknowingly involved in providing services and lending to the government' including the use of covert credit cards for undercover intelligence operations (TRC, 19998: 4 (2) 26). The Anti-Apartheid Movement archives noted manufacturers' admissions that they were engaged actively with apartheid but that they raised the living standards of employees, but that this argument could not be applied to the banks as they gave huge loans directly to the government in order to 'repress South African citizens, wage war against liberation movements and invade its neighbours' (TRC, 1998: 4 (2) 130).

Third order involvement covered those who had *benefited* from the apartheid economy *indirectly* by virtue of operating within the racially structured context of apartheid thus, argued the TRC, highlighting current inequalities in the distribution of wealth and income and challenging the liberal argument that business was harmed by apartheid.[13] Third order involvement, however, acts as a 'cover all' making first and second order findings redundant: 'third order involvement is the most problematic of all the levels of involvement because it proceeds beyond the bounds of intention and implies guilt by association' (Nattrass, 1999: 388). In addition, a third order finding makes no distinction between the complicity of different sectors of business, and makes commensurate the culpability of corner shop owners, for example, with that of the much more heavily implicated Armscor.

Overall, the TRC concluded that business was central to the economy that sustained apartheid whether it had been involved in designing and implementing apartheid policies, co-operating with state security structures, or profiting from the racially structured context of apartheid South Africa (TRC, 1998: 4 (2) 161).

Two clear views of the relationship between business and apartheid emerged out of the submissions, and these mirrored the liberal-radical debate. White business argued that apartheid raised the costs of doing business, eroded South Africa's skill base and undermined long-term productivity and growth.[14] It claimed that apartheid raised the costs of doing business as it engaged a set of politically inspired yet economically irrational policies that hindered rather than generated profit. By contrast, the ANC, COSATU and the SACP saw apartheid as a system of racial-capitalism that depressed black labor costs in order to maximize white profit. Their argument strenuously resisted the persistent liberal distinction between the economic and political spheres by emphasizing the intrinsic relationship between apartheid ideology and capitalism on the one hand, and the concomitant relationship of the black trade union movement to the struggle for democracy on the other. The ANC submission argued that white business had played no role in opposing the regime, and instead, at key moments in the re-emergence of the democratic movement 'business initial reaction was invariably one of opposition, victimization of activist and union officials, and recourse to the regime's security forces' in which 'many violations of human rights occurred as a consequence' (TRC, 1998: 4 (2) 19).

Some businesses resisted the TRC's investigation on its own terms. Old Mutual, a large mutual insurance fund, argued that it was excluded from making a submission by the TRC's mandate because it was not party to gross violations of human rights.[15] This complaint points to the limitations of a mandate that in fact circumscribed a full and proper enquiry into apartheid violence beyond the party political conflict at the heart of its investigations, an elision to which the lawsuit promised to answer.

Overall, the TRC noted a 'complex and contradictory' relationship between apartheid and business, and stated that industry remained divided on the question of black trade union rights and wage determination because higher wages leads to higher consumer demand. However, because apartheid created downward pressure on wages, all business benefited either by staying in business or because profits were boosted. International corporations were found to benefit most as they fell into a high-level profit category, but they also contributed to improved wages due to the intense pressure of international campaigns that created enough embarrassment for them to make some 'concessions'.

The TRC charged business with either direct or implicit collaboration: directly by arming and equipping the security apparatus, or implicitly by doing business with the state, paying taxes and promoting economic growth. It concluded that whilst business as a category was not homogenous and that there were varying degrees of complicity, economic power was in fact concentrated in the hands of a few conglomerations with enormous influence on state affairs that could have used their power instead to reform apartheid rather than strengthen and perpetuate it. It found that 'business was central to the economy that sustained the South African state during the apartheid years' and that many businesses were culpable either directly, or by omission, by failing to use their power to challenge apartheid policies and practice (TRC, 1998: 4 (2) 161).

For the TRC, the liberal-radical debate has a crucial bearing on the question of culpability because the different sides of the debate produce dramatically different interpretations of accountability. On a liberal account, business is cast as the *victim* of a regime that impeded profitability and growth, rather than as a beneficiary or collaborator with apartheid. But on a radical account white business is *inescapably culpable* since it profited directly from the exploitation of black workers and the constraints placed on black entrepreneurial activity by apartheid.[16] Further, because the lawsuit draws heavily on the TRC findings in fleshing out its justification, the liberal-radical debate also infuses the terms of the claims contained in it, which are strongly oriented towards the radical interpretation of accountability of corporate interests. The radical claim represents a repudiation of the discursive regime projected by the TRC because structural violence escapes its individualistic, self-referential logic, and cannot be subsumed by a mandate that sought to identify primarily the agents of party political violence.

Challenging the TRC's Reparations Policy and Provision

In spite of the fact that the TRC enquiry into business and labor was a sideshow to the main event, it is arguable that without it the apartheid litigation case would not have been possible. Whilst the TRC's central discursive regime—focusing on the victims and perpetrators of party political violence, and encouraging healing and forgiveness as reconciliatory foundations—fleshed out the imaginative terrain upon which reconciliation was negotiated, it did not answer to the very real material needs of many of the participants in the process. It suggested that the TRC reparations were meant primarily to be symbolic, facilitating victim stories, granting official recognition of their accounts, and thereby restoring dignity.

Interestingly, Tutu added his voice to contestations of the TRC in the wake of its work, contributing in important ways to the unraveling of the TRC apparatus.[17] He has supported the lawsuit and stated in an affidavit to the court that 'the TRC always took the view that its mandate was to consider *reparations* rather than *compensation* for victims of apartheid, and that sums of money granted to victims by the TRC were only ever meant to be 'symbolic rather than substantial'. Tutu suggested that, against this, 'proper' compensation was in fact necessary for reconciliation because it addressed the needs of those victims dissatisfied with the TRC monetary grant. He added that whilst he preferred victims to seek redress in South Africa, he would still support their right to seek redress in any country where the courts have the necessary jurisdiction.[18] By contrast, South African Justice Minister Dr Penuell Maduna pleaded for the case to be thrown out of court because, he claimed, the case in fact *threatened* the reconciliation process because it would deter foreign investment in the country.

The lawsuit was in fact thrown out of court on September 29, 2004. However, regardless of its failure to secure reparations, the case is important because it challenged the TRC's discourse by transforming the subjects, objects, and practices of reconciliation and showing how a different story about South Africa's past might be written. The case demonstrates the limitations of the discourse of reconciliation, showing how the TRC concentrated, problematically, on the narrower categories of victims and perpetrators of gross violations of human rights perpetrated in a political context and with a political objective, and promoted (cheap?) symbolic reparations as the means by which the wounds of the past might be healed and past divisions transcended. The effect of this was, according to Mamdani, to present all experiences of apartheid as victimization, which included apartheid's beneficiaries: "The TRC invited beneficiaries to join victims in a public outrage against perpetrators. If only we had known, it seemed to invite beneficiaries to say, we would have acted differently; our trust has been violated, betrayed, abused. So beneficiaries too were presented as victims" (Mamdani, 1998: 40). The lawsuit points up the particular ways in which the TRC's dominant story about reconciliation individualized the causes and effects of violence, privileging the effects of transacted violence over the effects of the structural imperatives of apartheid South Africa within which violence was an organizing factor of everyday life, and in which business was not simply com-

plicit, but out of which it actively profited. It undermined the importance of material redress of ongoing material inequality by prioritizing symbolic reparations.
In addition, the metaphor of the 'wounded nation' that the therapeutic regime of
the TRC engendered, worked to reconstitute the territorial boundary of the state
as the physical, and hence moral, boundary of reconciliation with the effect that
that international agents of apartheid violence were excluded from scrutiny, including multinational corporations. By contrast with the TRC, the lawsuit brings
into view the beneficiaries of apartheid (and indeed, suggests that they too are
'perpetrators' of a kind), the victims not of party political violence but of the
violent fabric of everyday life under apartheid, and suggests that a central practice of reconciliation should be financial compensation to those victims.

The debate between reconciliation as therapy and reconciliation as reparations that is embedded in this conflict between the TRC version of reconciliation
and that put forward by the Khulumani lawsuit becomes manifest in the question
of *when* reconciliation is said to occur. There is a profound and intrinsic difference between the time of therapy and the time of compensation, which has a
direct bearing upon the inauguration, indeed upon the possibility of reconciliation. Therapy implies a teleological adjudication of trauma that necessarily engages inner psychological and emotional processes, professing to be destined, at
some unknown point in the future, for wholeness or healing. By contrast, compensation, whilst it cannot fully address the harms suffered under apartheid and
its continuing legacy, engages directly the subjects of compensation—the past
and present beneficiaries and victims—in a negotiation that entails an acknowledgement of past harm enacted at the very moment that compensation is
awarded. This potential for acknowledgement and restitution is something that is
made possible retroactively by recourse to legal categories that may be activated
in the present to address harms perpetrated in the past.[19] However, it is important
to note here, in concluding, that financial compensation is not a panacea for the
redress of past harms in all contexts, but that it is subject to multiple and complex interpretations that are very much context dependent. For example, financial compensation has been rejected by victims in other contexts because it
represents, to some, an attempt by the state to 'shut down' calls for justice. Families of the disappeared in Chile and Argentina refuse state compensation because
for them, it represents an attempt by the state to 'buy' their silence. Their refusal
deliberately 'defers' any reconciliation with the state until a 'proper' accounting
has taken place. For these groups, to accept compensation would be to give up
the right to see perpetrators brought to justice, which for them is the only just
response to past violations. It is important to point out, however, that the material inequalities of South Africa are not comparable to other contexts such as
Chile, where compensation might perform a more overtly symbolic function—
compensation as acknowledgement—and the repudiation of which by victims is
perhaps a more affordable gesture. Thus the *type* of reparation required or demanded by victims in any one context may vary considerably from case to case
for multiple and complex reasons. Clearly, no one justice will satisfy multiple
and divergent claims.

The fundamental value of the apartheid lawsuit resides, overall, in the way that it challenges the dominant discourse of reconciliation by addressing the beneficiaries that profited from the racially structured social and political organization of the apartheid state, and the intrinsic web of exploitation and violations that this structure produced. It produces a different account of agency and responsibility for apartheid violence via a discussion of first, second and third 'orders of involvement'. In addition and crucially, the claim for material compensation alters fundamentally the *discursive image of claimants*, transforming them from victims to creditors, such that they are no longer seen to be seeking concessions or 'repair' for harms suffered, but are seeking what is rightfully due to them.[20] It subverts the reconciliatory story about healing the victims and perpetrators of party political violations by emphasizing the social and economic circumstances within which violations were made possible, and against whom, thus shifting the emphasis towards the *debt* owed to black South Africans by corporate beneficiaries of apartheid. As a result, it demands a rethinking of what drove racial domination in apartheid South Africa. The claim for financial reparations reconfigures reconciliation as a racial justice that partly answers to the profound and persistent economic inequality in post-reconciliation South Africa. It draws attention to the ways in which white supremacy was built on the pursuit of a wealth predicated on black exploitation, making central to reparations the relationship between racialized power and privilege and its continuing legacy, in ways that the narrative of reconciliation as therapy and theology cannot. The Khulumani campaign illuminates what I have discussed in this book as an important *disjuncture* between the 'symbolic' reparations instituted by the TRC and the expectations it generated, and the material processes by which applications for reparations and amnesty were administered. The TRC narrative sought to forge unity around the experience of violence and suffering by privileging symbolic over financial reparations, but instead, arguable, the TRC *displaced* the site of struggle and produced new conflicts around other issues such as reparations, a contest manifest in the lawsuit.

The lawsuit represents one amongst other alternative reconciliation narratives by highlighting a different story that might have been told about South Africa's past, a story that implicates multinational corporations in sustaining the apartheid regime and exploiting its repressive order for their own profit. This story is elided by the TRC's investigations because it cannot be integrated within the overall story about party political violence that the TRC seeks to emphasize, and indeed argues that is integral to, indeed conditional of, South Africa's apartheid history. International corporations represent different moral agents, or protagonists, from those engaged more directly in political struggle and as such, the interests of these agents alter considerably the kind of historical narrative that might have been written. The lawsuit presents the narration of this particular story as imperative, and thus challenges the official narrative.

However, South Africa is not alone in failing to implicate international agents, political *and* corporate, in the perpetration of human rights abuses in its investigation. This dimension has also been ignored by the vast majority of truth commissions and reconciliation processes to date in part because reconciliation is a nation-centered discourse which seeks primarily to reify the identity of the national community, to reinstate its boundaries, and to bolster political legitimacy.

Khulumani's campaign presents one powerful repudiation of the TRC's therapeutic and theological mandate by prioritizing financial compensation over psychological repair and contests the ambit of symbolic practices upon which reconciliation in South Africa was negotiated. The Khulumani case is a demonstration of one of the important ways in which the reconciliation projected by the TRC did not, could not, fully redeem the antagonisms of the past. It promises to have important ramifications for new reconciliation processes because they will have to attend more carefully to claims for financial compensation on the part of victims and incorporate provision within the reconciliation process. If not, and alternatively, the Khulumani lawsuit establishes a precedent for other class action lawsuits for reparations which may well be taken up by other victim groups in other contexts.

In conclusion, I have argued in this book that narrative is a discursive formation that seeks to transform and maintain meaning through emplotment, and I have demonstrated the way in which the TRC sought to construct a story about South Africa that highlighted and connected in a linear and causal way past violence, the present confessional and a future reconciliation. The TRC constructed events and relationships between key actors into meaningful wholes, not only between the events and actors themselves, but also by situating them within particular interpretations of the social and political context of apartheid violence and resistance to it. The central narrative logistic of the TRC centered upon its investigation of human rights violations arising out of the political conflict of the past, between, primarily, the ANC and the NP, and this became the ordering principle of the new historical narrative that the TRC sought to construct. This narrative connected people, events, and organizations by mapping out a network of relations between the three across a given period of time, seeking unity within diverse elements, making commensurate different perspectives on the past and putting forward a new foundational principle for the nation. Reconciliation-as-narrative constructed a universe of comprehensibility through which seemingly incommensurable views and experiences were mediated and synthesized. This point is illuminated, forcefully, by a consideration of contesting narratives such as that put forward by Khulumani, because it shows how and where the dominant narrative of the TRC *constrains*, in that it constructs the subjects (victims and perpetrators of political violence), objects (gross violations of human rights), and practices by which reconciliation is to be achieved (amnesty and truth-telling) and simultaneously *excludes* those subjects, objects and practices that do not fit within the matrix of reconciliation. Importantly too, however, the Khulumani case shows how the TRC's narrative *fails* to constrain because it points up the discrepancy between those agents who are incorporated within the narrative, and those who are excluded by it, those who conform and those who do not, and those practices that are deemed to be in the service of reconciliation (healing and forgiveness), and those that are not (the claim for financial compensation). It provides a moment of insight into the way in which the TRC forces a unity between conflictual and disparate elements. The lawsuit presents one (amongst other) possible contestations that might rewrite the story about South Africa's past in another way.

I argued earlier in this concluding chapter that it is perhaps surprising that reparations and not amnesty have become the key site of contestation of the TRC. Indeed, it might be argued that reconciliation in South Africa is continually haunted by its legal 'other'—the specter of retribution—and that this, rather than reparations, poses more of a threat to reconciliation, particularly as we enter a phase of post-reconciliation politics where trials of those perpetrators who did not seek amnesty have the potential to figure on the political landscape of South Africa. Retribution has always threatened the plausibility of the reconciliation narrative because it was constantly invoked as the transitional path that was being negated in favor of reconciliation. Whenever retribution was mentioned by the TRC and its officials, it was compared unfavorably with the more 'equitable', 'moderate', and 'rational' model of restorative justice. By contrast with what restorative justice seemed to promise, retribution was discredited by its constant, and erroneous, conflation with 'vengeance'. The suspended sentencing of Adriaan Vlok in August 2007 might well mark such a new post-reconciliation phase of prosecutions, but that remains to be borne out as yet.

However, it is notable that criminal prosecutions would not present a serious challenge to the *terms* underwriting the reconciliation process because they too would focus on party-political violence and upon human rights violations. In that sense they could be explained and understood on familiar terms, that is, terms familiar to the TRC and as such any future trials would be conducted *with the grain* of the TRC. Overall, the TRC was largely successful in pre-empting criminal prosecutions and rendered them unnecessary, and it was successful in securing a high degree of acceptance of its version of the past. However, the Khulumani claim demonstrates how this could only ever be *one* story about the South Africa's apartheid past. *Khulumani vs Barclays et al* presents a more radically re-focused challenge to the TRC's narrative and thus contests, profoundly, the TRC's whole approach. The fact that reparations and not amnesty became the key site of contestation to the TRC points to the fact that the TRC has had reasonable success in reconciling people to South Africa's violent past, but also, and crucially, to the fact that it has *not* reconciled people to its history of racialized economic exploitation.

Notes

1. The TRC's final and categorical statement about culpability falling to the state is somewhat haunted, however, by Malan's submission to the TRC in which he (astutely) relativizes morally the TRC's 'crime against humanity' finding against the regime. Malan argues that such 'moral imperatives are a phenomena of their times and locations' (TRC, 1998: 5). By implication, Malan suggests that another political order may well have made quite a different finding with respect to past state crimes.

2. *National Reconciliation Commission Ghana,* 2 (1) 2.1.2.1 and 2 (2) 2.6.1.1

3. The TRC recommended that reparations be granted on an individual basis. It received statements from 21,290 people of whom around 19,050 were found to be victims of gross violations of human rights. More than 2,975 victims emerged from the amnesty hearings although in some cases these were not found to be victims of gross violations of human rights. Relatives and dependents of dead or disappeared individuals were considered by the TRC as victims and were also recommended for financial reparations.

4. The case names from the oil sector, ExxonMobil Corp., Shell Oil Company, ChevronTexaco Corporation and Chevron Texaco Global Energy, Inc., British Petroleum P.L.C., Flour Corporation, Total-Fina-Elf; from the armaments sector, Armscor, Rheinmetall Group; from banking, Barclays National Bank Ltd., Citigroup Inc., Commerzbank, Credit Suisse Group, Deutsche Bank, Dresdner Bank, J.P. Morgan Chase, Union Bank of Switzerland AG; from transportation the Ford Motor Company, Daimler-Chrysler AG, General Motors Corporation; from technology, Fujitsu Ltd, IBM; and from mining, Rio Tinto. The lawsuit is one of a number of other such cases launched, with varying degrees of success, since the TRC began its investigations. In another example, British company Cape PLC agreed in March 2003 to a compensation settlement of £7.5 million to 7,500 South Africans affected by asbestos mining during the apartheid years.

5. Khulumani gave referrals to those in need of additional psychological care and supported families of the disappeared by organising special counseling. When the TRC stopped taking victim testimonies in 1998, Khulumani extended its programs to providing direct medical assistance to victims and their families, equipment such as wheelchairs to injured victims, and educational assistance to children.

6. The TRC's institutional hearings did, however, receive submissions from a number of South African companies. Khulumani argues that multinationals should also have made submissions to the TRC, with the implication that had they done so, they may not now be subject to legal petition.

7. Khulumani was working on these campaigns in collaboration with Jubilee South Africa, an organisation lobbying for the cancellation of Apartheid Debt. The case is based on common law principles of liability and on the Alien Tort Claims Act, 28 U.S.C. § 1350, which, under federal common law grants U.S. courts jurisdiction over certain violations of international law regardless of where they occur as long as the accused have some presence in the U.S., as is the case with the corporations concerned. The venue of the case is eligible because the defendants have offices in the New York district.

8. International Convention on the Suppression and Punishment of the Crime of Apartheid (UN 1973/1976), Article I.

9. The case gives legal historical precedents and examples on third party liability as 'aiding and abetting' from U.S. law, Nuremberg, the International Criminal Tribunal for the former-Yugoslavia (ICTY) and the International Criminal Tribunal for Rwanda (ICTR).

10. High profile reparations awards have been made to Holocaust survivors, to those of Japanese descent imprisoned in North America during World War II, and there is a well-organised movement in the U.S. for slavery reparations for African-Americans.

11. For a review of the historiographical dimensions of this debate see Saunders (1988).

12. For an excellent account of the way in which the terms of the TRC investigation into business culpability is conditioned by this debate see Nattrass (1999).

13. Some participants in the investigation questioned third order involvement. They wanted to know if payment of taxes was tantamount to involvement.

14. These included business organisations such as the Steel and Engineering Industries Federation of South Africa (SEIFSA), the South African Chamber of Business (SACOB), the Afrikaner Handelsinstituut (AHI), the Council of South African Banks

(COSAB) and the Textile Federation and the Johannesburg Chamber of Commerce and Industry; specific companies and corporations such as South African Breweries (SAB), the Anglo American Corporation, Old Mutual and Tongaat-Hulett (South Africa's sugar producer); and corporate executives such as Mike Rosholt of Barlow Rand and Anton Rupert of Rembrandt International (TRC, 1998: 4 (2) 15).

15. It might have added that commission with 'political intent' excluded the business community. Yet other parties refused to make a submission including the Mineworker's Union and the South African Agricultural Union. Yet others did not respond to the invitation including the multinational oil corporations (the largest foreign investors in South Africa), and white labor organisations.

16. However, this position does distinguish between white business agents and argues that some sectors of white business, such as banking, mining and armaments, profited more than other sectors.

17. Not only has Tutu supported the right of victims to pursue financial compensation in U.S. courts, stating that the TRC should have made more 'generous' financial reparations, but he has also stated—on South Africa's National Reconciliation Day—that the TRC had possibly contributed to a culture of impunity because it had failed to prosecute perpetrators (Carroll, 2005).

18. See Tutu's affidavit at www.woek.de/pdf/kasa_tutuaffidavit_dec_2003.pdf.

19. I am very grateful to Scott Veitch here for his perceptive comments on the time of therapy and the time of compensation.

20. Martha Biondi makes this argument in an excellent article in relation to the African American reparations movement (Biondi, 2003: 9).

Bibliography

Books and articles

Althusser, Louis. 1993. *Essays on Ideology*. London: Verso.

American Psychiatric Association. 1980. *Diagnostic and Statistical Manual of Mental Disorders*, Third Edition. Washington, D.C: APA.

Arendt, Hannah. 1958. *The Human Condition*. Cambridge: Cambridge University Press.

Asmal, Kader, Louise Asmal, and Robert Suresh Roberts. 1997. *Reconciliation Through Truth: A Reckoning of Apartheid's Criminal Governance*. Cape Town: David Phillips.

Biondi, Martha. 2003. "The Rise of the Reparations Movement." *Radical History Review* 87: 5–18.

Boraine, Alex. 2000. *A Country Unmasked: Inside South Africa's Truth and Reconciliation Commission*. Cape Town: Oxford University Press.

Boraine, Alex and Janet Levy, eds. 1994. *The Healing of a Nation?* Cape Town: Justice in Transition.

Boraine, Alex, Janet Levy and Ronel Scheffer, eds. 1994. *Dealing With the Past: Truth and Reconciliation in South Africa*. Cape Town: IDASA.

Borges, Jorge Luis. 1970. "Funes the Memorias." *Labyrinths*. London: Penguin.

Borneman, John. 1997. *Settling Accounts: Violence, Justice and Accountability in postsocialist Europe*. Princeton, NJ: Princeton University Press.

Botman, H. Russel, and Robin M. Petersen, eds. *To Remember and to Heal: Theological and Psychological Reflections on Truth and Reconciliation*. Cape Town: Human and Rousseau, 1996.

Carroll, Rory. 2002. "South Africa Shuns Apartheid Lawsuits." *Guardian*, November 27.

——. 2005. "Tutu bemoans failure to bring rights abusers to justice." *Guardian*, December 17.

Carver, Richard. 1990. "Called to Account: How African Governments Investigate Human Rights Violations." *African Affairs* 89, no. 356: 391–415.

Chidester, David. 1999. "Stories, Fragments, and Monuments." Pp. 132–141 in *Facing the Truth: South African faith communities and the Truth and Reconciliation Commission* edited by James Cochrane, John de Gruchy and Stephen Martin. Claremont, SA: David Philip Publishers.

Cochrane, James, John de Gruchy and Stephen Martin, eds. 1999. *Facing the Truth: South African faith communities and the Truth and Reconciliation Commission.* Claremont, SA: David Philip Publishers.

Cohen, Stanley. 2001. *States of Denial: Knowing about atrocities and suffering.* Cambridge: Polity.

Crocker, David A. 2000. "Retribution and Reconciliation." *Institute for Philosophy and Public Policy.* Maryland School of Public Affairs (Winter/Spring). http://www.puaf.umd.edu/IPPP/WinterSpring00/retribution_and_reconciliation.htm (accessed April 3, 2006).

Derrida, Jacques. 1992. *Given Time: 1. Counterfeit Money.* Chicago: University of Chicago Press.

——. 1994. *Spectres of Marx: The State of the Debt, the Work of Mourning, and the New International.* London: Routledge.

——. 1997. *The Politics of Friendship.* London: Verso.

——. 2001. *On Cosmopolitanism and Forgiveness.* London: Routledge.

Derrida, Jacques and Gianni Vattimo, eds. 1998. *Religion.* Cambridge: Polity Press.

Digeser, Peter. 1998. "Forgiveness and Politics: Dirty Hands and Imperfect Procedures." *Political Theory* 26, no. 5: 700–724.

Dillon, Michael. 1999. "Another Justice." *Political Theory* 27, no. 2: 155–175.

Douglas, Mary. 1990. "Foreword: No Free Gifts." Pp. vii–xviii in *The Gift: The Form and Reason for Exchange in Archaic Societies* by Marcel Mauss. London: Routledge.

Dowdall, Terry. 1996. "Psychological Aspects of the Truth and Reconciliation Commission." Pp. 27–36 in *To Remember and to Heal: Theological and Psychological Reflections on Truth and Reconciliation,* edited by H. Russel Botman and Robin M. Petersen. Cape Town: Human and Rousseau.

Dreyfus, Hubert L. and Paul Rabinow. 1982. *Michel Foucault: Beyond Structuralism and Hermeneutics.* Brighton, UK: The Harvester Press.

Elster, Jon. 2004. *Closing the Books: Transitional Justice in Historical Perspective.* Cambridge: Cambridge University Press.

Empson, William. 1984. *Seven Types of Ambiguity.* London: Hogarth..

Esterhuyse, Willie. 2000. "Truth as a trigger for transformation: from apartheid injustice to transformational justice." Pp. 144–154 in *Looking Back, Reaching Forward: Reflections on the Truth and Reconciliation Commission of South Africa* edited by Charles Villa-Vicencio and Wilhelm Verwoerd. Cape Town: University of Cape Town Press.

Feldman, Alan. 1999. "Strange Fruit: Torture, Commodification and the South African Truth and Reconciliation Commission." Paper presented at the "TRC: Commissioning the Past' conference," University of Witwatersrand, Johannesburg, South Africa (7–9 June).

Foucault, Michel. 1972. *The Archaeology of Knowledge.* London: Tavistock.

——. 1973. *Madness and Civilisation: A History of Insanity in the Age of Reason.* New York: Random House.

——. 1977. *Discipline and Punish: The Birth of the Prison.* New York: Pantheon Books.

——. 1978. *The History of Sexuality: Volume 1.* London: Allen Lane.

——. 1980. *Truth and Power, Power/Knowledge: Selected Interviews and Other Writings 1972–1977,* edited by Colin Gordon. Brighton, Sussex: The Harvester Press.

——. 1982. 'The subject and power' in Hubert L. Dreyfus and Paul Rabinow, *Michel Foucault: Beyond Structuralism and Hermeneutics.* Brighton: The Harvester Press.

Frost, Brian. 1998. *Struggling to Forgive.* London: HarperCollins.

Gadamer, Hans-Georg. 1998. "Dialogues in Capri." Pp. 200–211 in *Religion* edited by Jacques Derrida and Gianni Vattimo. Cambridge: Polity Press.

Guelke, Adrian. 1999. *South Africa in Transition: The Misunderstood Miracle.* London: I.B. Tauris.

——. 2000. "South Africa's morality tale for our time." *Review of International Studies* 26 no. 2: 303–309.

Guruita, Bianca. 1998. "The Shadow of Securitate." *Transitions* 5 no. 9: 37–45.

Gutmann, Amy and Dennis Thompson. 2000. 'The moral foundations of truth commissions.' Pp. 22-44 in *Truth v. Justice: The Morality of Truth Commissions* edited by Robert Rotberg and Dennis Thompson. Princeton: Princeton University Press.

Hamber, Brandon and Hugo van der Merwe. 1998. "What is this thing called Reconciliation?" *Reconciliation in Review*, 1, no.1. http:www.csvr.org.za/articles/artrcbh.htm (accessed April 10, 2007).

Hawkes, Terence. 1972. *Metaphor.* London: Methuen.

Hayner, Priscilla B. 1994. "15 Truth Commissions—1974 to 1994: A Comparative Study." *Human Rights Quarterly* 16, no. 4: 597–655.

——. 2001. *Unspeakable Truths: Confronting State Terror and Atrocity.* New York: Routledge.

Hegel, G,W.F. 1956. *The Philosophy of History.* New York: Dover Publications Inc.

Hinchman, Lewis P. and Sandra K. Hinchman, eds. 1997. *Memory, Identity, Community: The Idea of Narrative in the Human Sciences.* New York: State University of New York Press.

Holiday, Anthony. 1999. "Forgiving and forgetting: the Truth and Reconciliation Commission". Pp. 43–56 in *Negotiating the Past: The Making of Memory in South Africa,* edited by Sarah Nuttall and Carli Coetzee. Oxford: Oxford University Press.

Howarth, David R. and Aletta J. Norval, eds. 1998. *South Africa in Transition.* Basingstoke, UK: Macmillan.

Humphrey, Michael. 2002. *The Politics of Atrocity and Reconciliation: From Terror to Trauma.* London: Routledge.

——. 2003. "From Victim to Victimhood: Truth Commissions and Trials as Rituals of Political Transition and Individual Healing." *The Australian Journal of Anthropology* 14, no. 2: 171–187.

Ignatieff, Michael. 1996. "Articles of Faith." *Index on Censorship*, 25, no. 5: 110–122.

Jeffery, Anthea. 1999. *The Truth About the Truth Commission.* Johannesburg: South African Institute of Race Relations.

Kairos Theologians. 1985. *The Kairos Document—Challenge to the Church: A Theological Comment on the Political Crisis in South Africa.* Braamfontein: South Africa.

Kaminer, Dan Stein, Irene Mbanga and Nompumelelo Zungu-Dirwayi. 2001. "The Truth and Reconciliation Commission in South Africa: relation to psychiatric status and forgiveness among survivors of human rights abuses." *British Journal of Psychiatry* 178, no.4: 373–377.

Kearney, Richard, ed. 1996. *Paul Ricoeur: The Hermeneutics of Action.* London: Sage Publications.

Kermode, Frank. 2000. *The Sense of an Ending: Studies in the Theory of Fiction.* Oxford: Oxford University Press.

Kritz, Neil J., ed. 1995. *Transitional Justice: how emerging democracies reckon with former regimes, volumes 1–3.* Washington: United States Institute of Peace Press.

Krog, Antjie. 1999. *Country of My Skull.* London: Vintage.

Kundera, Milan. 1983. *The Book of Laughter and Forgetting*. Harmondsworth, UK: Penguin.

Lipton, Merle. 1985. *Capitalism and Apartheid*. Hounslow, UK: Maurice Temple Smith.

Lynch, Michael and David Bogen. 1996. *The Spectacle of History: Speech, Text, and Memory at the Iran-Contra Hearings*. Durham, NC: Duke University Press.

Macey, David. 1994. *The Lives of Michel Foucault*. London: Vintage.

Maluleke, Tinyiko Sam. 1999. "The Truth and Reconciliation Discourse: A Black Theological Evaluation" Pp. 101–113 in *Facing the Truth: South African Faith Communities and the Truth and Reconciliation Commission* edited by James Cochrane, John de Gruchy and Stephen Martin. Claremont, SA: David Philip Publishers.

Mamdani, Mahmood. 1996. "Reconciliation Without Justice." *South African Review of Books*. 46.

——. 1998. "A diminished truth". *Siyaya* 3: 38–41.

Mauss, Marcel. 1990. *The Gift: The Form and Reason for Exchange in Archaic Societies*. London: Routledge.

Mbeki, Thabo. 1996. Statement of Deputy President TM Mbeki, on Behalf of the African National Congress, on the Occasion of the Adoption by the Constitutional Assembly of "The Republic of South Africa Constitutional Bill 1996." Cape Town, 8 May.

McAdams, A. James, ed. 1997. *Transitional Justice and the Rule of Law in New Democracies*. Notre Dame, IN: University of Notre Dame Press.

McGreal, Chris. 2000. "Hitman links apartheid regime to massacre." *The Guardian*, 3 October.

Mendeloff, David. 2004. "Truth-Seeking, Truth-Telling, and Post-conflict Peacebuilding: Curb the Enthusiasm?" *International Studies Review* 6, no. 3: 355–380.

Minow, Martha. 1998. *Between Vengeance and Forgiveness: Facing History after Genocide and Mass Violence*. Boston, MA : Beacon Press.

Moll, Terence. 1991. "Did the Apartheid Economy Fail?" *Journal of Southern African Studies* 17, no. 2: 271–291.

Moon, Claire. 2006. "Narrating Political Reconciliation." *Social and Legal Studies* 15, no. 2: 257–275.

——. 2004. "Prelapsarian State: Forgiveness and Reconciliation in Transitional Justice." *International Journal for the Semiotics of Law* 17, no. 2: 185–197.

——. 2006. "Reconciliation as Therapy and Compensation: A Critical Analysis." Pp. 163–184 in *Law and the Politics of Reconciliation* edited by Scott Veitch. Aldershot: Ashgate.

Müeller-Fahrenholz, Geiko. 1997. *The Art of Forgiveness: Theological Reflections on Healing and Reconciliation*. Geneva: World Council of Churches Publications.

National Reconciliation Commission Ghana. 2005. *Report of the National Reconciliation Commission*.

Nattrass, Nicoli. 1999. "The Truth and Reconciliation Commission on Business and Apartheid: A Critical Evaluation." *African Affairs* 98, no. 392: 373–391.

Nolan, James L. 1998. *The Therapeutic State: Justifying Government at Century's End*. New York: New York University Press.

Norval, Aletta. 1996. *Deconstructing Apartheid Discourse*. London: Verso.

——. 1999. "Truth and Reconciliation: the Birth of the Present and the Reworking of History." *Journal of Southern African Studies* 25, no. 3: 499–519.

Nuttall, Sarah and Carli Coetzee, eds. 1999. *Negotiating the Past: The Making of Memory in South Africa*. Oxford: Oxford University Press.

——. 1999. "Telling 'free' stories? Memory and democracy in South African autobiography since 1994." Pp. 75–88 in *Negotiating the Past: The Making of Memory in South Africa* edited by Sarah Nuttall and Carli Coetzee. Oxford: Oxford University Press.

Ochs, Elinor. 1997. 'Narrative' in *Discourse as Structure and Process* edited by Teun A. Van Dijk. London: Sage Publications.

Olick, Jeffrey K. 1998. 'Memory and the Nation—Continuities, Conflicts, and Transformations'. *Social Science History.* 22, no. 4: 377–387.

Olick, Jeffery K. and Brenda Coughlin. 2003. "The Politics of Regret: Analytical Frames." Pp. 37–62 in *Politics and the Past: On Repairing Historical Injustices* edited by John Torpey. Lanham, MD: Rowman and Littlefield Publishers Inc.

Omar, Dullah. 1998. "Introduction to the Truth and Reconciliation Commission." http://www.doj.gov.za/trc/legal/justice.htm (accessed November 4, 2006).

O'Neill, John. 1999. "What Gives (with Derrida)?" *The European Journal of Social Theory.* 2, no.2: 131–145.

Onyegbula, Sonny C. 1999. *Seeking Truth and Justice Lessons from South Africa.* London: Centre for Democracy and Development.

Piglia, Ricardo. 1994. *Artificial Respiration.* Durham and London: Duke University Press.

Popkin, Margaret. 2000. *Truth without Justice.* University Park, PA: Pennsylvania State University Press.

Ricoeur, Paul. 1974. "Metaphor and the Main Problem of Hermeneutics." *New Literary History.* 6, no. 1: 95–110.

——. 1975. "The Specificity of Religious Language." *Semeia: An Experimental Journal for Biblical Criticism* 4: 107–145.

——. 1981. "Narrative Time." Pp. 165–186 in *On Narrative* edited by W.T.J. Mitchell. Chicago: Chicago University Press.

——. 1986. *The Rule of Metaphor.* London: Routledge and Kegan Paul.

——. 1996. "Reflections on a new ethos for Europe." Pp. 3–13 in *Paul Ricoeur:The Hermeneutics of Action* edited by Richard Kearney. London: Sage Publications.

Rigby, Andrew. 2001. *Justice and Reconciliation: After the Violence.* London: Lynne Reinner.

Ross, Fiona. 2003. *Bearing Witness: Women and the Truth and Reconciliation Commission in South Africa.* London: Pluto.

——. 2003. "On having voice and being heard: Some after-effects of testifying before the South African Truth and Reconciliation Commission." *Anthropological Theory* 3, no. 3: 325–341.

Rotberg, Robert I. and Dennis Thompson, eds. 2000. *Truth v. Justice: The Morality of Truth Commissions.* Princeton, NJ: Princeton University Press.

Sachs, Albie. 1990. *The Soft Vengeance of a Freedom Fighter.* London: Grafton.

Sacks, Sheldon. 1979. Chicago: University of Chicago Press.

Sarbin, Theodore and Karl Scheibe, eds. 1983. *Studies in Social Identity.* New York: Praeger.

Saunders, Christopher. 1988. *The Making of the South African Past: Major historians on race and class.* Cape Town: David Phillip.

Scarry, Elaine. 1985. *The Body in Pain: The Making and Unmaking of the World.* New York: Oxford University Press.

Scheper-Hughes, Nancy. 1998. "Undoing: Social Suffering and the Politics of Remorse in the New South Africa." *Social Justice* 25, no. 4: 114–142.

Shalev, Arieh Y. 1997. "Discussion: Treatment of Prolonged Posttraumatic Stress Disorder: Learning from Experience." *Journal of Traumatic Stress* 10, no. 3: 415–423.

Shepherd, Ben. 2000. *A War of Nerves.* London: Jonathan Cape.

Shriver, Donald. 1995. *An Ethic for Enemies: Forgiveness in Politics.* New York: Oxford University Press.

Soyinka, Wole. 1999. *The Burden of Memory, the Muse of Forgiveness.* Oxford: Oxford University Press.

Steiner, Henry J., ed., 1997. *Truth Commissions, A Comparative Assessment: World Peace Foundation Reports.* Cambridge: Cambridge University Press.

Summerfield, Derek. 2001. "The invention of post-traumatic stress disorder and the social usefulness of a psychiatric category." *British Medical Journal* 322 (13 January): 95–98.

———. 2002. "Effects of war: moral knowledge, revenge, reconciliation, and medicalised concepts of 'recovery'." *British Medical Journal* 325 (9 November): 1105–1107.

Teitel, Ruti. 2000. *Transitional Justice.* New York: Oxford University Press.

———. 2003. 'Transitional Justice Genealogy.' *Harvard Human Rights Journal*, 16: 69–94.

Theissen, Gunnar. 1997. 'Between Acknowledgement and Ignorance: How white South Africans have dealt with the apartheid past.' Johannesburg: Centre for the Study of Violence and Reconciliation.

Torpey, John. 2004. "Paying for the Past: the movement for reparations for African-Americans." *Journal of Human Rights*, 3, no. 2: 171–187.

Torpey John, ed., 2003. *Politics and the Past: On Repairing Historical Injustices.* Lanham, Maryland: Rowman and Littlefield Publishers Inc.

Tracy, David. 1979. "Metaphor and Religion: The Test Case of Christian Texts." Pp. 89–104 in *On Metaphor* edited by Sheldon Sacks. Chicago: University of Chicago Press.

Tremlett, Giles. 2002. "Bringing Franco's crimes to Light." *The Guardian,* July 17.

Tucker, Aviezer. 1999. "Paranoids May Be Persecuted: post-totalitarian retroactive justice". *European Journal of Sociology* 50, no.1: 56–100.

Tutu, Desmond. 1995. *Address to the First Gathering of the Truth and Reconciliation Commission,* December 16.

———. 1996. "Interview: Healing a Nation." *Index on Censorship,* 25, no. 5: 38–43.

———. 1996. "Foreword". Pp. 7–8 in *To Remember and to Heal: Theological and Psychological Reflections on Truth and Reconciliation* edited by H. Russel Botman and Robin M. Petersen. Cape Town: Human and Rousseau.

———. 1999. *No Future Without Forgiveness.* London: Rider.

Vattimo, Gianni. 1998. *Religion.* Cambridge: Polity Press.

Verdoolaege, Annelies. 2006. "Managing Reconciliation at the Human Rights Violations Hearings of the South African TRC." *Journal of Human Rights* 5, no.1: 61–80

Veitch, Scott. 2001. "The Legal Politics of Amnesty." Pp. 33–45 in *Lethe's Law: Justice, Law and Ethics in Reconciliation,* edited by Emilios Christodoulidis and Scott Veitch. Oregon: Hart Publishing.

———, ed. 2006. *Law and the Politics of Reconciliation.* Aldershot: Ashgate.

Villa-Vicencio, Charles and Wilhelm Verwoerd, eds. 2000. *Looking Back Reaching Forward: Reflections on the Truth and Reconciliation Commission of South Africa.* London: Zed Books.

White, Hayden. 1973. *Metahistory: The Historical Imagination in Nineteenth-Century Europe.* Baltimore: Johns Hopkins University Press.

———. 1978. *The Tropics of Discourse: Essays in Cultural Criticism.* Baltimore: Johns Hopkins University Press.

———. 1987. *The Content of the Form: Narrative Discourse and Historical Representations.* Baltimore: Johns Hopkins University Press.

Wilson, Richard. 2001. *The Politics of Truth and Reconciliation in South Africa: Legitimizing the Post-Apartheid State.* Cambridge: Cambridge University Press.

Zizek, Slavoj. 1994. "The Spectre of Ideology". Pp. 1–33 in *Mapping Ideology*, edited by Slavoj Zizek. London: Verso.

Documentation, cases and hearings transcripts

Argentina National Commission on Disappeared People. 1986. *Nunca Mas: (never again) a Report*. London: Faber in association with Index on Censorship.

Convention on the Prevention and Punishment of the Crime of Genocide (UN 1948/1951).

Convention Against Torture and other Cruel, Inhuman or Degrading Treatment or Punishment (UN 1984/1987).

Constitution of the Republic of South Africa. 1996.

Government Gazette Republic of South Africa [no. 16885, 15 December, 1995].

Interim Constitution of the Republic of South Africa Act [no. 200 of 1993].

International Convention on the Suppression and Punishment of the Crime of Apartheid (UN 1973/1976).

Kabbah, Ahmad Tejan. 2003. *Address by the President His Excellency Alhaji Dr Ahmad Tejan Kabbah at the Start of the Public Hearings of the Truth and Reconciliation Commission,* Freetown, Sierra Leone, April 14. http://www.sierra-leone.org/kabbah041403.html (accessed April 10, 2007).

Khulumani, et. al. v. Barclays National Bank, et. al. Case No. 02-CV5952 (S.D.N.Y. 2002).

Organization of American States. 2006. 'The Right to the Truth'. AG/RES. 2175 (XXXVI-O/06).

Promotion of National Unity and Reconciliation Act [no. 34 of 1995].

Truth and Reconciliation Act of Liberia. June 9, 2005.

Truth and Reconciliation Commission South Africa. 1998. *Truth and Reconcilation Commission of South Africa Report Volumes 1–5*. Cape Town: The Truth and Reconciliation Commission.

——. 2003. *Truth and Reconcilation Commission of South Africa Report Volumes. 6–7*. Cape Town: The Truth and Reconciliation Commission.

——. 1996. *Amnesty Application: Eugene De Kock* (AM0066/96). http://www.doj.gov.za/trc/decisions/1999/ac990349.htm (accessed April 10, 2007).

——. 1997. *Amnesty Hearing: Jeffery T. Benzien*. Cape Town, July 14. http://www.doj.gov.za/trc/amntrans/capetown/capetown_benzien.htm (accessed April 2, 2007).

——. 1997. *Armed Forces Hearings: Maj. Gen. B. Mortimer, Submission IRO The Former SADF: SA Defence Force Involvement in the Internal Security Situation in the Republic of South Africa*. http://www.doj.gov.za/trc.submit/sadf.htm (accessed April 7, 2007).

——. 1997. *Armed Forces Hearings*. Cape Town, October 7–10. http://www.doj.gov.za/trc/special/index.htm#afh (accessed April 7, 2007).

——. 1997. *Human Rights Violations Submissions: Bettina Mdlalose*, Vryheid, April 16. http://www.doj.gov.za/trc/hrvtrans/vryheid/vryheid1.htm (accessed April 19, 2007).

——. 1996. *Human Rights Violations Submissions: Dorothy Seatholo*. Soweto, July 22. http:// www.doj.gov.za/trc/hrvtrans/soweto/seatlhol.htm (accessed April 7, 2007).

——. 1997–1998. *Mandela United Football Club Hearings*. Johannesburg, November 24 to December 4, 1997 and Johannesburg, January 28–29, 1998. http://www.doj.gov.za/trc/special/index.htm#mufch (accessed April 7, 2007).

UN Commission on Human Rights. Resolution 2005/69. 'Human rights and transnational corporations and other business enterprises' (chapter XVII, E/CN.4/2005/L.10/Add.17). April 20, 2005.

Index

abduction: as category of human rights violation, 34, 53, 80. *See also* human rights violations; Infocomm

African National Congress (ANC): amnesty and, 12–13, 88, 103–104; armed wing and, 73; banning of, 74; capitalism and, 150; exile and, 74; founding of, 78; healing and, 130; human rights violations and, 76–80, 104, 111; Inkhata Freedom Party (IFP) and, 10, 77–78, 104; just war and, 12, 33, 139; Motsuenyane Commission and, 44n12, 111; nationalism and, 102; peace process and, 9, 27–28, 50; Skwekyiya Commission and, 44n12, 111; split in, 72; Stuart Report and, 111. *See also* amnesty; apartheid; *askari*; business corporations; Inkhata Freedom Party (IFP); human rights violations; just war; National Party (NP); Pan African Congress (PAC); peace process; perpetrators; Tutu; *Umkhonto we Sizwe*

African Youth League, 98

Afrikaner Weerstandbeweging (AWB), 13

Afrikaners: nationalism and, 102, 107

Algeria: truth commission and, 24

Althusser, Louis, 9, 48, 55–58; ideology as material practice, 56–57; Ideological State Apparatus (ISA) and, 55–57, 65n4; interpellation and, 57–58; subjectivity and, 57–58. *See also* confession; confessional; Foucault; perpetrators; testimony; victims

American Convention on Human Rights, 143

American Psychiatric Association, 138n7

Amin, Idi: Ugandan truth commission and, 23. *See also* Hayner; transitional justice; truth commissions

amnesia, 17–18, 26

amnesty, 2, 4, 5, 6, 12, 17, 15n5, 19, 103, 111; contestation of TRC and, 144, 145, 154–155, 156; forgiveness and, 122, 126–127; hearings and, 11; law and, 84; naming and, 105–106; objectives of the TRC and, 39; peace process and, 29, 31, 41, 50, 73; reconciliation and, 117–118; therapeutic discourses and, 117, 132–134; TRC Committee on Amnesty, 11, 41, 80, 106; types of, 15n5, 23. *See also* Ben-

About the Author

Claire Moon is Lecturer in the Sociology of Human Rights at the London School of Economics and Political Science where she is based in the Department of Sociology and the Centre for the Study of Human Rights. She is the author of a number of articles on the subjects of South Africa, reconciliation, forgiveness, political apology, reparations, trauma and therapy in war.